second edition

# The Parish Behind
# God's Back

second edition

# The Parish Behind God's Back

The changing culture of rural Barbados

Sharon Bohn Gmelch
George Gmelch

*University of San Francisco*
*and*
*Union College*

WAVELAND
PRESS, INC.
Long Grove, Illinois

For information about this book, contact:
  Waveland Press, Inc.
  4180 IL Route 83, Suite 101
  Long Grove, IL  60047-9580
  (847) 634-0081
  info@waveland.com
  www.waveland.com

10-digit ISBN 1-57766-775-1
13-digit ISBN 978-1-57766-775-9

Printed in the United States of America

7   6   5   4   3   2   1

*To anthropologist Jerome Handler,*
*pioneering scholar of Barbadian history and culture*

# Contents

# Acknowledgments

## First Edition

During the six years this book was intermittently in progress, many people helped out. We wish to thank our academic colleagues, Barbadian friends, and former students who offered ideas, read drafts of chapters, or provided critiques of the entire manuscript in one of its several forms: Jeff Broomes, Tracy Bush, Loran Cutsinger, Peter DiCerbo, Margaret Deutsch, Jerome Handler, Victor Johnson, Marcus O'Neale, Betsy Phelps, Barbara Scantlebury, Jeanette Springer, Karl Watson, Janice Whittle, and three anonymous reviewers. Susan Whitlock, our editor, gave us direction at an early stage and encouraged us toward final revision.

We are also grateful to Stephen Hackenberger, Colin Hudson, Wayne Hunte, and Robert Speed for teaching us about the history and environment of Barbados. Librarians Bruce Connolly and Dave Gerhan, at Union College, and Michael Gill and Alan Moss, at the University of the West Indies, Cave Hill, graciously assisted us over the years in various ways. Many thanks are due to Mary McKay, Janet McQuade, Megan Donovan, and Kerry Cassidy for their help in preparing the manuscript.

Much appreciation is owed the students we have taken to Barbados since 1983 on eight anthropology field programs supported by Union College. Their insights, experiences, and attempts to make sense of a new culture greatly contributed to our knowledge of the island. Our search for an up-to-date ethnography of an eastern Caribbean culture for the students' reading list first prompted us to think about writing this book. While the students are too numerous to mention individually, we wish to thank Johanna Campbell, Amy Dillenback, Siri Doble, Sara Finnerty, Dan Gilbert, Betsy Phelps, Annika Michaels, and J. J. Weiner for permission to quote from their field notes. Our son, Morgan, has added enormously to the pleasure of each of our field trips; he first went to Barbados when he was four months old. He is now fourteen and is as familiar with the back roads of St. Lucy as those of his hometown in upstate New York.

Our greatest debt is to the people of St. Lucy, especially the residents of Josey Hill, for their gracious acceptance of our presence there. Our neighbors Rudolph and Shirley Hollingsworth have made our time in Josey Hill especially pleasant; we thank them for their friendship, kindness, and help. We also want to thank all the families who have hosted our students over the years. Many of those in St. Lucy have become our friends and teachers as well: Siebert and Aileen Allman, Daphne Armstrong, Judy and Roosevelt Griffith, Valenza Griffith, Marcus and Janet Hinds, Uzil Holder, Gail and Victor Johnson, Marcus and Velma O'Neale, and Arlette Went. Without them this research would not have been nearly as pleasurable. This book is dedicated to them.

We use pseudonyms for most of the names of villagers who are quoted in the text. We have done this to protect their privacy and because the line between conversation and interview, between friend and "informant," was sometimes blurred. We realize that some people would have preferred to see their real names used, and we apologize to those who may be disappointed. The names we have substituted are common in Barbados. All place names and other personal names in the text—including the individuals profiled in chapter 4—are real.

## Second Edition

For this new edition, we are especially grateful to student research assistants Pearl Jurist-Schoen and Chelsea Tussing, who accompanied us to Barbados in 2010 and spent the summer doing fieldwork in St. Lucy. They contributed to the revisions in this new edition, especially to our understanding of teen and young adult perspectives on a range of topics. Several other student assistants, Carolyn Hou, Joan Piasta, and Diane Royal, read the first edition of the book and made valuable suggestions for revising. We thank anthropologist Jerome Handler for his thorough reading of the book, and especially for his many helpful suggestions for the history chapter. Tom Curtin at Waveland Press was, as always, a joy to work with, and Jeni Ogilvie was a master copy editor. We thank Robert Potter for updating information on return migrants. We also thank the University of San Francisco for funding our research, and Union College for funding our student research assistants though its Summer Research Fellowship Program.

Ermine Graves was our generous and delightful host in Checker Hall, St. Lucy. We are also grateful to Marsha and Findlay Cockrell for a place to stay while we were working in Bridgetown. We also benefitted from bouncing ideas off old friends and former neighbors Shirley Hollingsworth, Marcus O'Neale, Susan Mahon, and Janice Whittle.

second edition

# The Parish Behind God's Back

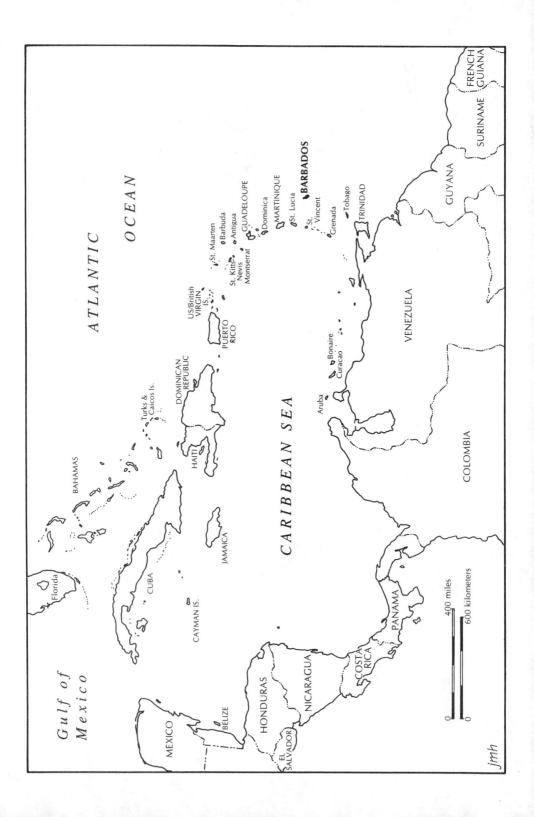

# Introduction

On the eastern Caribbean the expression "behind God's back" refers to a place that is remote or faraway. In Barbados the saying is used when speaking of the parishes or districts that are farthest from the capital city of Bridgetown. Although the rural parishes of St. Andrew and St. Philip are sometimes described as "behind God's back," the expression is most frequently applied to St. Lucy, the most distant and rural parish. St. Lucy has a population of about 10,000, spread over 30 villages. Nearly all of its residents are of African descent. Most people live close to the land, deriving some of their subsistence from gardening and livestock raising, while being tied to the wider economy through wage labor and salaried jobs and to the rest of the world through telecommunications, tourism, and travel.

Although this book focuses on life in one rural parish, what we find there holds true in large measure throughout the island. There is a certain uniformity to village life in Barbados. This contrasts with many other Caribbean islands, particularly mountainous ones, in which differences between highland and lowland environments and less-developed transportation links have produced greater variation. Even the contrast between rural and urban areas is less pronounced in Barbados than elsewhere in the region. Its small size, gentle geography, and extensive network of roads allow people to travel easily between country and town, village and city, producing a homogeneity in culture, although a few regionalisms in custom remain.

In describing life in rural Barbados, we are mindful of influences emanating beyond its shores. An important aim of this book is to reveal how connected Barbados and its people, even those in its most remote parish, are to the outside world. Barbadians may live in a distant corner of the Caribbean, but they are by no means isolated. One of the first things any visitor notices are youths wearing baseball caps and T-shirts sporting the names and logos of North American athletic teams: the Chicago Bulls and Oakland Raiders. Switching on the television, you are more likely to find an American sitcom or soap opera than a Caribbean program. In conversation with local people it

1

soon becomes apparent that nearly every family has a relative living overseas and that many people have themselves traveled to or lived in New York, Atlanta or Miami; Toronto or Montreal; London and beyond. Barbadians understand the extent to which their lives are influenced by the metropolitan countries of Europe and North America. They know only too well, for example, that the health of the US and European economies directly affects the number of tourists who arrive on the island and their expenditures. In the pages that follow we devote considerable time to discussing the impact of tourism and other global influences on the island. While the primary aim of this book is to provide a contemporary ethnographic portrait of rural Barbados today and its connections to the outside world, we also try to provide sufficient historical context to show how present-day patterns of village life came about. To understand any Afro-Caribbean society it is essential to know something of the historical processes through which a once enslaved people of African descent established their own communities and culture within the constraints imposed by a European colonial power.

The bulk of the data for this book were collected between 1990 and 2000 during six field trips, each lasting 11 weeks, as well as a shorter return visit in 2010. In the 1990s we lived in the St. Lucy village of Josey Hill; in 2010 we stayed in Checker Hall and the capital city of Bridgetown. A good deal of our understanding of Barbadian society, however, dates back to 1983 when we first began bringing American undergraduates to Barbados for a ten-week field training program in cultural anthropology. We returned with students nine more times, bringing nearly 100 students. They, as well as two student research assistants in 2010, have contributed to this book in several important ways. To begin, they lived individually in 15 different villages in the northern half of the island, about half of them located in St. Lucy. In the villages they carried out full-time field research that we supervised. Our visits to the village and home of each student contributed much to our knowledge of rural Barbados over the years and led to a network of friendships that extends across St. Lucy and into the neighboring parishes of St. Andrew and St. Peter. Much of our understanding of Barbadian culture has come from witnessing and assisting our students in their attempts to understand village life. The innocent mistakes they made often brought community norms into sharp focus. Through their friendships with Barbadians of their own age they also have given us insight into the problems, attitudes, and values of young Barbadians. It is partly because so much of our knowledge about rural Barbadian life has come from people and experiences across the entire parish that we have made the parish of St. Lucy, rather than the single village we lived in, the setting for this book.

Our fieldwork has extended beyond the parish as well. When investigating macrolevel issues such as the impact of tourism, we routinely have turned to experts and individuals directly involved, ranging from academics at the University of the West Indies, government officials, and journalists in Bridgetown to hoteliers, hotel employees, and foreign tourists along the tourist belt. While most of the village-level field data have come from daily observations and informal conversations with neighbors and other residents, when working outside the parish we have more often relied on formal, tape-recorded interviews. Our prior work—especially George's—on return migration to Barbados has also informed the present study.

This book was written with students in mind. In deciding, for example, how to organize it and what level of detail to aim for, we thought of the students we have taught. This was especially so in this new edition where we have dropped or relegated to endnotes material that was included in the University of Michigan Press' first edition of this book and that was primarily of interest to other Caribbean scholars, and less relevant to student readers in anthropology courses. Also with students in mind, we discuss in an appendix the impact that living in Barbadian villages had on the undergraduates in our anthropology program. While Caribbean villagers are not "exotic" tribal peoples, the staple of most introductory anthropology courses, their cultures are equally interesting and instructive. Barbados has been involved in the most significant trends that have shaped the modern world: the disappearance of an indigenous Amerindian population; colonization by a European power; the rise of European commercialism based on sugar production; the African diaspora; a complex pattern of out-migration and return; and incorporation into the global community through work, tourism and travel, and increasingly, telecommunications. Barbados, like the Caribbean generally, exhibits cultural and historical characteristics that clearly promote anthropological understanding of a broad range of issues.

The book begins with an introduction to the island and parish, followed by history and a macrolevel description of Barbados' economy, before turning to the local scene—patterns of work, gender relations and life cycle, community, and religion. Toward the end the perspective widens again to look at the global forces that influence, shape, and impinge on the lives of villagers today. Specifically, chapter 1 introduces Barbados and the parish of St. Lucy. Chapter 2 gives a historical overview of the English colonization of the island and its transformation into an agro-industrial plantation society based on slavery. Chapter 3 examines Barbados' economy, particularly the changes that have taken place with the decline of sugar and rise of tourism. Chapter 4 profiles six village households both as a way of exploring how local people make a living and, by getting to know a few individuals, contextualizing the later ethnographic material. Chapter 5 discusses the life cycle and gender relations. Chapter 6 looks at community and how it has been transformed in recent decades by modernization and new technology. The next chapter deals with religion, a major institution in rural Barbadian life. In chapter 8 we discuss Barbados' global connections, examining how outside influences introduced through the electronic media, travel, tourism, and emigration are affecting village and all Barbadian life. We conclude with some final thoughts about the country's growing regional ties and the pervasiveness and impact of American cultural penetration.

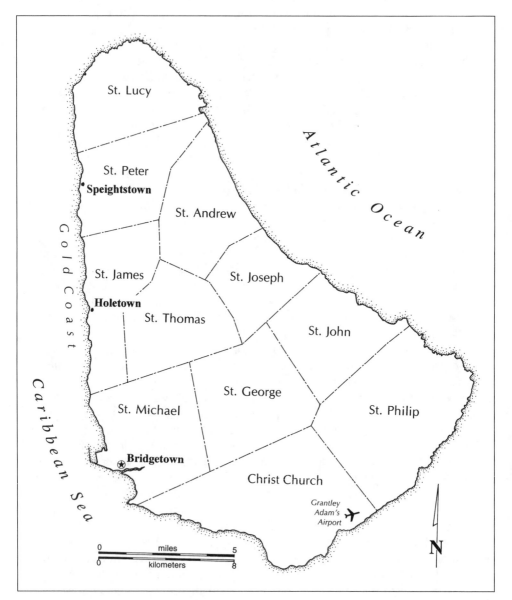

The parishes of Barbados.

# Chapter 1

# Island and Parish

*B*arbados is the most easterly of the Caribbean's islands, lying outside the great arc of volcanic islands that sweeps a thousand miles from the Virgin Islands in the north to Trinidad and Tobago in the south. Unlike these volcanic neighbors, which are steep and mountainous, Barbados is a coral island with a gentle terrain amenable to agriculture. The English who colonized it in the early 17th century, and the African slaves they later imported, quickly brought most of the island under cultivation. Barbados is also the only Caribbean country to have had a single colonial master. It became an independent nation in 1966, although like Canada and Australia, it remains a member of the British Commonwealth. Today, Barbados is widely known for its white sand beaches and tropical climate, which have made it a popular tourist destination.

The temperature varies little throughout the year, from an average of 77°F in January to 81°F in August and September. The proximity of all parts of the island to the sea ensures comfortable year-round breezes. The northeasterly trade winds that sweep over the land have traveled thousands of miles from Africa—one of the longest uninterrupted passages of wind on earth. This climate, combined with the purity of its groundwater, led one 19th-century English traveler to claim that Barbados was the healthiest place in the British Empire, which then included half the nations on earth. Indeed, the island's earliest tourists usually came for their health.

Currently, 285,000 people live on the island, which measures just 21 by 14 miles at its widest, making Barbados one of the ten most densely populated countries in the world.[1] More than half the population lives in the capital city of Bridgetown and its environs. Most people (93 percent) are dark-skinned, many being the descendants of the Africans who were transported to the island to work as slaves. The largest minorities are "whites"—the descendants of English colonists and their indentured servants as well as recent expatriates, predominantly from Britain and North America—and persons of "mixed" heritage (each at 3 percent). The remaining one percent of the population is mostly East Indian.[2]

Stretching outward from Bridgetown along the west and south coasts are strips of hotels, condominiums, restaurants, and other businesses catering to tourists—the mainstay of Barbados' contemporary economy. One of the main ways to reach St. Lucy from Bridgetown is to drive north along Highway 1, a two-lane road with no verge or dividing line, which hugs the turquoise waters of the Caribbean Sea. The west coast is referred to in Barbados' tourism literature as the "Gold Coast" or "Platinum Coast." The lush grounds of its hotels are planted in flowering trees and shrubs. Some of its hotels, like the Coral Reef Club and Colony Club, are single and two-story cottage-style resorts that evoke an earlier era and the exclusivity of a private club. The names of all its hotels and condominiums conjure the images the Barbados Tourist Board likes to foster—Golden Palm, Sandy Lane, Coconut Creek, Glitter Bay, Port St. Charles. A few miles inland, a second, newer highway built to alleviate traffic also heads north.

Just beyond the town of Speightstown, which lies on the coast ten miles north of the capital, the scene changes. The bustle of west coast tourist development gives way to small villages and open fields. Here the people waiting at bus stops or walking along the road are Barbadians, not tourists. Turning inland, the road climbs several hundred feet over ancient, uplifted coral reefs. Beneath Barbados the edges of two continental plates collide, one plunging beneath the other, the top plate, like the blade of a giant bulldozer, scraping off

Construction project cuts through Barbados' coral cap. (Photo by George Gmelch)

a mountain of oceanic sediment from the plate diving below. This sediment is the underlying land form on which the coral cap of Barbados rests. In places the road cuts deep, revealing white walls of limestone and ancient reefs.

# The Parish

Passing through the village of Mile and a Quarter—so named because it is exactly that distance from Speightstown—the main road swings north again toward the parish of St. Lucy. Shortly after the British established their colony in 1627, the island was divided into ecclesiastical and administrative units known as "parishes," with boundaries running from one plantation on the Caribbean coast to another on the Atlantic side. Another remnant of Barbados' plantation history are small wooden "chattel houses," more common in St. Lucy than elsewhere on the island. They developed in response to the insecure tenure of the newly freed slaves who became tenants on their former plantations. They were simple one-room wooden structures built to the dimensions that the imported timber boards arrived in and could be dismantled and moved (the word *chattel* refers to movable personal property) should their owners be evicted from plantation land or find a better situation on another estate. Some still perch on crude foundations of uncemented coral stone. They are steadily being replaced, however, by larger bungalows made of wood or by even larger "wall houses" made of concrete block. Just after reaching St. Lucy's imposing stone parish church—first constructed of timber in the 1620s—the road divides, heading further north across the flat coastal plain and east to the top of yet another uplifted terrace.

St. Lucy encompasses 13.6 square miles (8 percent of the island) and caps the entire northern tip of Barbados. It was one of six original parishes. As the population grew and new churches were built, five additional parishes were carved out of the originals. The creation of parishes reflected both the importance of the Church of England (Anglicanism) to early settlers and their familiarity with this form of local government. Originally, each parish formed a parliamentary constituency, with parish officials levying taxes and administering the roads, water supply, poor relief, and local education. When a British commission visited Barbados in 1939 while investigating social conditions in the British West Indies following a series of riots on several other islands, it noted "the extraordinary degree" to which the functions of government in Barbados were still decentralized and distributed among its parishes. Although local government was reorganized and parish councils dissolved in the 1960s, the parish remains the source of most Barbadians' geographical identity. When asked where they come from most Bajans (the colloquial term Barbadians use for themselves and for their dialect) usually give the name of their parish—St. Lucy, St. Andrew, St. Philip, St. Peter, St. George, and so on—rather than their district or village. Residents of Bridgetown and large communities like Speightstown are an exception.

Automobile license plates also identify parish; all cars registered in St. Lucy begin with the letter L.

To Barbadians living in the more urbanized, southern half of the island, St. Lucy is "country" and far away—"the parish behind God's back." When we first went to the island in the early 1980s, we met Bajans who have never been there, and even today primary schoolchildren in other parts of the island sometimes mistakenly refer to it as "St. Lucia," the name of a neighboring island. Before the era of modern communication, people in the southern parishes claimed that news was a day old by the time it reached St. Lucy. During a cold spell in January 1996, when temperatures at night fell into the low 60s, people joked that folks in St. Lucy and neighboring St. Philip, being so far north, must be suffering from frostbite. Historically, the relative isolation of Barbados' rural parishes resulted in different speech patterns; St. Lucy was said to have the most distinctive. Nowadays, radio, television, cell phones, e-mail, social networking websites, and the ease of movement and contact with other Bajans have all but erased them.

In a study of how Barbadians perceive different parts of the island, geographer Robert Potter found that most people dislike the north, viewing it as backward. St. Lucyians would not agree. The words they commonly use to describe their parish are *safe, kind, friendly, sharing,* and *quiet.* It is a place where most people still know their neighbors and where animals staked out to graze at night are safe from thieves (although people do carefully lock their doors). A neighbor of ours who spent half his life in Bridgetown put it this way, "In St. Lucy you don't find the competitive struggle that goes on in town. Here people are relaxed, and life is slow. You're surrounded by relations, and you have lots of people pulling for you." In 2000, nearly three-quarters of St. Lucy's residents had been born in the parish, although this represents a decline from the previous census.[3]

St. Lucy's terrain is divided between a flat coastal plane and a terraced, hilly interior. Ocean swells pushed by relentless trade winds pound the tall coastal cliffs pocked with small caverns and fissures, forming blow holes that send great jets of spray upward when the waves surge in. Because spindrift (sea spray) is blown inland, the land nearest the cliffs along the northeastern fringe of the parish is saturated with salt, and little vegetation grows there giving it a barren, lunar look. Farther inland, as the salt lessens and the soil thickens, palm, coconut, casuarina, and mahogany trees and clumps of sea grape green the countryside, although rainfall is low and the sour grass that mantles the ground is dry and brown most of the year.

Because Barbados was never physically connected to any other landmass—unlike Trinidad which was once joined to South America—all of the indigenous plants on the island reached the island as seeds carried by ocean currents or in the stomachs of migrating birds. St. Lucy's rolling interior is cut by steep gullies or ravines that were once underground caverns whose roofs have collapsed. Since villagers have stopped cooking with wood, the ravines have been reverting to bush and forest. Many contain native plants that some people still use to make "bush teas" or medicines. The reforested ravines also provide a rich habitat for vervet monkeys that originally arrived aboard ships from Africa. Seeing monkeys always brightened our day, but they are the bane of villagers whose fruit and vegetables they eat and destroy.

Gully vegetation. (Photo by Sharon Gmelch)

Vervet monkey, the bane of many farmers. (Photo by George Gmelch)

Most of St. Lucy's residents (98 percent) are of African descent. After emancipation in 1838, former slaves were free to settle anywhere. In reality, there was no place to go since virtually all the island's arable land was owned by existing plantations, few jobs in Bridgetown were available for the newly freed, and few people had the means to emigrate. Consequently, most people ended up working for their former plantation masters and living in settlements known as "tenantries," usually located within a kilometer of the plantation "Great House." They were given a house plot on marginal plantation land and a small wage in exchange for their labor. The anthropology students we have placed with families sometimes have been the first whites in memory to have lived in the community. And during their first few weeks many students are very aware of their skin color, often for the first time. They are inevitably the objects of curiosity and until they become known by name; many villagers refer to them simply as "white girl" or "white boy."[4]

A sizeable white population once lived in the parish; until the mid-19th century the owners and overseers of St. Lucy's 32 plantations were white as were the descendants of their indentured servants. Most had come to Barbados in the 17th century from Ireland, England, and Scotland, having been given passage to Barbados in exchange for signing contracts that tied them to a single employer for up to ten years.[5] After fulfilling their labor contracts, they were given a small parcel of land or enough money to buy it. Some St. Lucy place names, such as Glendalough Street near Josey Hill (named for Glendalough, Ireland) reflect this past.

# The Village

St. Lucy's villages are generally quiet places. The day often begins shrilly, however, with a rooster's crow, followed by a chorus of hungry cows and sheep. Soon human voices and music are added to the mix as windows are opened and radios and televisions are turned on, spilling the morning obituaries, gospel music, calypso, and pop into the streets. Although some people have been up since 4:30 AM, the village comes alive at about 6:00 with little seasonal variation. (Barbados lies so near the equator—13°5′ north latitude—that the sun rises and sets at about 6:00 AM and PM throughout the year.) The relatively cool hours of early morning are filled with activity. Passing by friends' homes, neighbors shout out greetings and check on the elderly: "Trotman! You there?"; "Mrs. O'Neale! How you spend the night?" Others greet one another in the street with "Mornin'," receiving an "Ah'right, okay" in return.

Some people are outside watering or weeding their gardens before the day heats up. Still others are out exercising: three or four women walking together at a brisk pace, single men running along the road. Others fork the land in preparation for planting, creating high furrows in the rich dark soil. Some make their way to the news seller's house or mini-mart to buy the *Nation* or *Advocate* before retiring to their porches to read. Meanwhile, boys feed and briefly exercise their families' dogs, while the women of the house cook breakfast, iron uniforms, and ready their other children for school. Before long, the children burst from doorways and make their way to the bus stop, where they stand color coded by school—blue uniforms for St. Lucy Secondary School, peach for St. James Secondary, and here and there a distinguished Harrison College grey and white. The luckier ones are driven to school or catch lifts in a neighbor's car.

Adults with jobs outside the village either drive to work or gather at the bus stop.[6] Women who stay at home soon disappear indoors to tidy up, prepare the day's meal, or work in the garden, while men without formal jobs work the land or gravitate toward the rum shop or the shade. During the day the main sounds are the deep-throated bleats of black-bellied sheep, punctuated by the honk of the bread man's truck, the buzz of the postman's motorbike, and the distant grind of a government bus. And so the day goes, until the second flurry of activity occurs in late afternoon with the return from work and school.

There are approximately 30 villages in the parish. More are named on the map, but many of these are tiny places, more place name than actual population center, while others are so close together as to meld into one another.[7] Most villages are former tenantries. Some still bear British names of the plantation they sprang from: names like Allmans, Babbs, Benthams, Fosters, and Harrisons. Other village names such as Seaview, Mount View, Rockfield, and Church Hill reflect location and landscape. Along St. Lucy's west coast, the villages of Half Moon Fort and Fustic developed as fishing and boat-building communities and are oriented to the sea. Fishing boats are still made on the beach just south of Half Moon Fort where the day's catch of flying fish, kingfish, and dolphin are landed and sold along the road. Most of St. Lucy's other villages are oriented to the land.

In some areas, sugarcane still dominates the landscape with fields lining both sides of the circuitous roads. Once the cane is harvested, the land takes on a different character. Its contours and shapes, previously hidden behind walls of grass-like cane, become visible. For the first time since the previous harvest oncoming motorists and buses can see each other at a distance rather than looming up unexpectedly around corners. The color of the land also changes from lush green to yellow and brown as the fields are covered with dried-out cane leaves, referred to as "trash."

The settlement pattern of Barbadian villages is an untidy affair. Some houses line the roadside; others are scattered beyond the road and reached by

Fishing boats (above); the flying fish (opposite), are one of Barbados' most popular foods. (Photos by George Gmelch)

footpath or dirt track. They lack recognizable centers. When we first arrived we sometimes had difficulty identifying villages, since our conception of what one looked like had been forged in Mexico and Ireland, where we had done our earliest fieldwork. Villages in the Mexican highlands, for example, are laid out in a grid, with a central plaza built around a large Catholic church. Nothing like this exists in Barbados, where the settlement pattern has been shaped by the piecemeal sale of plantation land over the years and by the division of private land into new house spots for sons and daughters. Nevertheless, there are places where people informally gather and social-ize—mini-marts, rum shops, bus stops, corners, shade trees, and, at night, under streetlights.

Village housing in St. Lucy. (Photos by Sharon Gmelch)

# Homes

One notable feature of village housing is its wide variation, from tiny chattel houses to small wooden bungalows (also known as "board" houses) to large, masonry "wall" houses. What is unusual from an American perspective is seeing the large and small side by side. In North American communities, especially in suburbs, homes in a given neighborhood are generally of the same size and price range—a pattern that reflects the de facto segregation of population by class and income. In Barbados, the distinction between "wood" and "wall" housing has been an important social marker. "Barbadian society," notes Barbadian historian Trevor Marshall, "divides itself into those that live in board and those who live in wall houses." Wall houses, because of their greater cost, size, and permanence, have higher status. It states for its owner, "I not only own this house, but I own the land on which it sits." We have met people in different parts of the parish who proudly told us that their parents or grandparents had built—often with money earned by working on the construction of the Panama Canal or in post–World War II England—the first wall house in their village.

The largest houses in St. Lucy usually have been built by return migrants or by families with substantial remittances from family members working overseas. The large wall house of one of our neighbors, Marcus Thornhill, is an example.[8] As a young man, Marcus made six trips to the United States as a migrant farmworker, picking apples in New York's Hudson Valley and beans in Connecticut. Living frugally, he saved two out of every three dollars he earned, which, with an additional loan from a relative, he invested in a taxi cab on his return to Barbados. For more than 20 years he has driven a taxi six days a week and is often away from home 12 hours a day. Nearly all of his savings from his first years back went into the construction of his house, which he built during vacations and on Sundays, with the help of family. It is always being improved and now boasts a new detached garage and work area, upgraded bathrooms, and a new kitchen with granite countertops, high-end appliances, and custom cabinetry. He also saved enough to help send his two daughters to university; one earned a PhD.

Most of St. Lucy's residents—like most Barbadians—still live in more modest, four- and five-room homes. Twice as many St. Lucyians (22 percent) as Barbadians as a whole live in houses with only one or two rooms;[9] their homes are simple and economically built with old roofing material recycled as fences and surplus cement blocks used to create raised garden beds. But St. Lucy is changing rapidly. New construction and large homes are going up throughout the parish. This was the most visible sign of change we saw in 2010, and when we asked friends and former neighbors how the parish had changed in the last decade, they all immediately said "new houses."

Despite differences in size and material, Bajan homes share certain features. The rigid separation between the indoors and outside, characteristic of housing in northern latitudes, is noticeably absent. This is particularly true of

Chattel house being converted into a wall house (top) and a newer village bungalow.
(Photos by George Gmelch)

board houses in which the thickness of a single one-inch plank is all that separates occupants from the outside. Inside you can feel strong winds buffet the house and hear the rain beating loudly against the roof. The sounds of bleating sheep, gospel singing from neighborhood churches, and tree frogs and crickets at night easily penetrate the walls. During the day, windows and doors are usually open, allowing the breeze as well as insects and other creatures inside. One village house we rented had four resident green lizards that we came to know well; each morning we would awake to find some portion of the group staring down at us from the wall above our heads. Homes tend to be noisy. The walls in board houses are thin. Some have partitions that do not extend to the ceiling and curtains rather than doors separating the rooms. Consequently, the sounds of television, radio, stereo, and conversation spread throughout the house.

Barbadians describe themselves as house proud, and St. Lucy's residents are no exception. Flowering shrubs and ornamental plants such as poinsettia, bougainvillea, and hibiscus border many front yards. People paint their wood homes regularly, often at Christmas, with their "galleries" (front porches) and windows trimmed in a contrasting color. They also sweep their homes frequently and do not wear shoes indoors. Interior walls are decorated with calendars, family photographs, and plaques with religious sayings such as "God is my copilot." The homes of older Barbadians sometimes have photographs of the British royal family. Souvenirs and other memorabilia reveal the places families have visited or the countries where sons and daughters now live—a statue of Big Ben or the Empire State Building, an ashtray from Blackpool, a pennant from Niagara Falls. And homes are always being upgraded; it would be difficult to find a village or even a single street in St. Lucy that did not have a new house going up or an older one being enlarged or improved.

## Land

The vast majority (87 percent) of St. Lucy's householders own the land on which their homes rest.[10] Land ownership is highly valued. Throughout the Caribbean, as many social scientists have noted, the ownership of land was once the most tangible expression of freedom. When villagers are asked about the importance of land, they often describe it in terms of security: "If you own land, you always have somewhere to live"; "As long as you have land, you will always be able to feed yourself"; "Land is better than putting money in the bank."

The importance of land, however, seldom translates into keeping other people off your land as is often the case in North America, especially in wealthier neighborhoods. Except for actual house sites, most privately owned land in the countryside is open, and people are free to cross it. Footpaths, worn down to the bare earth or coral rock, are evident in most fields and are frequently used as shortcuts. Fences—apart from those that separate two households' yards—are uncommon, and property boundaries are often difficult to make out. A hedgerow of *khus khus* grass may be planted along the border, but more often boundaries are marked only with a small iron stake driven into the ground and, formerly, by red painted rocks placed at each corner. Owners who are living abroad or who, for some reason, are not using their land often give permission to others to graze sheep and cows there, which also helps keep the land fertile. A piece of flat land below our village, on which the Ignatius Byer Primary School today stands, was once a large pasture. When its owner died and his heirs did not make use of the land, men and boys from the area played soccer and cricket there and some families grazed their sheep. The new owners had no objection as long as no one built a permanent structure that might have made it difficult for them to reclaim the land or sell it.

# Chapter 2

# Colonialism, Sugar, and Slavery

$\mathcal{B}$efore discussing contemporary life in St. Lucy, it is important to know something about Barbados' history. We begin with a brief discussion of the Amerindians who lived on the island for 2,000 years prior to its "discovery" by Europeans. Then we turn to the island's colonization and the basic patterns of Barbadian slavery and colonial life. By spanning two centuries of history in two dozen pages, we inevitably oversimplify patterns of considerable complexity and gloss over variations that occurred over time. We urge readers who want more than a brief overview to consult the primary scholarship, notably the writings of Hilary Beckles (1990), Jerome Handler (2009), and Handler and Frederick Lange (1978), for Barbados; and B. W. Higman (2011), Franklin Knight (1990), and Sidney Mintz (2010), for the Caribbean generally, to name just a few.

## European Contact and Amerindians

The first Europeans to visit Barbados early in the 16th century were the Spanish or Portuguese, who documented little about the island's indigenous population other than the existence of many settlements. When English mariners arrived in 1625, followed by an English settlement party two years later, the island was uninhabited although material remains pointed to its recent occupation. The question of what happened to the Amerindians continues to perplex archaeologists. It is well-known that elsewhere in the Caribbean and Central America, Amerindian populations died rapidly of European diseases such as the flu and measles, for which they had no immunity; others were taken by slave raiders. Still others fled.

19

Although there were no Amerindians living on Barbados when the English colonized it, small numbers were brought from South America during the early years of settlement.[1] Anthropologist Jerome Handler suggests that both Europeans and later, enslaved Africans learned fishing and intertidal gathering techniques from Amerindians, including using poisons to fish and harvesting sea turtles by turning over the females as they came ashore to lay eggs.[2] It is also likely that hammocks, used widely by the English from the earliest days of the colony and later by African slaves, were acquired from them. Richard Ligon, who lived on the island from 1647 to 1650 and provided the most thorough descriptions of Barbadian life in this period, notes that by tarring "the strings of our hammocks . . . we avoid [ants] better than in beds."[3] (Early Barbadians also lit smoldering fires under their hammocks to ward off ants and biting insects.) But the greatest contribution of Amerindians to the development of Barbados was probably domesticated plants, notably sweet potatoes, tobacco, maize, cassava, pineapple, and cotton. Cotton and tobacco were to become the colony's first major cash crops, until they were supplanted by sugarcane. Whatever borrowing of ideas occurred between Amerindians and the colonists did not last long, however, as Amerindians again disappeared from the island.

Barbados' earliest English settlers relied on indentured servants and laborers from England, Scotland, and Ireland to work their small tracts of land. Most were men and women with poor prospects at home who had signed labor contracts of two to ten years in exchange for a promised parcel of land or a start-up sum at the end of their term. Some had been kidnapped and forced into servitude. The harsh living conditions they endured in Barbados probably differed little from the later treatment of African slaves, although the whites only sold their labor for a period of time and their children did not inherit their status.

The economic objective of the English in Barbados was to produce an export crop. The colonists first tried tobacco. High prices on the London market incited "tobacco fever" throughout the Caribbean. For a short time, tobacco dominated the island's economy so much that Barbados was once described as "wholly built on smoke." But Barbadian tobacco was of poor quality; it was described by one European observer as "the worst that grows in the world."[4] Once the London market became saturated with high-quality tobacco from the American colony of Virginia, Barbados could not compete. By the 1630s its colonists had switched to cotton, which was also in great demand in England. A visitor to the island in 1632 wrote that "the trade in cotton fills them all with hope."[5] But, as English planters on other islands planted cotton, glutting the London market, prices plummeted. Barbadian planters then turned to indigo, a plant from which a rich blue textile dye is extracted. Like tobacco, indigo was grown on small holdings that could be managed by one person using the labor of only one or two indentured laborers. Before long, however, oversupply again led to declining profits and the search for yet another export crop.

# The Sugar Revolution

In the early 1640s Barbadian planters turned to sugarcane, a decision that revolutionized the island's economy and environment. Some sugarcane had been grown previously as a minor subsistence crop, cattle feed, and fuel. But it was the Dutch—some of them Sephardic Jews who had been heavily involved in sugar production in Brazil—who helped Barbados' colonists with the capital, technology, and markets to get large-scale sugar production off the ground.

With sugar, Barbados' planters believed that they had found, at last, a truly profitable staple and one that wasn't hostage to short-term price fluctuations. Sugar was in great demand as a sweetener; with the colonization of India and the Far East, coffee and tea had become popular drinks in Europe. Sugar cultivation did not require great skill, nor did the crop deplete the soil as did tobacco and cotton. The relatively gentle topography of Barbados, in contrast to the mountainous terrain of neighboring volcanic islands, was also ideal for its large-scale cultivation and for transporting the crop and its products to port for shipment to Europe.

Sugar did more than make many colonists prosperous. It radically transformed the landscape, the size of landholdings, the class structure, and the demographics of the island. Sugar for an export market could only be grown profitably on large estates; hence, wealthier planters bought out the smallholders. In just 30 years the number of smallholdings declined from a high of 11,200 in the mid-1640s to 2,639 by 1679. Some sugar estates, however, were formed by the opposite process. Very large holdings were broken up into more manageable, but still large, parcels of 300 to 500 acres. Sugar was so profitable that most of Barbados' arable land was put into cultivation, growing a combination of sugarcane and food crops. Within a few decades after the introduction of sugarcane, Barbados had lost most of its original forest; Turners Hall Wood, located in the hilly center of the island, is said to be the only remaining area (ca. 40 acres) of indigenous flora.[6]

Sugar cultivation and the manufacture of rum and molasses required an enormous amount of unskilled manual labor during "crop time" to cut, transport, and quickly process the cane. Few laborers, however, were needed during the off-season. Since there were not enough white indentured workers in the West Indies to meet the labor demand, planters began buying African slaves, who, because they did not receive a wage, were cheaper to support during the off-season. Dutch merchants were then the leading traders in the Caribbean, and the Dutch West Indies Company was the major purveyor of slaves. By the mid-1600s the growing efficiency of the slave trade also made African slaves an economical alternative to indentured labor. Planters could buy the lifetime services of an African and their offspring (although mortality rates were high) for a little more than they paid for a seven-year contract for a European. Furthermore, the length of service required of indentured laborers

Detail of St. Lucy from early 17th century map of Barbados designating plantations by name of owner—there were a total of 285. The vignette at the top depicts a planter chasing runaway slaves. Richard Ligon is believed to have redrawn the map from an original made by John Swan, the island's leading surveyor of the time. (From Richard Ligon, *A True and Exact History of the Island of Barbadoes* [1657]; Courtesy British Library Board)

was steadily being reduced, and their interest in coming to Barbados was waning since little land was available for acquisition after their period of servitude was over.[7]

Despite high mortality rates, Barbados' slave population grew dramatically, from about 6,000 in the mid-1640s to nearly 50,000 by the end of the century. Meanwhile, more than 30,000 whites left the island. At the beginning of the sugar revolution in the 1640s Europeans outnumbered Africans by as much as five to one. Four decades later Africans outnumbered Europeans by three to one. Barbados changed from being over 90 percent white, including indentured servants, before the sugar revolution to being 70 to 80 percent black and slave within a century. Not all blacks were slaves, however. A decree issued in 1636 by the governor of the Barbados and his council

Bridgetown laborers tighten hoops on casks of molasses in 1940. (From Anne Langley, "British West Indian Interlude," *National Geographic* [1941])

stated that "Negroes and Indians, that came here to be sold, should serve for life, unless a contract was before made to the contrary." This suggests that a few Africans may have had the same legal status as white indentured servants. It also points out that Amerindians were also brought to the island to work on its plantations.[8]

The spread of sugar estates transformed colonial Barbados into a classic monocrop plantation society, with thousands of enslaved Africans producing sugar, molasses, and rum for the markets of Great Britain and North America. So successful was sugar production that the value of the island's exports to England exceeded that of any other West Indian island. Furthermore, by 1697 "Little Barbados, with its 166 square miles," wrote historian (and later, the prime minister of Trinidad and Tobago) Eric Williams in *Capitalism and Slavery*, "was worth more to British capitalism than New England, New York and Pennsylvania combined."[9] How Barbados and the other New World colonies were viewed by their European masters can be seen in British philosopher and economist John Stuart Mill's observation that "Our West Indian colonies . . . cannot be regarded as countries, with a productive capital of their own . . . [rather] they are the place where England finds it convenient to carry on the production of sugar, coffee, and a few other tropical commodities."[10] In short, the colonies were looked on as outlying agricultural or manufacturing estates that belonged to the home country.

With power rooted in its ownership of the island's sugar estates and in its control over commerce, Barbados' planter class, or plantocracy, put its stamp on society. On other sugar islands it was typical for landowners to set up their estates so that they could be run by others—namely, a resident manager, bookkeeper, and "attorney"—which allowed them to return to England. Their income gave them a comfortable life, and they enjoyed a higher social standing in England than they could have if they had remained in the islands. In Barbados, however, a greater proportion of owners lived on the island and managed their own plantations.

Barbadian planters, states Barbadian historian Hilary Beckles, "were proud of their English ancestry and held firmly to what they understood to be English values . . . they dressed in the finest of English clothes which were wholly unsuited to the tropics."[11] But, they were isolated and conservative in their ways, and each generation became more acculturated to the creolized ways of the colony. Thus, on their visits to England, they were often received as "distant cousins who had been amputated from the trunk of civilization."[12] They had developed a distinct dialect of English, and in England they were talked about as having been "Africanised." In Barbados, of course, political power was concentrated in their hands, and their belief in white racial superiority and their God-given supremacy shaped most of their attitudes and guided most of their actions toward their African laborers. They were "colonists," with a status accorded to them in Barbados that they did not and could not have in the "mother country."

# The Slave Trade

An estimated 492,729 Africans were shipped to tiny Barbados between 1641 and 1807. This exceeds the number of Africans shipped to North America during the same period, although it is unknown how many of these persons were transshipped to other Caribbean or North American areas.[13] They came primarily from present-day Ghana, Togo, Dahomey, western Nigeria, and neighboring territories in West Africa. The better-known ethnic groups from which they came include the Ashanti, Edo, Ibo, and Yoruba. It is nearly impossible, however, to determine the precise origins or the proportions of slaves from each ethnic group; the slave traders recorded only the numbers of slaves shipped from each port, not the locations where they were captured.

In the early years of the slave trade some Europeans formed raiding parties to capture Africans, sometimes luring them onto ships and then sailing off. In later years the Europeans relied on Africans, who had practiced a type of domestic slavery before the arrival of white traders, to provide captives. As historian John Thornton notes in *Africa and Africans*, "The institution of slavery was widespread in Africa and accepted in all the exporting regions. And the capture, purchase, transport, and sale of slaves was a regular feature of African society. This pre-existing social arrangement was as much responsible as any external force for the development of the Atlantic slave trade."[14] The raiders were paid for their services with European "trade goods": brightly colored woolen and cotton cloth, firearms, tallow, powder, tools, brass kettles, lead bars, tobacco, rum, and beads.

Firsthand accounts of ship captains give testimony to the extraordinary efforts of Africans to resist capture and enslavement. In the words of Thomas Phillips, the captain of the *Hannibal* which set sail for Barbados in 1694 with a cargo of enslaved Africans:

> The Negroes are so willful and loath to leave their own country, that they have often leap'd out of the canoes, boat[s] and ship[s], into the sea, and kept under water till they are drowned to avoid being taken up and saved by the boats, which pursued them. They have a more dreadful apprehension of Barbadoes than they can have of hell . . . we have likewise seen divers [diverse] of them eaten by the sharks, of which a prodigious number kept about the ships in this place. . . . We had about twelve Negroes did wilfully drown themselves, and others starv'd themselves to death: for 'tis their belief that when they die they return home to their own country and friends again.[15]

The ships sometimes spent several months on the coast collecting a full cargo of slaves before setting sail across the Atlantic. While trade goods were being off-loaded, the ships' carpenters constructed extra decks where the slaves were to travel, "lying prone all night and most of the day, for there was no room to stand upright."[16] During the first century of the slave trade conditions were particularly horrible. The captives had little space and no choice but to foul their own place; by the time they arrived in Barbados many people were covered in sores. On many ships the crew "danced the slaves" once or twice a day, a form of forced exercise that involved bringing the captives on deck, often temporarily removing their chains, and forcing them to jump up and down to the accompaniment of African musical instruments, primarily the drum, in order to restore their circulation.

To prevent mutiny, security on the ships was tight. A recent study estimates that during the transatlantic slave trade about one in ten ships experienced a revolt of some kind.[17] Most revolts took place within a week or so of leaving the African coast. Twice as many took place on the coast as during the long "Middle Passage" between Africa and the Caribbean itself, but since ships usually spent twice as long on the coast gathering slaves as they did crossing the Atlantic, revolts were equally likely to occur during any phase of the voyage. The "flux," or amoebic dysentery, also caused many deaths. The English slave ship *Hannibal* lost 320 slaves to flux during its two-month, 11-day voyage between the island of St. Thomas and Barbados.[18] The African death rate during Middle Passage varied. On the 35 ships surveyed by historian David Galenson, mortality ranged from 1.5 percent to a high of 26 percent on one ship destined for Barbados.[19] The mean proportion of slaves who died in transit for all thirty-five ships was 12 percent, a figure roughly consistent with the overall average mortality rate on all ships throughout the several centuries of the transatlantic slave trade.[20]

On arrival in Barbados, Africans were sold directly from the ship. Olaudah Equiano, an Igbo who was captured at the age of 11 by slave raiders near his village in present-day Nigeria, described his arrival in Barbados:

> At last we came in sight of the island of Barbados, at which the whites on board gave a great shout and made many signs of joy to us. We did not know what to think of this . . . many merchants and planters now came on board, though it was in the evening. They put us in separate parcels and examined us attentively. They also made us jump, and pointed to the land signifying we were to go there. We thought by this we should be eaten by these ugly men, as they appeared to us; and when soon after we were all put down under the deck again, there was much dread and trembling among us, and nothing but bitter cries to be heard all the night from these apprehensions. . . . They told us we were not to be eaten but to work, and were soon to go on land where we should see many of our country people . . . and sure enough soon after we were landed there came to us Africans of all languages. We were conducted immediately to the merchant's yard, where we were all pent up together like so many sheep in a fold without regard to sex or age. As every object was new to me everything I saw filled me with surprise. What struck me first was that the houses were built with storeys, and in every other respect different from those in Africa: but I was still more astonished on seeing people on horseback.[21]

In a subsequent passage Equiano describes the sale of his shipmates to a local planter and his astonishment at the callousness of his buyers, who "without scruple" separated husbands from wives and parents from children, "most of them never to see each other again." Richard Ligon described Africans being sold in Barbados in his *A True and Exact History of the Island of Barbados:*

> The planters buy them out of the ship, where they find them stark naked, and therefore cannot deceive in any outward infirmity. They choose them as they do horses in a market: the strongest, most youthful and most beautiful yield the greatest price. Thirty pounds sterling is a price for the best man Negro, and twenty five, twenty six, or twenty seven pounds for a woman; the children are at easier rates.[22]

Contemporary accounts suggest that slave owners in the 18th century expected up to one-third of their new recruits to die within their first three years in Barbados. Since the mortality rate in these early years was so high, plantation owners relied on a steady supply of African captives. By 1780, however, enough children were being born to slave mothers and surviving to meet Barbados' plantation labor demands. The slave trade was also coming to an end, leaving planters little choice but to wean themselves off their dependence on it.

# The Sugar Plantation

Barbados' sugar estates were agro-industrial enterprises that grew sugarcane and then processed it into marketable products: sugar, molasses, and rum. Plantations were fairly self-sufficient. They grew most of their own food, had enough artisans to produce and maintain their agricultural and manufacturing technology, and were able to transport products to port. During most of the period of plantation slavery in Barbados (1650s to 1834) there were on average 400 medium to large plantations. Slightly over 50 percent of plantations were between 100 and 300 acres; only 6 percent were larger than 500 acres. Most of these plantations had slave contingents of between 100 and 200 people. A significant number had slave populations in the 200s, but plantations with more than 300 slaves were relatively rare. There were also many hundreds of smaller plantations or farms, depending on the time period, with under 50 acres, and these had far fewer slaves.[23]

On a typical plantation the planter and his family lived in the "great house" or "mansion house." Nearby were the quarters of the overseer and bookkeeper. Grouped around the central "plantation yard" (also called the "mill yard" or, simply, the "yard") were the sugar mill (usually a windmill),

A typical plantation yard drawn around 1840—after emancipation. From left to right, it shows laborer or ex-slave houses, the pond from which both slaves and livestock drew their water, the plantation house, the boiling house, and the windmill. ("Ashford Plantation, Barbados, 1830s to 1840s"; courtesy, Mildred Hart Higgins and Jerome Handler)

boiling house, storerooms, workshops, and often stables, cattle pens, and other small buildings serving a variety of needs. Near the plantation yard was the slave village or settlement—the so-called Negro yard. Nearby was a pond that served as a water supply for both slaves and livestock. But the most visible feature of the plantation was the windmill, the source of energy, which turned massive rollers that crushed the cane squeezing the juice out. The juice then passed through gutters to the boiling house where it was processed through several "coppers"—huge cauldrons—all the while being stirred by the slaves, until it was reduced to a thick brown mass of sugar crystals and molasses.

About 75 percent of a plantation's slaves worked in the fields. These "field slaves"—the backbone of the plantation economy—were typically divided into three gangs. The first, or "great gang," composed of the most able-bodied men and women, performed the hardest physical labor. During the five-month harvest season, they cut the cane and transported it to the mills for processing. In the off-season they tilled the fields, dug cane holes for a new crop, planted cane and food crops, and collected animal dung and carried it to the fields for fertilizer. The second gang, composed mostly of adolescents, performed lighter tasks such as weeding the fields and planting corn and other food crops. The third gang, often known as "grass gatherers" or the "meat pickers gang" (*meat* meaning "fodder"), was composed of children. They did the lightest tasks, such as collecting grass and fodder for livestock and tending the sheep, goats, and fowl. Older women, whose age or infirmities had led to their retirement from the gangs, were assigned to do domestic chores for other slaves. They tended infants for mothers who were in the fields, cooked meals for the small children, and served as midwives and as "sick nurses" in the plantation's infirmary.[24]

During the harvest season most field slaves worked six days a week, sun up to sun down, with two breaks during the day when a meal, usually consisting of yams or potatoes, corn, salt fish, and a pint of molasses and water was served. It is important to remember that, while there was a general understanding of how plantations should be run, each owner or planter had his own way of doing things, and, consequently, there were differences in what planters expected of their slaves and in how they treated them. Not all slaves worked in the fields; there were also skilled artisans and domestics. The latter two groups generally had more ample food rations, some privileges, and generally better treatment. Blacksmiths, carpenters, coopers, and masons performed highly valued jobs in the sugar manufacturing process. Domestics such as butlers, doormen, cooks, maids, washers, nurses, and attendants ran every aspect of a large household. William Dickson described the distinctions or ranks among the slaves on the Barbadian plantations he observed in the 1770s: "Although slavery, properly speaking, admit[s] of no distinction of rank, yet some slaves live and are treated so differently from others, that a superficial observer would take it for granted they belong to classes of men who hold distinct ranks in society."[25] Some skilled workers and domestics, he claimed, lived in such comparative ease and plenty that they did not "feel any of the hardships of slavery." The inequalities were such that for a domestic slave to be sent from the great house to work in the fields was not only a demotion but also a severe form of punishment.

> The great body of slaves . . . are generally treated more like beasts of burden than like human creatures; since they cultivate the land with no assistance from cattle and suffer every hardship which can be supposed to attend oppressive toil, coarse and scanty fare, bad lodging, want of covering in the wet season, and a degree of severity which frequently borders on, and too often amounts to, inhumanity.[26]

Like planters elsewhere, Barbadian estate owners preferred slaves born in Barbados to new imports from Africa. Those born into slavery, largely because they had known no other life, were regarded as more tractable and useful. New captives from Africa, many of whom were wrenched away from family, kin, and community, knew well what freedoms they had lost and had to be "seasoned" into slavery, a process that involved, in Dickson's words, "getting over the heart breaking transition to a state so new and distressing to them as West Indian slavery."[27] Africans were more likely to rebel and run away, and their mortality rate was higher than locally born slaves. The preference for Barbadian-born slaves was reflected in market prices; an island-born slave, male or female, was valued up to twice that of an imported slave. By the late 1700s the vast majority of slaves were Barbadian born.

Barbadian plantations maintained a more even ratio of men to women than was true for other Caribbean islands. The sex ratio on the 89 Barbadian plantations that Jerome Handler and Frederick Lange analyzed stood at 48 males for every 52 females.[28] Many planters made a deliberate choice to maintain an even sex ratio, perhaps realizing that not only were women productive fieldworkers but also that having an ample supply of women could mean less competition among the men, less tension, greater social stability, and more offspring. In the words of Richard Ligon, "We buy them so as the sexes be equal: for, if they have more men than women, the men who are unmarried will come to their master and complain, that they cannot live without wives. And he tells them that the next ship that comes, he will buy them wives, which satisfies them for the present."[29]

In the African societies from which the slaves came, polygyny—in which men may have more than one wife—was often the ideal, although it was usually achieved only by older and wealthier men. On Caribbean plantations slaves maintained their preference for polygynous unions. Men and women, notes Beckles, "had no reason to believe this norm should not continue," and, consequently, men kept one "wife" on their plantation and sought others on other plantations.[30] It is evident from the advertisements planters placed in newspapers when they sought help in locating a runaway that they knew of this practice. Ads often mentioned the names of a male runaway's "wives" on other estates as clues to his possible whereabouts. The *Barbados Mercury* on 3 May 1783, for example, stated that a runaway named Grigg had "a wife at Mrs. Ann Walker's called Binah, and another at the Pool Plantation of Mr. Graemes."[31]

By the early 18th century on most Barbadian sugar estates there was some continuity in slave life. Generations were born, raised, and died on the same plantation. This "allowed for the emergence of grandmothers and great-grandmothers as matriarchal figures on estates, empowered with tremendous moral and social authority in the slave yards."[32] It also meant that black Barbadians could know their family lineages and traditions. Toward the end of slavery some planters also promoted Christian marriages; unions sanctified by the Anglican Church were, of course, meant to be monogamous. Many whites opposed blacks being married in the church, since it would mean the couple was Christian and no longer "heathen," which would make it more difficult for planters to justify enslaving them.

The lives of slaves were controlled by "slave codes," a series of acts passed by the Barbados Legislature whose members were elected on the narrow franchise of race, property-ownership, gender, and religion. It was composed, in other words, of white male Christian merchants and large landowners. Their main concern was to protect the economic and political interests of their class. In 1661, "An Act for the better ordering and governing of Negroes," which was to influence the early slave codes of South Carolina, Virginia, and Maryland, formed the legal basis of slave–planter relations and sought to structure the social order of the plantation. Its racist preamble described slaves as "heathenish," "brutish," and a "dangerous kind of people" whose "wicked instincts" needed to be repressed. The codes tried to control many aspects of the slaves' existence, from prohibiting them from beating drums and blowing horns to restricting their travel off the plantation, which in early years was allowed only if they obtained a pass or written testimonial from the planter. The code even went so far as to require that every slave house be "diligently searched . . . once every week," presumably to prevent theft and foil plans of rebellion. Slaves were legally defined as "real estate" and therefore could not own property. Yet, what the codes required and what was actually done in everyday life often differed considerably.

The codes gave planters the right to punish slaves in almost any way they deemed fit—branding, whipping, splitting their noses, or removing a limb. Under a later revision of the slave code a master could willfully kill his slave and receive no sanction other than a fine of fifteen pounds. If the slave died in the course of being punished without the planter's intent to kill there would be no fine at all. Slaves who stole property or who struck or threatened a white person could be put to death, and many were. They received no protection from the courts, and it was not until the early 19th century that they were even allowed to give testimony against whites.

# Resistance to Slavery

Just as Africans resisted capture, slaves in Barbados resisted enslavement. Running away, or "marronage," was a fairly common individual response to the ill treatment of an abusive driver or overseer or when the general hardship of their lives had become intolerable. Others ran away to join lovers and children on other estates. Some ran away with the intention of permanently escaping, while others needed temporary respite and left with the knowledge that they would be recaptured. Notices in Barbadian newspapers seeking information on missing slaves suggest that running away was a common form of resistance. The following is a fairly typical advertisement, published in the *Barbados Mercury* on 3 March 1783: "Runaway from Ashton Hall, St. Peter, one Negro wench, Sarah Clarke. Has been seen in B'town several times with a tray of clothes on her head, she is working as a washer woman . . . reward for her return."[33]

Slaves could escape to plantations where they had spouses or friends who would conceal and look after them. Barbados' gentle terrain and limited forest cover, however, provided relatively few places for "Maroons" or runaway slaves to hide. On a larger island, like Jamaica, runaway slaves could more easily hide in the mountainous interior. Some Barbadian slaves ran to Bridgetown and tried to "disappear" in the crowds. Men were more likely to run to the towns, while females favored the country, presumably seeking refuge in the slave villages of other plantations. Their chances of permanently escaping slavery were greatest if they had some skill, which would make them employable. A third, but more difficult, runaway option was to flee to another island aboard one of the interisland boats.[34]

If a runaway dressed well and spoke "good" English, he or she might pass as a "freedman." Ads placed by planters in the *Barbados Mercury* often mentioned the linguistic ability of runaway slaves. One public notice placed by Benjamin Pemberton for a runaway "wench" noted that she "speaks very good english" and was likely to pass as free. Some whites in Bridgetown knowingly hired runaway women as domestics. Conversely, an advertisement for an African-born runaway informed the public that she could "speak little or no english, having been purchased from a Guinea ship about ten months ago."[35] She enjoyed two months of freedom before being captured.

Some blacks and mulattoes of mixed African and European ancestry had been freed since the early years of plantation society. Many were former slaves who had been set free by their owners; others had been born free. In either case they were never numerous. In 1748 there were little more than 100 free blacks and mulattoes in Barbados; by the end of slavery they constituted only about 6 percent of the total population. Moreover, most free blacks lived in Bridgetown and its immediate environs.[36] There would have been very few in St. Lucy or other distant parishes.

Most runaways were eventually recaptured, usually within three months. The captives were taken to Bridgetown and placed in "cages"—prisons especially constructed for runaways—until they were picked up by their owners. While in prison, they were sometimes sexually and physically abused by poor white guards. Despite the high rate of return and the floggings and brandings they received on their recapture, some slaves chose to run away repeatedly. That one in every five runaways managed to avoid detection and escape permanently is testimony to the solidarity and support networks that must have existed in the black population. Their success also gave hope to others.

Resistance also took the form of acts of violence against whites. A slave woman was convicted and executed in 1768 for trying to kill her master, with whom she had had a sexual relationship. There are other accounts of household slaves poisoning or attempting to poison their owners. Resistance to slavery also involved sabotage and the destruction of plantation property. In 1815, for example, a domestic slave, "set fire to the bed and curtains" of the great house on the Griffith estate, with the intention of burning it to the ground. Slaves sometimes set fire to cane fields. But the most common acts of defiance were feigning sickness to avoid work or stealing plantation property, which was then sold at weekend markets and on street corners in town.

## Organized Slave Revolts

Several alarms of possible slave revolts (1683, 1685, and 1702) and two major conspiracies (1675 and 1692) on Barbados were discovered before the insurrections could take place. In 1675, for example, African slaves on several estates plotted to overthrow the plantocracy and seize control of the island. The rebels had been planning their revolt for three years, but just eight days before the insurrection, a few whispered words were overheard by a house servant, who reported the scheme to her master. An inquiry led to the arrest and eventual execution of 100 people for their participation in the conspiracy. After the alarm of 1702, the nature of black protest changed, and there were no more attempted revolts until 1816.[37]

The strength of Barbados' military system, which included local militia regiments, made organized resistance difficult. Every plantation was required to employ one white tenant to serve in the militia for every twenty black slaves it owned. Some slaves who whites considered "trustworthy" also served in the militias.[38] Frequent visits by both the British imperial army and navy to the island also acted as a deterrent to slave rebellion. Other factors were Barbados' good network of roads, which reached every corner of the island and its settlement pattern with plantations spread fairly evenly across the landscape, each within sight of another. This made mustering and moving the militia across the island easier, if and when needed.

Factors internal to the slave community, notably improvements in living conditions, also may have lessened the urgency of revolt. William Dickson, a reasonably informed observer, was fascinated by the refusal or inability of slaves to organize violent rebellions during the 18th century. He gave 11 reasons for slave quiescence, the first being the greater patience of island-born slaves, who outnumbered "imported slaves." He also believed the large white female population (much larger than on the other islands), "who are on the whole more lenient than men," produced a more civilized treatment of slaves and a more contented population.[39] Black Barbadians were certainly not happy with their lot during the 18th century, but they were relatively better off than in previous generations. They adapted to slavery as best they could while extracting concessions and freedoms from their masters whenever possible. They fought the system in a variety of ways but did so individually rather than collectively. The reduced threat of violence was welcomed by whites, who no longer felt the same acute fear—"the corporal dread of blacks"—that had been a part of planter–slave relations in Barbados in the earlier era.[40]

This respite from violence ended, however, with the slave revolt of 1816. Carefully planned by enslaved men and women on several estates and plantations, the rebellion began on the evening of April 14—Easter Sunday—when cane fields were set afire at the Bayley plantation in the southeastern parish of St. Philip. This attack on the economic basis of the plantocracy quickly spread to most of the southern and central parishes (Christ Church, St. John, St. Thomas, St. George and parts of St. Michael), eventually destroying one-fifth of the crop. The government declared martial law, and local militia and imperial troops stationed at the garrison in Bridgetown launched a joint counteroffensive the following morning. Colonel Edward Cobb described the insurrection in a letter to James Leith, the governor of Barbados, on April 25:

> On arriving in the Parish of St. Philip, I found that the system of plunder and devastation, which had been pursued by the Insurgents had been very alarming in its extent and ruinous in its consequences. Canes, Plantations, Provision grounds, a few dwelling houses and works on some of the states, in that and the neighbouring Parish of Christ Church having been involved, in a general flame whilst household furniture of every description, Rum, Sugar, Wine, Corn, and every species of food which had been stored were promiscuously scattered in the Roads and Fields near to the dwelling house, with a rapidity and destruction that evinced the fury of the insurgents . . . [41]

In the end, the revolt was put down. One white civilian and one black soldier from the West India Regiment—an all-black branch of the British Army—were killed as were 120 slaves; another 144 slaves were later executed and 132 were sent away to the British colony of Belize.[42]

# Slave Life Outside of Work

Although the daily routine and much of the behavior of slaves was circumscribed by the colonial state, slave masters, and the requirements of plantation work, slaves did manage to have lives of their own. Music and dance were two essential aspects of life in the Negro yard, and slaves arranged dances, especially on weekends and on holidays such as Christmas and Easter. Other diversions became possible as planters realized that many laws could not be enforced and that their slaves worked better after entertainment; as one contemporary account asserts, "They went through work with greater cheerfulness without expression of any weariness than if they had rested all night long in their huts."[43]

Not surprisingly, many features of slave culture reflected African traditions. Often noted examples include the veneration of ancestors, certain mortuary rites and burial practices, belief in evil magic, spiritual practices used in healing, and basic beliefs about the afterlife and the way the world functions. African traditions were also reflected in the architectural style of the early houses that slaves were forced to build for themselves on the plantations and in child rearing, cooking and dietary practices, and weaning and naming practices. Slave music was influenced by African patterns in its use of drums, rattles, and the rhythmic clapping of hands. Dancing was very similar to West African dance in its explosive nature and physical expressiveness, involving body contractions and strong pelvic movements. Barbadian slave culture, however, was no more wholly African than white planter culture was wholly English. The beliefs and practices of slaves were increasingly syncretic. That is, they combined and blended elements from their African homelands, from the creolized slave plantation community, and the creolized English planter society that controlled much of their daily life.[44]

The shift from a population with a majority of Africans to a Creole population in which Barbadian-born and raised slaves were predominant, occurred earlier in Barbados than it did in most other islands. By 1817 only 7 percent of Barbadian slaves had been born in Africa; the comparable proportion was 36 percent in Jamaica and 44 percent in Trinidad. A likely result is that Afro-Barbadians adopted many European cultural norms quicker than Afro-Jamaicans or Afro-Trinidadians. Two examples often cited are the smaller proportion of African words in the Barbadian vocabulary and the absence of African-derived religions such as Haitian *voodoo* and Trinidadian *orisha*. The Anglican Church also discouraged blacks from following practices that were alien to Europeans or that appeared pagan. The slaves selected for higher-status jobs in plantation houses and for specialized training in a skill most likely came from the ranks of those who had, outwardly at least, become acculturated to European customs.

# Emancipation

After years of agitation by British humanitarians, with support from some economists who argued that slavery was inefficient and wasteful, the British Parliament passed a law in 1833 calling for the freeing of all slaves in Britain's colonies on August 1, 1834. Slave resistance, culminating in open

These thatched wattle-and-daub houses in the Scotland District of Barbados in the early 20th century (top) are similar, if not identical, to the most common type of slave housing on the island in earlier periods (Library of Congress, Prints and Photographs Division, Frank and Frances Carpenter Collection, LC-USZ62-95078). A plantation yard (bottom) with windmill-powered cane crushers and piles of cane refuse or "bagasse" in 1940. (From Anne Langley, "British West Indian Interlude," *National Geographic* [1941])

revolts in several islands, including the slave revolt in Barbados in 1816, also convinced legislators that the time for emancipation had come.

How the transition to freedom was to take place was left up to each colonial legislature. The Barbadian legislature, not surprisingly, opposed the British Parliament's plan to free all slaves. Slavery was still profitable, and white planters feared that they would be bankrupted if they no longer had slaves to operate their estates. As a result, a compromise was reached with Parliament in which slaves over the age of six would become "apprentices" for several years after emancipation, during which period they would acclimate themselves to wage labor and continue to work on their plantations for three-quarters of the workweek. During the remainder of the week they were free to work for wages. The compromise produced widespread discontent on both sides. Some planters drove their former slaves harder than ever, giving them inadequate food rations, since they were no longer concerned about their long-term health. Many owners refused to support children under age six, since they were granted immediate freedom under the emancipation act and owed no labor to the plantations. Slaves, it was said, became insolent, insubordinate, and slack in their attitudes toward work. Recognizing the problems of apprenticeship, the Barbados House of Assembly, in May 1838, agreed that all apprentices should be declared free. In August over 70,000 Barbadians of African descent celebrated the end of slavery. As the lyrics of a then popular folk song attest: "licks" (whippings) and "lock-up" (jailings) were "done wid," "jin-jin" (the young Queen Victoria) had "set we free."

It could be expected that, once granted their freedom, the former slaves would scatter and seek work far away from their former plantations. But 50 years after the end of slavery most black Barbadians still lived on plantations and worked in agriculture. Their choices were limited. Most arable land on the island in 1838 was already owned, and jobs in Bridgetown were scarce. Emigration was an option for some, but it was fraught with uncertainties and meant separation from community and kin who remained in Barbados. Also, legislation was passed in the 19th century that made immigration difficult to impossible for many. As a result, most blacks were forced to stay on the same plantations they had worked on as slaves. Usually, they received a small wage and a house spot in a "tenantry" (a collection of houses) on marginal land in exchange for their labor. Many present-day villages in rural Barbados, including those in St. Lucy, were originally tenantries.

# Chapter 3

# From Sugar to Tourism

$\mathcal{S}$ugarcane is a giant perennial grass. Domesticated in New Guinea, it is currently grown in many parts of the world. Together with sugar beet, it supplies "every inhabitant of the globe . . . with more than 50 grams of sucrose per day," the equivalent of about 8 percent of the average individual's total food energy intake.[1] Sugarcane and its primary products—sugar and rum—have dominated Barbados' economy for more than three centuries. As recently as the 1970s, a majority of St. Lucyians worked on nearby plantations, and many cultivated small plots of sugarcane and vegetables at home. Today, few work in sugar, and most young people disdain all agricultural work. Nationally, sugar's contribution to Barbados' gross domestic product (GDP)—the cumulative value of all the goods and services the country produces—has declined dramatically, from 21 percent of the country's GDP in 1960 to just 1.5 percent in 2000.[2] When we returned in 2010, just two sugar factories were in operation and there were noticeably fewer fields planted in cane.

The sugarcane harvest officially begins when the island's remaining sugar factories notify growers that they are ready to receive cane. The timing is based on laboratory analysis of the sucrose content of cane samples taken from the fields of each plantation. Sugarcane is harvested by machine and by hand. Manual cutting yields more cane per acre, since machines inevitably waste some of the crop by not always cutting the stalks low enough to the ground. Mechanical harvesters, which can weigh 10 tons, also compact the soil, thereby reducing future yields. But machine harvesting has the advantage of speed and lower labor costs. It also avoids the problem of finding labor. Once the harvest begins, the factories run round-the-clock until it is completed several months later. For those living near or passing by a sugar factory, the molasses and burnt caramel smell of refining sugar is pungent and unmistakable.

In our anthropology field programs we always arranged for students to cut cane with a plantation crew. Spending a few hours in a cane field gave

Student tries her hand at cutting cane with two Barbadians. (Photo by George Gmelch)

them an understanding of the work that no amount of reading could. It is hot, sweaty, and onerous. To protect their skin from "prickers" (cow itch), insects, and the sharp edges of the cane blades, fieldworkers wear gloves, long-sleeved shirts, and long pants with the cuffs tucked into their socks despite the heat. Using a machete-like knife called a "collins" or "bill," they cut the stalk off at its base with one swift blow, then strip the stalk of its blade-like leaves, and lop off its top. Cane cutters often suck on chunks of cane as they work for energy and liquid. By the end of the day they are exhausted, especially during the first few weeks of crop season before their bodies have become accustomed to the exertion.

Traditionally, only men cut cane while female fieldworkers "headed," or carried, bundles of cut cane to where it would later be picked up. Once enough cane has been stacked in piles, a "loader" (a tractor with a mechanical arm) drives through the fields to load it into trucks or "carts" pulled by a tractor. Invariably, some canes fall off on the trip to the factory; during crop time, rural roads are littered with crushed stalks.

An average worker can cut about three to four tons or about half a truck-load of cane per day. Typically a small group of men, seldom more than five, work together as a "gang" and divide their earnings. When one person cannot keep up, takes a longer break, or does not return promptly from lunch, there is inevitably friction, and the gang may dissolve. "You don't really make that much money in a group," explained Junior Brathwaite. "People might just be a body, and not really work hard. It's not easy out there in the hot sun, and some people can't handle it. Then what happens is that the ones that work

Unloading cane in the yard of Portvale sugar factory. (Photo by George Gmelch)

hard carry the ones that don't work hard, and you make less money." Today, there are far fewer cane workers and harvesting is now largely mechanized.

On reaching the factory, the trucks and tractor-drawn carts bulging with canes drive onto a scale to be weighed. Their loads are then lifted off by an overhead crane, the cane stalks making their way onto a conveyor belt that carries them inside the mill. Although Bajans speak of "sugar factories," what actually takes place is not so much a manufacturing process as a conversion process, in which canes are crushed to produce a liquid, which is then converted to a solid (sugar). The process yields sugar, molasses, and two by-products—dried cane fibers, known as "bagasse," which fuel the factory's boilers, and "mud" (foreign matter), which is returned to the fields as fertilizer. The yellowish sugar is loaded into tank trucks and, just as in colonial times, taken to the port for export to Europe for further processing. Molasses is transported in tank trucks to rum refineries on the island like Mt. Gay, which is located in St. Lucy, where it becomes the raw material for making Barbados' famous rums. Molasses is also used in cattle feed and to make industrial alcohol.

## The Decline of Sugar

In 1961 there were 244 sugar plantations in Barbados and nearly 28,000 small farmers,[3] of whom about 90 percent grew sugarcane. At independence in

1966, sugar was still the most important source of foreign exchange. By 2000, the number of small farmers growing sugarcane had dropped more than ten-fold. Residents of Josey Hill—which is located on an uplifted terrace providing a panoramic view of St. Lucy's coastal plain—who previously could sweep their arms from west to east while describing the cane fields that lay below, in 2010 could point to only a few. Throughout Barbados, once arable land lies idle or is being taken out of production for housing and tourism developments.

Agricultural work holds little appeal for the youth today. "Working on the land is now considered beneath young people," a disgruntled 60-year-old villager told us. "They dream of landing a job in New York City." Reflecting on his youth, Marcus O'Neale—now in his 80s—said:

> Back then, there used to be more workers than work. Now there is more work than workers. The young just don't want to work in the fields. In my day that was all you could do. The only choice you had was which plantation you were going to find work on. You couldn't get further away than you could walk, because there was no way to get there other than on foot or bicycle. There was no other opportunity for employment, no stores, no restaurants, and no hotels like there are now.

When 20-year-old Rudolph Hinds was cutting cane for the first time in 1994, he explained why he had no plans of ever doing it again. "People think that cane cutters are stupid. . . . You can come onto a girl, talk to her in a deep voice, and tell her nice things, then you tell her what you do, that you cut cane, and suddenly she ain't interested no more. People have no respect for you." Nowadays, most of St. Lucy's younger residents would rather be unemployed than work in the fields even if jobs were available.

What happened to sugar? Beginning in the mid-1960s—which some refer to as "the era of cane fires"—sugar's profitability began to decline. Most fires were intentionally set at night by cane cutters to make harvesting easier. But fire hastened the loss of sucrose and destroyed the cane trash that acted as mulch and protected the soil from moisture loss and erosion. By 1981, many estates were losing money due to declining crop yields and rising costs. Much needed wage increases for cane workers demanded by the Barbados' Workers Union also increased the cost of production. Larger plantations overcame this to some extent through mechanization, but small farmers were left in the lurch. The fickleness of overseas markets also reduced the profitability of sugar. Many small farmers abandoned sugarcane cultivation, switching to livestock or vegetables or else leaving the land idle or selling it to developers. Many larger planters also sold to developers, and today, a number of former plantations are housing estates, golf courses, polo grounds, or other tourism developments.

The expansion of educational opportunities in Barbados also contributed to sugar's decline. Since independence, successive Barbadian governments, regardless of the party in power, have emphasized the importance of education. In 2010, Barbados spent 6.7 percent of its gross domestic product on education. (The United States spent 5.5 percent.) Secondary school students are exposed to a curriculum and values that are antithetical to agriculture. Newspaper editorials periodically complain about the neglect of agriculture in the schools, yet the problem goes beyond the curriculum. The aim of secondary education for many rural parents is to provide their children with the means to avoid the toil, low wages, and stigma associated with agricultural work. "In the old days colored people had to do agriculture work," explained one villager. "They toiled hard for low wages. . . . After a man pass down that road, he don't want his children to pass that road too." Errol Barrow, the country's first prime minister, contributed to such attitudes following independence. In a May Day speech he gave in King George Park in the parish of St. Philip, he told the crowd that he hoped to see the day when he could look from the park all the way to the St. Lucy lighthouse (metaphorically, the entire length of Barbados) and not see a single blade of cane. His sentiments were taken by many to mean that sugarcane was beneath the aspirations of a new nation and that the country's future depended on tourism—which was then booming.

Barbadians' negative attitudes toward agriculture to some degree have been around as long as slavery. Anthropologist Jerome Handler, writing about freed slaves in the 18th century, noted that they shunned agricultural work because it was the "hallmark" of slave status; in the words of one 18th-century observer, "In no instance will [parents] entertain the idea of agriculture as a pursuit for their free children, the thought appears humiliating to them."[4] The association between agriculture and slavery was highlighted in the postindependence era, as the history taught in Barbadian schools became less Eurocentric and began dealing more with the Caribbean. As teachers devoted more time to colonialism and slavery, contemporary agriculture's relationship to former plantation work became even more apparent. "It has reached the point," explained one shopkeeper, "that kids are embarrassed if their parents are farmers. Some kids today won't even eat yams and potatoes because they think they're slave food, food that slaves grew and ate."

The stigma attached to agricultural work was such that villagers in St. Lucy were often reluctant to admit that they worked in the fields or once had. A student of ours described the attitude he encountered in the 1980s when asking people in his village what their occupation was as part of a survey he was conducting:

> When I asked about their previous forms of employment I found that almost no one would volunteer that they had cut cane. However, when I asked directly, "Did you ever cut cane?" many people admitted that they had and told me something like it was so long ago that I needn't write it down. . . . It was part of their past that they weren't proud of or, at least, didn't want me to record.

Some experts regret the demise of sugar. According to then Deputy Governor of the Central Bank of Barbados DeLisle Worrell, writing in 1996:

The revulsion against sugar production which seems to be fixed in the Barbadian psyche by long and bitter historical association is set to deliver a mortal blow to agriculture. . . . A modern skill-intensive agro-industry based on sugarcane, producing a range of competitive and exotic products could, with creative marketing, be a major foreign exchange earner and the center piece of diversified agriculture.[5]

The government today is working to revitalize the sugarcane industry—and agriculture generally—in a variety of ways, including marketing specialty sugars abroad, producing more molasses for the rum industry, and using sugarcane to produce bioethanol and electricity.

# Tourism

In the 1960s as growing numbers of Europeans and North Americans began to travel with the advent of jet travel, more disposable income and vacation time, and affordable package tours, the Barbadian government began actively promoting tourism. A coral island, Barbados is endowed with miles of excellent white sand beaches (unlike its volcanic island neighbors). Its low relief also means that nearly constant trade winds moderate its sunny, tropical climate. The country was also politically stable and had a high level of basic services—airport, deepwater harbor, paved road system, pure water, ample electricity, telephones—which are always important to tourists, most of whom want to travel to an "exotic" place without losing the security or

View of Carlisle Bay near Bridgetown. (Courtesy Barbados Tourism Board)

comforts of home. By 1968, 111,000 tourists were visiting the island each year. Just six years later the number had doubled, and tourism surpassed sugar as Barbados' main earner of foreign exchange. In 2006, more than a million tourists visited the island by plane and cruise ship.[6]

Tourism has had an enormous impact on the island, including the people of St. Lucy. At the present time, it is the country's largest source of income and represents nearly 20 percent of its GDP.[7] It is the most important growth-inducing factor in Barbados' economy and helps to maintain the national income in the face of oscillations in other sectors. A labor-intensive industry, it has created a significant amount of new employment.[8] On the whole, people who work in the industry as maids, waiters, gardeners, security personnel, and kitchen staff believe their jobs are good. They like the clean environment and enjoy their social interactions with tourists, although one survey conducted in 1987 found that most were not keen to see their children go into tourism as an occupation.[9] Since then, however, tourism work has become increasingly professionalized, wages have improved, and there are more opportunities for upward mobility in the industry. The Barbados Community College Hospitality Institute, which opened in 1997, offers several educational tracks each of which requires students to learn a foreign language in addition to the specific skills of their specialty—French for culinary arts, Spanish and Italian for receptionists, Spanish and German for hospitality, and the like. It also sends Barbadian students abroad on tourism internships in other countries.[10]

Proponents of tourism often talk about its "multiplier effect," pointing out tourism's indirect contribution to the economy by fostering a demand for other goods and services. For example, farmers, fishers, and merchants benefit from tourism because hotels and restaurants need to feed the large number of visitors, which creates a demand for fish, meat, poultry, eggs, vegetables, and fruit. Similarly, tourists' desire for curios and souvenirs, and increasingly for fine art, generates work for local artisans and artists. In the 1960s the largest ripple effect from tourism was in construction. Hotels, guest houses, restaurants, and other structures related to tourist services had to be built for the growing number of visitors; over half of all the construction on the island in the mid-1960s was associated with tourism.

Although there are only two small guest houses currently in St. Lucy, many parish residents work in tourism. A survey of residents' occupations in four St. Lucy villages, conducted in 1994, found that 15 percent of employed adults worked directly in tourism as maids, waiters, gardeners, security men, cooks, beach vendors, desk clerks, and hotel activities staff.[11] The nearest hotel employing people from the parish was then the 288-room Almond Beach Village, located in nearby Speightstown. Since then, additional tourist developments have been built in Speightstown such as the Port St. Charles marina. Other villagers travel farther south to work in one of the many hotels and private vacation homes that line the west coast's beaches. Still other people work in affiliated occupations such as taxi driving and construction. In

2010, the government announced a major development project for Pickerings, St. Lucy, to promote growth in the northern part of the island. It would convert 220 acres of cane fields into a large residential development, hotel, and shopping complex. Once completed, new job opportunities will open up in the parish.

# Offshore Operations

Tourism is not the only new influence changing Barbados' former plantation economy. Since the 1950s, Barbadian governments of both parties have encouraged foreign companies to set up shop on the island in an attempt to diversify the economy, reduce its dependence on sugar, and generate foreign exchange. An Industrial Development Act (1969), for example, gave foreign investors a "ten-year tax holiday, duty free concessions on raw materials and production equipment imported from outside the region, and provision of subsidized factory shells."[12] The typical export assembly operation in Barbados, however, employed young women at low wages in jobs that required minimal training and capital investment but did not bring in much foreign exchange to the country. A number of "offshore" operations have been attracted to Barbados—electronic component assembly operations, garment manufacturers, and data processers.[13]

One such operation was Wacoal, a Japanese-owned corporation headquartered in the United States that opened a factory in St. Lucy. When we visited the large cinder-block building—constructed at government expense—with our students in the late 1990s, 160 local women were sewing women's undergarments for the US market. An additional 40 employees supervised, inspected, and maintained the factory's physical plant. The garments were sold not only under the Wacoal label but also under designer names such as Donna Karan. The seamstresses earned between Bds$3.00 and Bds$4.50 (US$1.50 and US$2.25) per hour—not much more over the course of a 40-hour week than the retail cost (US$53) of one of the high-end bras they stitched. While the women earned less than American seamstresses earned or even workers at the company's plant in Puerto Rico, they earned twice that of seamstresses at Wacoal's third plant in the Dominican Republic. At the time of our visit, local management worried that the parent company would move its operation to another country if the St. Lucy plant's reputation for high quality slipped even marginally or wages rose. Sure enough, the company left the island in 2001 for a still cheaper location, citing high production and labor costs.

State-of-the-art satellite technology, which allows information to be transmitted between "offices" all over the world, has allowed Delta Airlines and Multitext, a text entry operation that is a subsidiary of a British telecommunications giant, to employ Barbadians to enter their data on computers. Barbadians now handle airline ticketing, foreign insurance claims, consumer warranty cards, and magazine subscriptions. Some companies, like Offshore

Keyboarding Corporation based in California, employ Barbadians to enter manuscripts written by North American authors into computers. Anthropologist Carla Freeman, studying women, work, and "pink collar identities" in the 1990s, found that 11 data processing firms in Barbados employed over 2,000 workers.[14] These companies were attracted by Barbados' shared time zone with the eastern United States, modern telecommunications facilities, its satellite earth station, and low-cost custom-designed office spaces and other government incentives.

For Barbados, offshore companies create jobs and bring in much needed foreign exchange. For foreign corporations, Barbados offers low wages relative to the metropolitan countries in which the corporations are based, less stringent environmental and labor regulations than North America and Western Europe, a well-educated English-speaking labor force, modern communications and physical infrastructures, and proximity to the US market. Yet, there is always competition—as the Wacoal case shows—from lower-waged Caribbean territories, including the Dominican Republic, St. Lucia, St. Vincent, and Jamaica, as well as from less-developed countries in Asia and Central and South America, where, as Carla Freeman has noted, the strikingly high accuracy rates for keyboard operators and still lower wages will likely attract business away from Barbados.[15] Low-level data entry work for Multitext has moved from Barbados to lower-wage sites, including China. "There, double and sometimes triple keying (by three typists) insures high quality work at still lower rates than in Barbados or the United States."[16]

# Work and the Local Economy

One of the most salient characteristics of work in rural St. Lucy is the extent to which households rely on several sources of income to make ends meet. The term occupational multiplicity was coined to describe this phenomenon.[17] Our students were always struck by this pattern of work because it differed so much from the middle-class American households most came from, in which one or both parents had a single occupation or profession. A student from Boston, whose father is an engineer and whose mother is a schoolteacher, found himself living with a family in Pie Corner in which his host father was a postman, a Pentecostal preacher, and a part-time farmer, while his host mother ran the family's mini-mart and looked after its many pigs, chickens, and sheep.

Having multiple skills and multiple sources of income allows many villagers to earn enough money to live comfortably. It also offers them a measure of economic security; if one job fails or is no longer very remunerative, they can turn to something else. This is amply illustrated in the household profile of Judy and Roosevelt Griffith in the next chapter. When Judy was laid off from her government job as a cleaner, she expanded her baking, which she had previously done on a casual basis, into a business. One of our students, then living with the Griffiths, expressed surprise at how calmly Judy accepted the loss of her job, describing her as "unruffled." In contrast, she claimed that her own mother in Wellesley, Massachusetts, would "have freaked out." Over the next few days she discovered that Judy's calmness was due not only to her naturally easygoing personality or even to a certain fatalism that many villagers share but also to the fact that she had economic alternatives including baking, growing vegetables, and raising pigs.

Esther Cumberbatch demonstrates how even middle-class villagers in comparatively secure positions learn additional work skills in order to have greater economic security. Esther was promoted to a top-level administrative position in the Bridgetown company for which she worked. Nonetheless, she took time out to learn a new trade:

> When I got the promotion, lots of people [at work] were jealous. Some of them wanted to know why I had been promoted when I was working there only a short time. They didn't say anything to me directly, but I heard the gossip. They talked down about me, and the least little thing I do somebody complain. I was afraid that some of their talk might get to my bosses and they might start believing it. So I decided to have a back-up, and I started a course with this hairdresser, which normally takes three months if you go every day. But I am working and can only go every Saturday, so it took me two years. Now I am finally finished. I've got it if I need it, and I can do the hairdressing on the side when I need extra money to pay a bill or want to buy something for Sandra [her daughter].

The person we usually rented a car from was a schoolteacher who supplemented his teaching salary by maintaining a small fleet of rental cars.

The economic uncertainty that villagers feel is fueled in large part by the island's dependence on the global economy. For most of its history, Barbados' fortunes were determined by world demand for sugar. Currently, they are shaped by international tourism and the operations of multinational corporations. The number of tourists who visit the island and the amount of money they spend, for example, is influenced largely by the health of the economies from which they come as well as world events over which Barbados has no control. The terrorist attacks of 9/11, for example, which fueled a worldwide financial slump and concerns about the safety of international travel, caused a 7 percent drop in visitor arrivals to Barbados in the year following the attack. While tourist numbers in Barbados eventually returned to their pre-9/11 levels, in 2010 the US precipitated worldwide recession had once again curbed tourism, raised unemployment, and, in turn, adversely affected all related economic activities such as construction and trade. So, when people learn a second trade or devote a quarter-acre of their yard to cultivating a kitchen garden, they are, besides earning a little extra income, cushioning themselves from a future recession, natural disaster, or terrorist threat in North America and Europe.

Another aspect of village life that is readily apparent is that most people work long hours. A student living in Pie Corner described the daily routines of the men and women he got to know: "No one here comes home from work, pours himself a Scotch and puts up his feet and watches the news like at home. First, there are crops to look after and animals to bring in from pasture." Although their hours are long, many Barbadians approach work differently than most Americans. To begin with, the climate is hot and the pace of life is generally slower. "When it comes to getting a job done, Bajans like to take their sweet, sweet time about it," complained a returned migrant who had spent two decades in England and become used to a different pattern of work. Moreover, as is common in many small-scale societies, people know many of the people they interact with during the course of a day and consequently mix socializing and conversation with work. North Americans and other urbanities in large-scale societies more typically treat work and non-work as separate spheres of activity.

Many household incomes in St. Lucy are supplemented by "remittances"—money sent home from family members living and working abroad. At the national level, remittances are Barbados' third largest source of foreign exchange earnings, following tourism receipts and domestic exports. In 2004, they accounted for 4.3 percent of the country's GDP.[18] Friends and relatives living abroad also help many local families save money by purchasing consumer goods for them abroad and shipping them to the island. This is a long-standing practice; many older Bajans fondly remember the parcels of clothing (much of it second hand) they received at Christmas in years gone by from family in North American and England.

Another striking characteristic of St. Lucy's villages is the wide variety of occupations its residents have, from maids to social workers, masons to mechanics, bakers to barmen, carpenters to schoolteachers and civil servants (see appendix B). This represents an enormous change from earlier generations when nearly every adult worked in the fields of nearby plantations or in sugar factories. Not that long ago nearly everyone also walked to work; today, more than 80 percent of St. Lucy's residents commute, leaving the parish each morning by bus or car. Although agricultural work has been declining steadily for Barbadians for decades, when we conducted a household census in four St. Lucy villages in 1994, nearly 17 percent of the adults continued to work in this sector as small farmers, agricultural laborers, vegetable wholesalers, or street vendors. One woman we knew bought vegetables, herbs, and eggs from neighboring farmers and delivered them to customers in the parishes of St. James and St. Michael; she also raised pigs, which she sold to hotels and supermarkets.

Many people in St Lucy maintain "kitchen gardens," growing cucumbers, beets, lettuce, cabbage, and beans for home use. Other popular crops are peas, potatoes, yams, squash, carrots, sweet peppers, "ground nuts" (peanuts), cassava, okra, *eddoes* (a variety of taro), and herbs. Popular "tree crops" include coconuts, bananas, papaw (papaya), mango, sugar apple, and breadfruit. Breadfruit trees were introduced to the West Indies from the Pacific to provide a staple food for slaves; they produce large green starchy fruits that are eaten as a vegetable and have a potato-like flavor. Which crops are grown varies from village to village, depending on microclimate, soil, and tradition. One of our students lived with a family who had a breadfruit tree and was served boiled, steamed, roasted, or baked breadfruit on 16 of his first 17 days in their home; other students never tasted it. Monkeys cause considerable crop damage, resulting in some villagers abandoning gardening. About a third of village households in 1994 raised livestock—chickens, black-bellied sheep, and pigs and, occasionally, goats and cows. Fewer did in 2010, although it was still quite common. Animals supplement the diet and save the household money, and they can be quickly converted to cash in a financial pinch. "I keep them in case of an emergency," explained Rudolph Griffith. "If the economy presses down on me, I can turn around and sell a sheep or a cow and be back on top again." Some villagers regularly butcher their own animals, taking orders from neighbors for cuts of meat.

Nearly 12 percent of the surveyed adults in 1994 worked directly in the tourist sector, primarily in hotels as maids, waiters and waitresses, bartenders, gardeners, and security guards. This figure was comparable to the national average, but higher than expected for a parish that has only one commercial tourist attraction—Animal Flower Cave, a sea-eroded cave containing sea anemones. (St. Lucy's other tourist attractions are its coastal views.) As stated earlier, many people commute out of the parish for work, often in tourism. The 31 percent of parish residents who worked in the service sector (in 1994) were also employed in jobs that catered largely to tourists. Nearly all of

Student and her home-stay mother, a resident of Josey Hill, tend her cattle. (Photo by George Gmelch)

the fares of a taxi driver we knew, for example, were tourists. Similarly, most of the sewing that seamstress Aileen Allman (profiled in chapter 4) does is for the tourism industry—making uniforms for hotel staff.

Only 5 percent of the men and women in the village surveyed in 1994 held jobs in the manufacturing sector. This was about half the figure for Barbados as a whole and reflects the virtual absence of factories in St. Lucy and adjoining parishes. With the exception of the Arawak Cement plant and the Mt. Gay rum distillery, most industry on the island is located in the industrial estates around Bridgetown, a considerable commute away. When the government built the cement plant in St. Lucy in 1985, many homes in the village of Checker Hall had to be moved. Most villagers tolerated this and the degrading of their local environment since the plant promised much needed employment. Far fewer jobs materialized than expected, and the plant lost money. Ten years later the government sold it to a Trinidadian corporation at a considerable loss. It is profitable today, however, and about 75 percent of its employees live in the parish. Its buildings, which loom above the cliffs on the northwest coast, are also used by local fishermen to get their bearings at sea. The Mt. Gay rum distillery also employs a small number of local people. The Japanese-owned Wacoal garment factory, which previously employed 160 seamstresses, as mentioned earlier, left the island in 2001 in its search for cheaper labor; its St. Lucy facility is now occupied by a small company that makes windows and doors. The Superchick processing plant that previously employed local workers is also gone.

View of the Mt. Gay rum distillery in St. Lucy. (Photo by Sharon Gmelch)

Several small businesses in the parish including some mini-marts and rum shops, a few funeral homes, two small restaurants, and a gas station provide employment for a modest number of service workers. There are no tourist hotels and only one small guest house in the parish, although the new development planned for Pickerings, noted earlier, would change this by transforming 220 acres of agricultural land into 1,161 homes, a 200-unit hotel, a care center and primary school, a bus terminal, an amphitheater, and recreational facilities. But currently, most people must leave the parish to work.

# Women and Work

At one time, all women in Barbados, except the wives of white elites, worked outside the home. It was not until the 20th century that the idea that women should confine themselves to domestic tasks at home was introduced to the black population, which some scholars attribute to the influence of the West Indian Royal Commission of Inquiry, or Moyne Commission, of the late 1930s.[19] The commissioners who came to investigate social conditions and to propose reforms, following a series of riots in the British Caribbean, brought their biases with them including a paternalistic and protective view of women. In their view, Caribbean women should be trained for marriage and should work outside the home only when necessary and then at "suitable" careers such as teaching, nursing, and social work. Women's work, they thought, should be supplemental to that of the male household head. In Barbados these "ideals" were unrealistic for most people.

The workplace is, however, similarly gendered. In tourism women are overrepresented in hotel services (maids, food servers, and reception) which are the least-skilled and lowest paying.[20] Most parish women in paid blue-collar work are usually found in domestic jobs such as sewing, cooking, and cleaning. When St. Lucy's Wacoal garment factory was still operating, all of its 160 sewers were women. The only male employees were managers and the mechanics who maintained the plant's sewing machines. Likewise, in the parish's Superchick processing plant the vast majority of poultry workers were women. Managers at both plants told us in the 1990s that few men would consider applying for these jobs because they were considered women's work. Most career women in the parish are found in traditionally female professions, the so-called caring professions of nursing and teaching. All but one of the 13 nurses and teachers in the 1994 household survey were women. At the present time, however, younger and better-educated St. Lucy women are moving into a wider range of jobs and careers, contributing to a growing gap in the experience and standard of living between older and younger women in the parish. In the country as a whole, the fact that more women than men are graduating from university has prompted talk of the need for reverse affirmative action for men. According to the World Economic Forum, Barbados had 241 females to every 100 males in tertiary education in 2005.[21] (In comparison, the United States has about 140 females to every 100 males in higher education.)

The poorest village women often work in the informal economy. This includes hair braiders and beach vendors selling homemade beachwear and cover-ups to visiting tourists. Uzil Holder, profiled in chapter 4, after working

Woman carries dried cane stalks home for fuel, crocheting as she walks (c. 1940). (From Anne Langley, "British West Indian Interlude," *National Geographic* [1941])

A woman hawker sells fresh bread from door to door in Speightstown (c. 1940). (From Anne Langley, "British West Indian Interlude," *National Geographic* [1941])

for many years in the formal economy, found herself having to make do by selling homemade bread, chicken, fish cakes, and rotis (curried potatoes or meat wrapped in a flat unleavened bread) from her home and on the streets of Speightstown. Most of the "hawkers" or vendors in Speightstown and Bridgetown who sell vegetables and fruit from sidewalk stalls are women. Hawking is attractive to some rural women because of their access to vegetables and fruit and the flexibility of the work. In a few cases, hawking is a family tradition—something grandmother, mother, daughter, and granddaughter have done. Women working in the informal economy also make do by taking seasonal and part-time work, such as picking cotton, and by pooling their resources with other household members (e.g., sons and daughters, mothers, aunts) and "boyfriends."

## Unemployment

Although we do not have reliable statistics for unemployment in St. Lucy, in 2010 the official jobless rate island-wide was just under 11 percent. The jobless rate for youths between the ages of 16 and 24, however, is about

25 percent. This high rate of unemployment among youths, according to the government, reflects a structural problem, namely, the lack of core skills in communication, numeracy, problem solving, and knowledge of information technology, as well as the lack of more technical, job-specific skills. But many youths have high aspirations after graduating from secondary school and are disappointed with the type of work and wages available to them, so choose not to work instead. While waiting for something better to come along, they live at home with their parents, helping out in small ways around the house, in the garden, and with the livestock. Some go without employment for months or years before surrendering their aspirations and accepting a job they once considered beneath them. Others eventually find acceptable work, while some emigrate to further their education or get special training.

Village elders frequently complain about the large number of young adults—primarily males—who seem to have nothing better to do than "lime" or spend their time "on the block" (hang out together). Older adults remember how hard they had to work when they were young; "It was work in the fields or don't eat," claimed 83-year-old Ralph O'Neill. Sitting with Esther Cumberbatch one morning, she "chupsed" (an expression of disgust made by sucking air in through the teeth) and pointed down the road to a derelict house where a half-dozen young men were playing cards and gambling while next door a middle-aged woman and two older men cut cane in a small field. "The young people will not even take a job for the moment," she claimed,

> like cutting cane or pickin' cotton, and put a few dollars into their pocket. No, they will not do that. They sit on the road all day, and they interfers with the young girls passing on the road in an abusive way. The only time they go into a cane field is to take cane for themselves to chew. Just look at the road, and you'll see all the peelings from the cane they've taken from the field and the field is not theirs. . . . You won't ever see them asking for work in their fields. It's so bad that the plantations now have to get workers from St. Lucia and St. Vincent because these boys here don't want to work.

Trevor Hind, 23 years old and unemployed, responds to the criticisms of older people, expressing the sentiments of many youths: "It's hard to find work now. . . . The old people say that we all just lazy, that we don't want to do no work. When they were young, there was work for all. They worked in the fields because they didn't know no better. . . . There is still some jobs cutting cane, but I didn't go to school all these years to cut cane. If there be real jobs, I'd be working."

Joblessness in Barbados has not produced social turmoil or strife. The reasons, which are complex and not easily disentangled from one another, relate to points discussed earlier. Many young unemployed adults are able to live in reasonable comfort at home. Extended households are common, and kitchen gardens and a variety of fruit-producing trees make it possible to eat relatively cheaply. There are also fish in the sea. The profile of Eric O'Neale in the next chapter, which describes the accommodations one young man made to unemployment, is instructive. Most Barbadians are also charitable and willing to help each other out. The climate also helps; temperatures seldom fall below 75°F, making clothing requirements minimal and the expense of heating unnecessary. It is also fairly easy for jobless youths to occupy themselves at little or no cost in street corner groups, playing dominos or cards, gambling for small stakes, or participating in village-organized football (soccer), cricket, and basketball. Competitive village team sports, in particular, siphon off pent-up energy and engage males in a socially valued activity, while drug dealing and drugs pull some in the opposite direction. And there is always talk. Finally, the younger unemployed seem to believe that if they just wait long enough a decent job will appear.

Dramatic changes have occurred in Barbados since independence. It is no longer dependant on sugar production. Instead, its economy relies heavily on tourism and financial services and in general is more robust and resilient. The country survived a deep recession in the late 1980s and early 1990s and the loss of 3,000 government jobs in 1991 as part of a structural readjustment agreement with the International Monetary Fund, yet it managed to repay its IMF loan in five years and is now doing quite well despite a leveling off in the growth of tourism and competition in its off-shore business operations from lower-wage countries like the Dominican Republic. Despite unemployment rates of about 11 percent for several years, Barbados has the lowest level of poverty in the Caribbean. In 2010, it became the only Caribbean and Latin American country to be categorized by the United Nations as having a "very high human development index" (HDI). The index, which measures performance on health, education, income, and other quality-of-life indices, ranked Barbados 42 out of the 169 countries for which there were comparable data.[22] The need, however, to strengthen the skills and employability of all sectors of its population—particularly young men in places like St. Lucy—remains.

# Chapter 4

# Farmer, Fisher, Baker, Maid

$\mathcal{I}$n this chapter, we introduce some of the people behind the generalizations that follow and personalize the economic patterns we have just discussed. These profiles show the hard work and creative enterprise, as well as good humor, of many Bajans. They also reveal their many ties to the global economy.

## Selwyn and Barbara Greaves: Small Farmers

Selwyn and Barbara Greaves are farmers in Peterses, a neighborhood at the edge of the village of Josey Hill. Both are tall and lean, with bodies like marathon runners. Selwyn, who also drives a truck, wears aviator-style wire-rimmed glasses and has large sideburns. Barbara has a slender face with fine features. They have two children, Damian and Richelle, and when this profile was written, May Hinds, Barbara's 80-year-old grandmother, also lived with them. Peterses has an isolated feeling to it; the only sounds are those of farm animals, the wind rustling the trees, an occasional car passing by, or the radio coming from the open window of a neighbor's home.

The Greaves live in a modest, four-room wall house. A color television sits prominently on a table between the small kitchen and the living area; it can be watched from either room, whether cooking or relaxing. They also have Nintendo, which 11-year-old Damian plays after school. Barbara was born in Leicester, England, where her mother had immigrated in 1950 at age 18 to study nursing. In 1958, when Barbara was just five months old, her parents sent her back to Barbados to live with her grandmother. "Fed up with the cold," her mother returned home three years later; her father remained in England. Although Barbara has never seen her father, he occasionally phones, and once a year he writes her a letter. She does not expect to meet

Selwyn and Barbara Greaves. (Photo by George Gmelch)

him in person, since he has never expressed any interest in visiting Barbados, and she does not wish to spend her savings on airfare to England.

Barbara and Selwyn are devout Seventh Day Adventists. Selwyn is a deacon, and both sing in the choir of the Chance Hall Seventh Day Adventist Church, a 20-minute walk from their home. They spend Saturday morning in church attending Sabbath school and the worship service; they are back again on Wednesday for an evening service and on Thursday for choir practice. As conscientious Adventists, they try hard to adhere to the church's teachings, by not working on the Sabbath (from sundown Friday to sundown Saturday), not drinking alcohol or caffeinated drinks, and not eating pork and other meat. The church also discourages its members from eating chicken and fish, which Barbara and Selwyn have not yet managed to give up entirely.

After leaving St. Clements Senior School at age 16, Selwyn learned carpentry by working with his father, but he didn't like it and soon took a job as a gardener at a complex of private guest houses along the beach in St. James parish. Three years later he was offered a job in St. Lucy, less than a 10-minute walk from his home, milking cows on a former sugar plantation that had been converted to a dairy farm. For the past eight years Selwyn has been employed as a truck driver, delivering cement, lumber, sand, and stone to building sites. But his chief interest is farming. When asked about farming,

Selwyn's eyes brighten and his voice and manner exhibit an enthusiasm that he doesn't have when talking about driving a truck or his earlier occupations.

Selwyn and Barbara are typical of the half-dozen larger-scale small farmers in the Josey Hill area. They grow vegetables on a half-acre of land behind their house and are currently looking for an acre plot to rent so they can expand their farm. Beans, sweet peppers, and cucumbers are their major crops, but they also grow okra, cabbage, and carrots. Around the perimeter of the field Barbara's grandmother grows pigeon peas; she also keeps chickens in the yard. Her hens produce about 25 eggs each day, which she sells to a baker in the village. To determine which crops to plant and how much space to allot to each, Barbara and Selwyn talk to their wholesaler and to other farmers and examine the wholesale prices being offered for different crops, which are listed each week in the island's two newspapers. Their chief strategy is to plant crops that are yielding low prices at the moment, because, explains Barbara, "By the time the price has risen back up, your crop will be ready, and you'll get a good price for it." Until this year they did everything by hand, including the heavy work of "forking" (turning over the top soil with a pitchfork). They now hire a "contract plow," that is, an individual who brings his tractor to prepare their land—plow, furrow, and "rotivate." The government also has a plowing service for small farmers, and Barbara says they could save a few dollars using it but don't because "it doesn't always come when you need it."

They have been fortunate in not losing much of their crop to monkeys. They attribute this to the farms on either side of their land producing "ground nuts" (peanuts) and potatoes, crops that monkeys prefer. Both neighboring farms lose a sizable percentage of their crop to monkeys, despite their owners' efforts to keep them away by spreading newspaper in the furrows and tying plastic bags to sticks in the ground in the hope that the noise they make in the wind will scare the monkeys off.

Both Barbara and Selwyn farm six days a week, only taking Saturdays off—their Sabbath. On most days Barbara is in the field pulling weeds, loosening the soil, and watering and tending her plants from 8:00 AM until noon, when the sun is overhead. She then comes inside to get lunch and does housework until mid-afternoon, when she returns to the field until "night closes in," around 6:00 PM. Selwyn does not get into the field until he returns home from his truck-driving job around mid-afternoon. But on most days he is able to work several hours until dusk; he is also in the field on Sunday. Together they put about 60 hours a week into their farm.

For Barbara, farming is more profitable than the clerical job she once held, and, since the garden is near home, it allows her to be close to her family. Although the work is tiring and both Barbara and Selwyn are usually exhausted by the end of the day, they find it satisfying. "The beautiful part," says Barbara, "is watching the crops grow. Sometimes you just have to stand up and admire them." Selwyn likens gardening more to a "hobby" than to a job. "With farming you always have something to do. It keeps your mind occupied, and it keeps you out of mischief. And at the end of the day you get a good bath, and you go to sleep in a hurry."

Barbara and Selwyn sell their produce to a wholesaler in the village of Bishops on the coastal plain below Josey Hill, who in turn supplies hotels. Selwyn calls the wholesaler a week before the crop is ready to be "reaped." There is no haggling, since the wholesaler always pays the price listed in the newspaper or better. The Greaves keep some of their crop for the family freezer, and, occasionally, they give or sell vegetables to neighbors.

May (Barbara's grandmother) picks, shells, bags, and sells the pigeon peas that grow on bushes bordering the field. They are a staple of Barbadian cooking, a necessary ingredient in rice and peas. She loads them in a large sack and takes them by bus to Bridgetown, where she "hawks" them, sitting on Swan Street in a place where the congestion causes pedestrians to slow down and take more notice of the hawkers' produce. On a good day May can sell 25 pints of peas at five dollars per pint and even more around Christmas, when demand is greatest. Altogether, farming yields about one-third of the family's income.

In the mid-1990s Barbara earned extra income picking cotton from January until May on a nearby plantation. Usually starting at dawn, she and a group of four or five neighbors walked to the "cotton ground" at the top of the village. They were joined in the fields by other women and some children to pick the sea island cotton that was exported to Japan, where its high-quality fibers were spun into cloth used in expensive garments. The women worked steadily, plucking the chest high cotton pods, or bolls, and placing them in a burlap bags they trailed with them as they moved down each row. The women rarely talked while picking, except when the cotton was thin. "When the cotton is good," explained Barbara, "you don't want to form a conversation because then you lose concentration on what you're doing and you pick less. And, if you pick less, you make less money. But when it's thin, you crack a joke and laugh with one another." "Fast pickers" could pick 50 to 60 pounds a day, while "slow pickers" might end up with 25 to 30 pounds. In the field Barbara worked steadily until lunch, stopping only briefly for a sip of the "frozen water" she brings with her. At noon she joined other workers in a lunch of rice and peas, macaroni pie, and bread or biscuits. Their meals were always high in carbohydrates, since they "keep you heavy so you can work for a long time." They drank homemade lemonade or *mauby*—a refreshing sarsaparilla-like beverage made from the bark of the mauby tree (*Colubrina elliptica*) and spices like cinnamon and allspice.

Barbara laughs at the stigma attached to fieldwork and joked that her nonagricultural neighbors called her "Queen of the Crop." Most villagers, she admitted, were "ashamed to be seen on the cotton ground, even though they'd like to have the money." Barbara quit after two years when cotton prices fell due to competition from other countries and fewer Barbadian farmers planted cotton.[1] Barbara could have found work outside of agriculture if she wished. She completed two years at the Barbados Polytechnic, having taken courses in typing, bookkeeping, and commerce. She also took a three-month training program to be a receptionist. And in 1989 she worked for a year in an offshore data entry house, as a "keyer"—or, in the company's vernacular, a "text operator." Barbara was one of 100 young women and one man who, grouped into clusters of four at different work stations scattered throughout a large "open office," typed manuscripts from North America— reference books, dictionaries, medical texts, and scientific journal articles— into computers. Barbara remembers becoming adept at glancing at a line of text, committing it to memory, and then typing it in without having to look back at the page. All the keyers worked fast, since "incentives" were paid if their average hourly productivity exceeded a certain number of keystrokes.

Her employer at that time, Offshore Keyboarding Corporation, is a California-based company that also has overseas operations in Sri Lanka and Grenada. Like other offshore companies, it operates in Barbados to take advantage of low labor costs. Anthropologist Carla Freeman, who studied Barbados' offshore pink-collar sector, describes the work setting:

> Their fingers fly, and the frenetic clicking of keys fills the vast and chilly room [air conditioned, for the computer technology] as Walkman-clad women work . . . at video display terminals—constantly monitored for productivity and accuracy—typing to the latest dub, calypso, or easy-listening station. The muffled clatter of keys creates a sort of white noise, and the green glow of a sea of computer screens lends a sort of Orwellian aura to the tropical setting outside.[2]

Barbara earned only twenty-four dollars for a seven and a half hour shift (or about US$1.60 per hour); the trip from Peterses to the company's plant near the deepwater harbor in Bridgetown took at least an hour each way. Only by working overtime could Barbara make the job worthwhile; she routinely worked an extra half-shift (four hours) and occasionally double shifts, in which case, after 15 hours of typing, she would take the midnight bus home, getting to bed at 1:00 AM only to rise four hours later to start a new workday all over again. When Barbara first applied for the job, she was excited, and it still looked appealing when she first started—the workplace was tidy and air-conditioned and the corporate offices were plush and gave the workers pride in being employed by a "corporation" and an American-owned one at that. Her workmates were neatly dressed and looked "middle-class" in appearance (a company requirement). But what appeared to be a good "clerical job" in the beginning was, in reality, a repetitive, semiskilled, and low-paying job only marginally better than traditional factory jobs or working in the garment industry. Before the year was out the glare from the video display terminal caused eyestrain; she had difficulty focusing, and her eyes were tearing.[3]

Barbara is content with her life at present but hopes that in the future she will "have to work less hard and be able to relax." She also hopes that her children will have things "a little bit easier."

# Sandra Broomes: Maid

Sandra is short and slender with a coffee-colored complexion and a broad, frequent smile. She has been cleaning the rooms of North American and European visitors for most of her life and seems sincerely to enjoy meeting tourists. At 31 she is the mother of two teenage girls, Fontaine and Kareen, and has never married. Never having been able to save enough money to buy a house of her own, she and her daughters live with an aunt and her sister's two sons in a humble, three-room board house on the edge of the village of Half Moon Fort. They do not have electricity. The land the house sits on is rented and is located 50 yards back from the road and the electric lines. It would cost them a thousand dollars to have a "pole" put in, which they cannot afford and have little motivation to do, since the land is not theirs. An unusual feature of Sandra's house, especially considering its small size and the absence of electricity, is a bookshelf overflowing with children's books. "I didn't get much schooling," Sandra explained. "I say that what I didn't have my children must get, and that was learning. So from the time they able to read, whenever they have a birthday or Christmas, I always buy them books."

Sandra went to school until age 14. She began work when she was 12, weighing produce and packing bags in a grocery store. During crop time she helped her mother work in the sugarcane fields "tying canes" (tying the cut stalks into bundles before they were loaded on trucks for transport to the sugar factory). She wishes she could have stayed in school longer, but her mother needed help to support her 13 children. Sandra's father was absent much of the time and contributed little to the support of the family, eventually developing a relationship with another woman. Having seen the hardship her mother endured, with little support from a man, combined with her own disappointments with men, has made Sandra skeptical about marriage or becoming permanently involved. The father of her first child went to the United States and never came back. Despite promises to the contrary, he has never written or sent money. The father of her second child comes by the house sometimes to visit their daughter: "He comes to the curb and blows the horn, and she goes out to him." He doesn't contribute to her support. As she puts it, "You got too many men here in Barbados who only want you for being their maid, to do their dirty work, and for their bed. I don't want my life to be so. I saw how tough my mother had it, and it ain't for me."

Sandra began working as a maid at age 16, in a guest house on the west coast. She stayed only a year and a half because the guest house was hidden in the trees and was always being broken into, and after a time she didn't feel safe there. She then became a maid at Heywoods Holiday Village, a 288-room hotel complex spread over 30 acres of beachfront property in nearby St. Peter, which was once a sugar plantation. For the first five years Sandra worked full-time as a maid, being responsible for 12 rooms:

Sandra Broomes.
(Photo by George
Gmelch)

You always make up the bed first, then you do bathroom—the sink and faucet, tub and toilet—the tub is sometimes not so good when people don't drain it and you have to put your hand down into their dirty water to open the stopper. Then you sweep the floor, pull the drapes, spray scent, leave, and close the door. If anything bad happens in your rooms, like the light or the froster [air conditioner] doesn't work, then management calls you to the desk and you have to answer for it.

The only part of the job that really bothered Sandra was "having to pick up peoples' dirty whatnots. Some people leave their things lying all about; even their dirty sanitary pads. That makes me very uneasy." An occasional tourist also misplaces a camera, cash, or jewelry and reports it stolen at the front desk. She is certain that some of these claims are fraudulent, that some guests do it to make an insurance claim and collect money. While she likes most of the guests she deals with, some women can be very difficult: "I don't know what it is, but nothing is ever right for them." She recounts how some female guests will claim that the sheets aren't clean and request that they be changed, when Sandra knows she changed them that very day: "I don't know what their problem is, but they can annoy you. I try not to let it enter my mind. It's better if you don't let them bother you."

Sandra takes pride in doing her job well. Most days for Sandra start at 5:30 AM. She gets up to prepare breakfast, pack a lunch for her daughters and nephews, and get them ready for school and then catches the bus down the coast three miles to work. After "clocking in," she changes into her uniform. Each hotel staff member is issued three uniforms, which are washed and pressed each night so they always look neat for the guests. Once changed, Sandra reports to her "station," the towel room, where she issues and collects 100–200 towels a day. Although the guests are only entitled to one beach towel per day, some always want two. Sandra can see no reason why anyone would need two beach towels, but rather than argue, she gives in, but with a warning that they must return both or be charged. There is much free time in the towel room, and Sandra fends off boredom by doing crossword puzzles, by reading *In and Out* (a newspaper for tourists) and religious pamphlets, and by talking to the guests. She tells them interesting places to visit, things to do at the hotel, and where not to walk at night.

After the Heywoods Holiday Resort was sold to the Barbados Shipping and Trading Company, remodeled, and reopened as an all-inclusive resort under the name "Almond Beach Resort," Sandra was kept on and returned to being a maid. She gets off work at 6:00 PM and goes directly home to prepare dinner for her kids. Often she sits on the back steps for a while and helps her aunt clean and bone flying fish, which bring in a small amount of cash during the flying fish season (December through June). Dinner is usually rice and peas and steamed flying fish. Canned corned beef substitutes for flying fish when the fishing season ends. Like most Bajan households, the family does not sit down to eat together, except on Sunday; rather, the food is left on the stove, and each person eats when he or she is ready. Without electricity they have no refrigeration and no way to preserve leftovers, so Sandra tries to prepare no more than what the family will eat in one sitting. After dinner the children often go two houses away to the home of a relative to watch television; her aunt goes off to her sister's, while Sandra reads by a kerosene light or lies down on her bed to rest and say her prayers.

On her days off—Wednesdays and Sundays—Sandra walks across the road to the ocean for a "sea bath" (dip or swim in the sea). She goes either early in the morning or late in the day to avoid the midday heat. Unlike many villagers, she can swim; she likes the feeling of the water on her skin and thinks it's healthy for her body.

Sandra's household has only her paycheck as income. She earns about twenty-five dollars (US) per day but takes home much less after taxes and other deductions. What little money is left after paying for food, daily bus fares to and from school, and clothing and shoes for her daughters goes into maintaining the house. Over a period of five years Sandra had saved enough money for the airfare to New York to visit her sister in Brooklyn: "I heard so much about America from the guests that I really wanted to go see it, and to see my sister." Her two daughters were able to travel to Florida to see Disney World with their school class, but Sandra was twice denied a travel visa by the US Embassy in Bridgetown and is now losing hope of ever seeing the States. Being denied a visa was a "major upset." She cannot fathom why Americans are able to come to Barbados so easily, while she is unable to travel to their country. Curious about why she had been denied a visa and thinking that we might be able to help, we inquired on her behalf at the US Embassy. We were told that Sandra was probably turned down because she didn't have a bank account or own land in Barbados and, therefore, "didn't have sufficient ties to the country" to convince officials that she would return to Barbados. A couple of years later, Sandra was finally granted a visa to visit her aunt in Brooklyn, but when we last spoke to her, she had not yet made the trip.

Overall, Sandra is satisfied with her life and says she will work at the hotel as long as there is a job for her. "My mother used to tell us," Sandra recalls, "never hang your hat higher than you can reach, because you could fall. If I'd tried to go too high, I might get into situations that I can't handle. And I don't want to fall." The only other kind of work that Sandra has ever considered was as a telephone operator. Her attitude, which ambitious middle-class Americans or Bajans might dismiss as fatalistic, is in fact quite realistic. With her limited formal education in an environment in which so many Bajans now have a secondary education, Sandra would have difficulty obtaining a job above her present level. Unfortunately, the low pay she receives will make it difficult for her ever to save enough money to buy a house of her own, and, financially, as she readily recognizes, life will continue to be "tough." But she genuinely enjoys going to work, where she has many friends, and she likes her job, which she asserts is more than most people can claim in Barbados or the United States.

## Eric O'Neale: Mason, Fisherman, Unemployed

Eric O'Neale, age 26, fishes and works as a mason when he can find work, which isn't often. He is of medium stature, with an athletic build and a quiet disposition. As a schoolboy, Eric never had any particular career ambition, although, he says, "For a time I fancied being in the army or the police. But, as I grew older, I learned the things they did to other people just from a simple order, and I thought it wasn't for me."

After leaving St. Lucy Secondary school at age 16, Eric learned masonry by working with his older brothers, Timothy and Malcolm. They built houses, although the work was never steady. He shared an apartment in Bridgetown with one brother and some friends. At night he would sometimes hang out in the nightclubs and pick up or be picked up by a female tourist. Most of the women he left with were German, many allegedly having come to Barbados in hopes of having an affair with a local. He sometimes moved in with them for the duration of their two- or three-week stay. "But I stopped

Eric O'Neale. (Photo
by George Gmelch)

that after a while," he said, "because of the emotions. Even though these are
short-term relationships, you get into people's lives. You develop feelings for
them and them for you, and then they have to go home. It can be hard to separate. For some guys it's an ego thing—how many women they can sleep
with. Some guys do it for the money, but I never got into that."

Having grown up in rural St. Lucy, Eric had difficulty adjusting to the
city and has vowed never to live in Bridgetown again:

> The streets are dirty, there's pollution, there is theft, and people can be
> selfish. They don't know one another, and they don't care about anyone
> but themselves. In the morning, when you are trying to sleep, people will
> drive up and beep their horn. I consider that selfish. And then there is all
> the break-ins and theft. You couldn't pay me money to live in Bridge-
> town today.

With long stretches between jobs, Eric returned home to St. Lucy to live
with his parents:

> Renting an apartment was very expensive, you have to pay around $600
> (Bds) a month, and, with what I was making, I didn't have much left
> over for anything else. My parents were getting older, and they could

use someone to help them out around the house and in the kitchen garden with things they can't do so easily anymore like forking [turning over the soil].

At home Eric doesn't pay rent, but he does help out with the family's bills.

Today Eric does home maintenance and looks for work as a mason, mainly building house extensions such as bedrooms and washrooms. He earns about Bds $75 a day, but it is often months between jobs. His passion, and a supplemental source of income, is fishing. He fishes from the cliffs, a mile from his home, beginning at dusk and not returning home until sunrise. With a large shank hook baited with a moray eel, a 200-pound test line, and a steel leader, he goes after "smooth skin" and nurse sharks. On most nights he will get at least one, usually between 50 and 80 pounds in weight. At low tide or when the sea is calm regardless of the tide, he spears fish on the reef just offshore. With a snorkel and a mask, a four-foot Champion spear gun, and a float from which he suspends a mesh bag, he swims out from one of the small bays that dot St. Lucy's rugged, precipitous coastline. Ever mindful of the treacherous currents and undertow, which keep most villagers from ever going into the sea along the north coast, Eric hunts for fish in "white holes"—large holes, or breaks, in the reef with white sand bottoms that reflect the light and contrast with the surrounding dark-colored reef. His prey are porgies, blue barbers, and chubs, generically known as "pot fish" because they are more commonly caught in fish traps or "pots." Aiming for the head and firing his spear gun within ten to 15 feet of his quarry, Eric hits his target two times out of three. He avoids the much larger and stronger tarpon or albacore, which are able to swim off with gear, unless he is very close to shore and confident of a head shot. On a good day Eric may spear 30 pounds of fish. He sells most of his catch to local families, some of whom have placed orders with him in advance. "I sell some for six dollars [Bds] per pound," he explained, "but some I sell cheaper to older people who don't have the money. I always give some to two kids who do favors for me and whose moms are unemployed [and fathers are absent]."

Eric once joined two friends in cutting cane at the nearby Spring Hall plantation, but as new cutters they were assigned the worst fields and could not cut enough tonnage to make the job worthwhile. Moreover, a work slowdown at the sugar factory meant that the canes they had cut sat in the fields for days, drying out in the hot sun and losing weight—the basis on which workers are paid. Earning little for arduous, sweaty work, they quit, and Eric returned to fishing and looking for small masonry jobs.

With his free time Eric hangs out with friends near a coral stone wall in the village. There he and his age-mates listen to music (dub, reggae, calypso), play dominoes and cards (harps, rummy, cricket), drink beer, and talk. Frequent topics of conversation are money (who has it and how it's spent or invested), women (who looks good, differences between local and tourist women), sports (cricket and football, depending on the season), family (behaviors and characteristics of village families, family problems), and jobs (who has them and how good are they). They may also watch the Pie Corner or another parish team play football (soccer) or cricket on the nearby field. And they play road tennis—a sport developed in Barbados and played with a homemade wooden paddle and a tennis ball on a small court marked out on the street. The game is halted, and the net—a plank—is removed whenever a vehicle passes. Like street corner groups in all villages, Eric and his friends also have "cookouts":

> The guys will say, "Let's cook out tomorrow." We might go over to Patrick's house and everyone brings something. I'll catch some fish; Jefferson will bring some breadfruit. We roast the fish and breadfruit over the fire and throw everything else into a saucepan and stir it together. When you're hanging out, you are trying to find things to occupy your mind, so you do little things to get your mind away from what you are not doing—working.

Eric says he is seldom bored. And, while he is able to live comfortably, although simply, at home, he prefers to be working and earning money. "When I am working and the day comes to an end, I feel better because I have done something, achieved something. It makes me feel more independent, too."

Eric says he has never had a "craving" for money, but he does dream of someday being able to save enough to own a fishing boat:

> If I had my own fishing boat, I could make up to a thousand dollars a day. Most fishermen in Barbados are very lazy. Some fish to buy luxury, but lots fish just for enough money to buy rum or their other dirty habits. In other parts of the world people catch fish by the ton; here we catch fish by the pound. If I had a boat, I'd be making real money.

His ambition suffered a setback in 1994, when his savings were wiped out by an ill-fated trip to London with his Bajan girlfriend:

> When we got off the plane [at Gatwick Airport] the English immigration man asked where I was from, why I was coming to England, and how much money I had. I tell him all the answers. It seemed okay, but then this other immigration guy came over and took charge. He asked all the same questions, all over again. Then he asked me to come to this room. I sat there for three hours—it was really cold. Then he came back and asked me all the same questions all over again. I told him all the answers—that I was with my girlfriend, who lived in London, and that I was on holiday with her—but he say he didn't believe me, and he left the room again. Maybe an hour later he came back, and I said, "Listen, if you are going to send me back, send me back now, but don't keep me in this room." He said, "Okay, I am sending you back." The trip cost me $2,100 [Bds], and I never saw England . . . except the airport.

Eric also hasn't seen his girlfriend since, though they did talk on the phone on Valentine's Day.

# Judy and Roosevelt Griffith: Bakers

Judy and Roosevelt Griffith make and sell baked goods, raise vegetables, and tend a few livestock. Until recently, Judy also had a part-time job cleaning a community center in a neighboring parish. They are in their mid-40s and have been together since she was 16 years old and he was 22. They have raised two sons and a daughter. The eldest, Trevor, is a constable in the police force; the second child, Shernell, lives in New York, where she is a caregiver to several elderly women; and the youngest, Donny, drives a van that picks up vegetables from small farmers and transports them to hotels and stores.

Judy has a soft voice and a gentle manner. Though serious and somewhat shy, she is quick to see the humor in things and likes to laugh, despite having endured a good deal of hardship. Her father died when she was four and her mother when she was seven. Before their deaths the family had been prosperous, living in the first wall house in Josey Hill, which her grandfather

Judy and Roosevelt "Griff" Griffith and student Sarah Finnerty. (Photo by George Gmelch)

had built with "Panama Money," savings from the years he spent working on the Panama Canal. After the loss of her parents, Judy was raised by her eldest sister, who today owns a rum shop at the top of the hill. But the loss of both parents, both breadwinners, impoverished the family.

Judy is one of several women of her generation in the community who take it on themselves to help elderly neighbors who are in need. She frequently stops by the homes of several old widows and a widower to visit and offer assistance. She may bathe them or run errands or shop for them when she goes to town, and, if repairs are needed on their homes, she will arrange for a tradesman to come. At Christmas she brings them each a little present, and she helps the elderly widower with his wash. "When I pass by in the road," she explains, "some people just shout out to me. They call me and ask me to do things for them. Things they can't do for themselves." People like Judy who selflessly give their time to look after people who are unrelated to them, say other villagers, are a vanishing breed. Judy and those like her are a vestige of a time when the village was a close-knit community, when people worked on the same plantations or at least at the same jobs, socialized together, and, to varying degrees, looked out for one another's welfare.

Roosevelt, better known as "Griff," has an open, friendly disposition and a fondness for greeting others with "Yeah man, how you doing? That good, good, good." He has a handsome face, with gray hair at the temples. He is missing two teeth on the right side of his mouth from an auto accident, which occurred at night near the Mt. Gay plantation. His passenger was killed, and, although the accident was not Griff's fault, friends and relatives of the deceased are still bitter toward him. The memory of the accident has caused Griff to avoid that road, even though the alternative is a longer route to town.

Griff was raised in the village of Cave Hill. Like many village boys, his ambition was to drive a bus or a truck, because, as he says, "as young boys that was mostly the only kind of work you saw outside of plantation work. You didn't know nothing else, so that's what you wanted to be." After completing secondary school, however, Griff went to the Barbados Technical Institute to study engineering and, after earning his City and Guilds certificate in 1972, found work with a Bridgetown manufacturer, Barbados Packers and Canners. There he serviced and repaired machinery and rose to the position of chief engineer before a dispute with his superior resulted in his dismissal in 1985. For the next two years he worked at home raising 35 pigs, tending a large garden, and taking people to town in his car.

When the Arawak Cement Plant on St. Lucy's western coast was completed, Griff found a job there doing maintenance. At the cement plant Griff met a fellow worker who had recently returned from a job on a Shell oil tanker. "I didn't see much opportunity to progress at the cement plant . . . there was a bottleneck [barrier]; you had to be in a certain clique to move ahead," explained Griff, "so I made inquiries about going to sea. I thought the experience would be good for me and that I'd see some of the world too." Griff applied at Shell's recruiting office in Bridgetown and, after passing the medical exam, was offered an eight-month contract on a VLCC (very large crude carrier). A week later he was on a plane to Spain and then to Gibraltar, to meet his ship, the SS *Leona*, which was hauling oil from Iran and Iraq to the West. The 35-man crew was composed of about a dozen English officers and 20-plus Barbadian seamen—cooks, stewards, pump room mechanics, greasers (motor mechanics), deckhands, and the like. As a pump room mechanic, Griff's work station was the engine room, where in the Middle East the temperatures could reach 130°F. The ear protectors all crewmen were required to wear only partially muffled the noise of the engines. The work was hot and dirty, and the hours were long, as Griff worked all the available overtime. It was not uncommon for the crewmen to put in 12- to 14-hour days. Between overtime and working on his "off-days," Griff earned about a thousand pounds a month, or three times what he had been making at the cement plant in St. Lucy. And with nothing to spend his money on during the long stretches at sea, and his food provided for, he was able to save 80 percent of his earnings. "I had a vision," he says, "that I could save enough money to finish the house." He and Judy had begun construction five years before on a wall house that sits on the shoulder of the hill with a panoramic view of the northern coast of St. Lucy, from the Caribbean Sea on the west all the way around to the Atlantic Ocean on the east.

Griff's hopes to see the countries he sailed to were frustrated by few opportunities to get ashore. Unlike freighters, which usually dock in port cities, large oil tankers, having twice the draft, must take on and discharge their cargo in deep water. "In the Gulf of Mexico," explained Griff, "the jetty is so far out to sea that you can't even see land." In many places the distance to shore, the red tape in getting a shore pass to clear immigration and a refinery pass to get back onto the vessel, and the cost of a taxi from the terminal to town made it impractical for Griff and his sea mates to go ashore. Before starting his first "contract," or voyage, however, he had a week in London on his own and was able to visit many of the places—Buckingham Palace, 10 Downing Street, St. Paul's Cathedral—that he had learned about in the British-based school curriculum that was taught in Barbadian schools during his youth. During the two years he spent at sea on Shell tankers, he was also able to spend a few days in Singapore, Rotterdam, Dubai, the Bahamas, and several cities in Malaysia and the United States.

It was during his third trip that Griff saw an advertisement in an English magazine, *Exchange and Marts,* for a home securities business, etching identification numbers on personal possessions. Interested in the idea of having his own business and being his own boss, and growing weary of life at sea, he wrote to his sister-in-law in England and asked her to buy the equipment he would need—an air compressor and a small sandblasting gun that could etch ID numbers on TVs, cameras, VCRs, automobile windshields, and the like. He called his new business Airline Security Systems and placed ads in Barbados newspapers and on radio and television. With crime on the increase, especially burglaries, he reasoned there would be considerable demand for his services. But the timing was wrong, as Barbados was entering a recession. "People seemed excited about it," Griff says, "but there was very little business. Very little."

After a year Griff stored his equipment away, never having recouped his investment. He thought he might start up his business again once the economy picked up, but since then an East Indian in Bridgetown has started a similar business, and Griff believes he would have a hard time competing against him: "In Barbados if you see a Bajan and a foreign guy both start business, more people will go to the foreign guy. We still have a small island mentality that the big country guy is better . . . and Bajans don't like to see one another get ahead." The end to Griff's hopes of restarting his business came when the Barbados police began to offer a similar identification marking service to all residents for free.

While Griff's business was failing, Judy was laid off from her cleaning job at the Belleplaine Community Center. Like most rural households, the Griffiths had always depended on several sources of income. To make up for the loss of one income it is often possible to expand into another area, just as Griff had done by raising pigs and increasing the size of his garden after being dismissed by Barbados Packers and Canners. They considered several options. At one time Judy had made handicrafts—table mats and doormats from "khus khus" grass (*Andropogon muricatus*, an East Indian grass with fragrant roots) and baskets and table mats from cane lilies—and sewed women's hats and bags, which she sold in a handicraft store in Speightstown. But the demand for them was seasonal, as many of her goods were bought by tourists during the winter months, and, besides, the store was not doing well. Judy had always made a little extra money by baking, selling her breads to the local rum shop and some villagers. She has a knack for baking, and people especially like her salt bread—the dense, un-sweetened rolls or buns that Bajans use to make sandwiches known as "cutters." So she and Griff decided to try baking on a large scale and selling beyond the village.

Working together, they have now been baking for four years. On Tuesdays and Fridays they bake all day, while on Wednesdays and Saturdays Griff sells the baked goods from the back of his hand-painted orange Toyota van. The hours are long; on baking days Griff is up at four in the morning mixing the ingredients (flour, sugar, butter, eggs, lard, essence, spice, baking powder, yeast). Judy gets up an hour later to begin shaping the dough and placing it in their homemade oven. All through the day they load and unload the oven.

Once the baked goods cool, they put them into plastic bags and load them into the van. By 3:00 PM Griff is ready to start out on his regular circuit that takes him through most of the villages of the parish—Crab Hill, Grape Hall, Pie Corner, Rock Hall, and more. Over the next six to seven hours he cruises slowly through each community honking his horn, pausing longer in front of houses of regular customers, always waiting a "reasonable amount of time," he says, to see if they appear. By 10:00 PM Griff's route has brought him full circle back to Josey Hill. Usually, he will have sold all 100 turnovers, 70 salt bread packages, 80 small coconut breads, and the several dozen cassava pone, rock cakes, and light sweets that he started out with. The surplus, if there is any, is used at home, fed to the pigs, or shared with children who pass by the house on their way to school.

Like many Josey Hill residents, Judy and Griff also have a garden and raise a few cows, pigs, and goats. They graze their cows and goats on pasture land on the coastal plain below the village. Like most livestock, they are staked out, tethered with a long rope to keep them from wandering off. Each morning Griff goes down the hill to move them to fresh grass and give them water. When the cows and pigs grow to full size, Griff has them butchered, earning upward of $1000 per cow and $500 per pig. They may keep some of the meat for home use, but they usually sell the bulk of it. Sometimes they sell the animals on the hoof, before they have been butchered, all except the goats, which, as Griff says, "You get so little money ($75 per goat) that it's not worth you sellin' them. You do better to eat them yourself." Griff and Judy grow peas, cassava, pumpkin, potato, seasoning, thyme, and peppers. The crops are mostly grown for home consumption, but they give away any surplus to neighbors. If they have a sufficiently large harvest, they will sell it to a wholesaler.

Over the next couple years, Judy and Griff expanded their baking business by adding an extension onto the house and hiring help. They also had their own label: "J & R Bakery—Quality Is All We Bake." They were proud of having gotten the business off the ground and liked being independent, but, Griff added, "Baking is not my love, not 100 percent. If someone told me a year ago that I'd be selling bread today, I'd have laughed. No, I'd rather be doing engineering, working with machines."

When we visited Judy and Griff in 2010, they had finished their house but were no longer baking. In the end, it was too much work for too little profit. Griff has returned to machinery and is experimenting with wind-generated electricity and biofuel using manure from the pigs Judy now raises. He relies on his 14-year-old granddaughter to do the research he needs on the Internet.

## Siebert and Aileen Allman: Emigrant and Seamstress

Siebert and Aileen Allman are in their late 50s with five grown children. They live in a large house in Sutherland on St. Lucy's western coast. Siebert is a modest, private man who prefers his own company and television to the rum shop or a social gathering. Some neighbors have mistaken his reserve for snobbery. Aileen is loquacious and buoyant. They come from humble origins. Siebert, for example, lost his father when he was six; his mother supported him and his sister by working as a maid in the Blackrock mental hospital. Emigration and years of hard work and saving have enabled them to enter the ranks of the middle class. Indeed, they own one of the nicest homes in the village of Sutherland.

Like many Barbadians, Siebert sought to get ahead in life by emigrating. When he was 25 he left his work as a cabinet maker and went to England. "I thought there would be more opportunities there," he explained. "With all the people here going to England, you had to think it must be good. . . . In those days you could just buy a ticket and go, since we were a colony belonging to Britain." Like most migrants of the time, he left his family behind until he

Aileen and Siebert
Allman. (Photo by
George Gmelch)

could assess what the conditions were like and determined whether they would
all benefit by being there. Soon after arriving, he obtained a job as a bus conductor with London Transport, a major employer of West Indian immigrants.

Siebert worked Route 134 from Victoria Station and Route 43 to Lon-
donbridge, each route extending about 15 kilometers out before retracing its
journey back into the city. Taking fares on double-decker buses, he remembers, was very tiring. "It was up stairs and down stairs all the time . . . [and]
you'd have to deal with people who didn't like you just because you were colored. I remember this one lady who put her fare on the seat. She wouldn't
hand it to me because she didn't want me, being a colored person, to touch
her hands." Siebert learned to ignore such racist acts, reminding himself that
there were similarly narrow-minded people back home in Barbados. The
"teddy boys" and punks, however, who got on his bus late at night after
drinking were more menacing. Some liked to intimidate immigrant conduc-
tors. After one Barbadian conductor was badly beaten by teddy boys, Siebert
did his best to avoid them, even to the point of sometimes not asking for their
bus fare. While in England, Siebert worked all the overtime he could get, as
his sole purpose in emigrating had been to earn money and improve his family's standard of living at home. With overtime he could make £30 per week;

he kept £10 for his own meals and lodging and sent the rest home. While the money was better than what he had been making in Barbados, he sorely missed the company of his family. "To put away the loneliness, I used to travel on the bus after I finished work," he recalls:

> I'd go to Trafalgar Square, Hyde Park, and places like that—anything to distract me. When I was tired I'd go home, just to lay down and sleep. Otherwise, it was too lonely. Some of my friends got involved with other women and started families in England, but that wasn't for me.

The loneliness caused him, after two years in England, to return home to Barbados. He wasn't home long, however, when London Transport's recruiting office in Barbados asked him to go on the radio and speak about working in England, to help them recruit Barbadians. To set an example, and concerned that Siebert being home in Barbados might create the wrong impression, they encouraged Siebert to return to England, offering him free airfare, his old job, and other incentives. By then (1963), however, an economic recession and rising unemployment was creating resentment in England toward immigrants. That the British government and some private corporations had actively recruited tens of thousands of Siebert Allmans to fill the jobs needed to get postwar Britain back on its feet seemed unimportant to the British working-class men and women who believed they were in competition with West Indians, Pakistanis, Indians, and other "colored" immigrants. "Things had really deteriorated for colored people in England," recalls Siebert. Some of his bus passengers were now openly hostile, and he began to overhear people call him derogatory names, including "nigger." This hostility, and loneliness for his family, caused him to return home after just one year. At home he returned to making cabinets, with limited prospects for growth in his business in a stagnant Barbadian economy.

Five years later, in 1968, Siebert and Aileen together applied to the Canadian High Commission to emigrate to Montreal. They had been encouraged by newspaper advertisements for artisans that Barbadian friends in Montreal had sent. Siebert, a skilled cabinet maker, and Aileen, a seamstress, decided they would earn more money in Canada, and, besides, Siebert said, "Aileen had never traveled before, and I wanted her to see how the other side of the world lives." They arranged for neighbors to look after their four children until they got settled and could send for them over a year later. Siebert remembers, "Aileen used to cry every day over being away from the kids. We should have brought all the kids with us . . . the Canadian government would have let us, but we didn't know that then. We thought we had to do just what the man [immigration official] said." When they arrived in Montreal, neither of them were able to find skilled work. Instead of making cabinets, Siebert ended up working on a conveyor line inspecting desks for scratches; instead of making clothes, as she had done in Barbados, Aileen now merely sewed pockets on shirts. They worked all the overtime available and sent most of their salaries home for deposit in their Barbadian account at the Canadian Imperial Bank of Commerce branch in Speightstown. With the money out of reach, they reasoned, there would be no temptation to spend it. They saved for the day they would return home and build a new house. Aileen recalls that Siebert complained a lot about the cold. Every evening at six o'clock, she remembers, "He'd turn on the TV to see what the weather was in Barbados. He'd say, 'What am I doing here? If I was home now I could go to the beach. . . .' He used to annoy me so."

But the high wages, at least relative to what they had been earning in Barbados, kept them in Montreal. It wasn't until they returned to Barbados on a holiday in 1974 that Siebert decided it was time to come home for good. They had brought along a French-Canadian friend of theirs, recalls Siebert. "When she came here and saw our home and all our family, she said, 'What are you living in Montreal for?'" She loved the climate here, the sea bathing, and all the different foods. She'd say, 'What are you trying to achieve? You have everything here.' Well, hearing that made you think different. It was then that we decided to really come home."

For three years they planned their return. Aileen wanted to stay in Montreal, but Siebert was determined that the entire family should come home together, and in the end he prevailed. They had saved enough to build a large wall house, the ambition of every migrant Barbadian. Their four-bedroom house with a veranda is perched on a bluff overlooking the quiet fishing village of Half Moon Fort and the Caribbean Sea. Like a beacon, it signals to the community below the Allmans' success as migrants. Inside the house the kitchen accessories, wall-to-wall carpeting, drapes, and sliding glass doors are pure North American. With the money they saved the Allmans have also sent all five children to college; two have done graduate work, and their son, Hugh, making use of the French he learned in Quebec's public schools, worked in Barbados' embassy in Belgium as a foreign service officer until moving back to the Caribbean.

Like many successful migrants who resettle in their home villages, they have encountered people who were jealous of their new wealth. Aileen says, "When you have traveled, people think you're rich, and they try to see how much they can get out of you. They don't know how hard you worked for your money." Malicious rumors circulated that the Allmans had won the lottery or that they gained their wealth illegally.

Siebert and Aileen opened a small general store near their home, but they had few customers, because, says Aileen, "They thought we were already too rich . . . we had a big house and two cars." After two break-ins, and with their insurance company refusing to cover their losses, they closed the shop. Aileen returned to sewing full-time, just as she had done in the years before they went to Canada. Siebert had several different jobs in Bridgetown, eventually becoming a supervisor with Rayside, a large construction firm.

Today Aileen is still sewing hotel uniforms for the doormen, bellmen, and maids at Sandy Lane, Barbados' most exclusive resort. She also sews other apparel, such as wedding dresses, for individual customers. Inured to hard work, she still rises before dawn to begin sewing and, when deadlines approach, will work late into the night. She uses some of her earnings to visit three of her children who are living abroad and to travel with them on vacations. When we visited in 2010, she had recently returned from an extended trip to Africa with her daughter.

## Uzil Holder: Roti Maker

Uzil Holder, 48, is a single mother of three children. She has a wide, pleasant face and an open, friendly disposition. She is an immigrant from Guyana, one of over 2,500 Guyanese living in Barbados, 60 percent of whom are women. There are six Guyanese households in the Josey Hill area, four of them headed by Uzil's siblings. Barbados and the former British colony of Guyana have been linked since the 19th century, when British Guiana became one of the first destinations of freed slaves in the decades following emancipation. Uzil's story is intimately tied to her immigration to Barbados and her struggle to forge a new life there.

Both Uzil's mother and paternal grandfather were Barbadian. They had migrated to Guyana in 1921, when, explains Uzil, "Things were better there than in Barbados. There were jobs in the gold fields, in bauxite [aluminum ore], in cutting cane, and there was lots of land for farming." Uzil's mother had ten children, all of whom were raised in the district of Uitvlugt (pronounced "Eyeflot"), an area of many small villages whose inhabitants rented their house plots from a single sugar plantation, the second largest in the country—"a plantation," says Uzil proudly, "half the size of Barbados."

> When we were growing up [in Guyana] all us kids were aware that our mother was Barbadian and our father's father too. We didn't have no connections with relatives in Guyana, and like all kids we wanted to know our family. The only grandparents we had, and nearly all our aunts and uncles and cousins as well, were in Barbados, so naturally you are curious about them . . . every kid wants to know his grandma and grandpa. But we were a happy family in Guyana, and as time went by my father, who was a logger, and my mother, who worked washing and ironing other people's clothes and doing home baking, improved our lives to a comfortable middle-class style with a two-storied house.

After Uzil left school at 16, she did needlework and made baskets and Sunday hats for people in the district. But it wasn't enough:

> The money was too slow in affording me my dreams of what I wanted to achieve in life. So I got my mother to purchase me a sewing machine on hire purchase [installments], and I started cutting patterns for clothing on old newspaper. I made a skirt suit which made me the envy of so many. Friends came from other districts to get me to cut patterns for them. What I earned by dressmaking afforded me the fee to attend evening classes in the city [Georgetown] in accounts.

After the course ended, Uzil obtained a job with the Booker Sugar Company as a telephonist and payroll clerk on the same plantation where she had grown up. She had a relationship with a supervisor at Bookers, and they had a child, Yolanda. They were together for six years before Uzil left him. "He didn't have a settled mind or a future that would be secure. When he joined the Defense Force, I thought it would be a lifestyle—partying, getting involved with other women—that I wouldn't like, so I broke it off."

Uzil's job at Bookers gave her the income to make several trips to Barbados to get to know her grandmother and relatives and "to see the place where my mother had come from." Every five years each employee of the sugar company was given free passage to any destination in the region, and Uzil used hers to come to Barbados. But Uzil never expected that she would settle there. Like so many emigration decisions, her moving to Barbados resulted from a series of unforeseen circumstances. It began in 1959, when her mother returned to Barbados for the first time. Uzil went along and stayed for six months, getting to know her relatives. In 1977 her mother was asked by family members to return to Barbados to look after Uzil's grandmother, who was now ill and bedridden. As Uzil remembers, "There was no one there to look after her as all the other sisters were working in the fields, and the grandchildren who were living with her were all males. There were no female children around, so they asked my mother to come. She left us, her husband, and a good house in Guyana to go to Barbados. It was a big sacrifice for her, which I don't think the relatives in Barbados ever understood."

At home in Guyana, Uzil, then 33 and with a three-year-old daughter, was trying to get out of an unhappy relationship:

> We had broken up, but he wouldn't stay away; he wouldn't leave me alone. He tormented me. I thought my temper might get the better of me and that I might do something to him that I'd regret for the rest of my life. I had Yolanda to look after. I thought the best thing was for me to get away. I thought maybe I will meet someone who will cut me out of this bad luck. I was young, and when you're young a little change can be great.

Uzil planned to stop in Barbados for a while to visit her mother, and to leave Yolanda with her, and then go on to New York. In New York she hoped to get a job as a domestic and to save enough money to do a course in cosmetology and, if that wasn't possible, to continue her training in accounting. In Guyana she had begun a correspondence course at the Rapid Results College in "accounts and commerce," but a shortage of funds and spare time had prevented her from completing it. If things worked out in New York, she would send for Yolanda. Uzil never got further than Barbados, however.

Once in Barbados her cousins persuaded her that she could do just as well there as in New York and that she wouldn't have to deal with winter. They said she would be among family. So Uzil decided try it for awhile and see how things worked out. She saw an opportunity to start a small village shop. The house in which she was living with a cousin was an ideal location for a shop—a spot where the bus turned around before heading back toward town. The bus usually stayed there for a while; its passengers would have a few minutes to come into the shop to buy something to drink or eat. More-over, there were no other shops in the village of Rock Hall at the time. Uzil and her cousin started the business together, building a wall addition onto the house. While the cousin owned the property and put up most of the capital to get it started, Uzil ran the shop. It was an instant success, and they soon expanded their inventory. Their "cake shop" soon became a small mini-mart, selling dry goods as well as baked goods and soda. As Uzil explains:

> The money we made was more than my cousin ever imagined, and that was the start of the trouble. She began to think that, with all the money coming in, maybe I was holding back some for myself—that I was cheat-ing her. One day she tells me that she wants me to record every little sale in a book, right down to five-cent candies that the children buy. Every-thing has to go into a book. Now I had 12 years experience working in an office in Guyana, while my cousin had worked in the fields. I told her we could do stocktaking every month, but she didn't know anything about running a shop. She didn't want to hear it.

Uzil Holder. (Photo by George Gmelch)

Tensions increased between them, Uzil resenting her cousin's suspicions and her attempts to exert more control and intervene more in the running of the shop. "She started calling me up at all hours to check and see if the shop was open," recalls Uzil. "She'd call at 10:00 in the evening to ask if the shop still open, and then she'd call early in the morning to see if the shop be open yet." When her cousin brought several pigs and chickens for Uzil to look after in the yard behind the shop, Uzil had had enough. "Because I was an immigrant from Guyana, even though I was a relation, she thought she could boss me around, that she could have me do whatever she wanted and that I wouldn't mind, that I would be grateful for being able to live in Barbados." Uzil believes her Barbadian relatives assumed that, because she had left her home in Guyana, her living conditions there must have been bad and she should be grateful for anything they did for her. When in fact, she says, "In Guyana we lived in an upstairs house with electricity and running water that was superior to some of my relatives' homes in Barbados. In Barbados you had to walk down the road to the standpipe to get water, and the light was a kerosene lamp. My relations had never come to visit us in Guyana, and they didn't know what we had there."

At about this time Uzil's cousin from New York City returned to Barbados, dashing any plans Uzil had of emigrating. "Even if I was to go, I now had no one to stay with," she explained. "I started looking for a job as a clerk in town." In 1980 Uzil's grandmother, who Uzil's mother had been looking after since her return to Barbados three years earlier, died. No one told Uzil's mother when the will was to be read. Only weeks later did they learn of its contents, that they—the Guyanese side of the family—had largely been left out. The house, in which Uzil, her daughter, and mother were living, had been left to a relative who had been living in England for nearly 20 years and never once returned. She came back to claim her inheritance, nevertheless, and asked her Guyanese kin to vacate the house immediately. Her attitude toward Uzil's mother and family was, recalls Uzil, "'You were asked to come to Barbados to do a job, and, now that you've done it, you should all go back to Guyana where you belong.' What really bothered me, too, was that she didn't acknowledge my mother as a Barbadian. When my grandmother died, we discovered that my family didn't mean anything to our Barbadian relatives." When Uzil, her daughter, and mother didn't immediately leave, their English-Barbadian cousin got a court order to have them removed from the house because she was concerned that if her relatives were allowed to remain, they might have a legal claim to the property. The suspicious circumstances surrounding the will made Uzil determined to stay in Barbados to make inquiries and also to help support her mother. The process dragged on for months. In the end Uzil was rebuffed by the lawyer and by the person who had signed the will as a witness. But in the meantime she had found a new job as a clerk in the shoe department of N. E. Wilson and Company, a general store in Bridgetown, and was gradually settling in.

Several of Uzil's siblings also moved to Barbados in search of better economic circumstances. "Things were getting tight [in Guyana]," explained Uzil. "The economy was going bad, and the cost of living was getting out of hand. So we grouped together and helped pay the passage of my brothers and sisters." Together the family rented a three-bedroom house in Peterses, not far from Barbara and Selwyn Greaves. The arrival of her brothers and sisters contributed to Uzil's decision to stay in Barbados.

For the past 14 years Uzil's main source of income has come from making and selling rotis (curried potato and beef or chicken wrapped in a tortilla-like shell), which was introduced into Barbados by East Indians. Much like the circumstances that led Roosevelt and Judy Griffith into baking, making rotis was not something that Uzil had planned to do. It began when she was working as a clerk in the shoe department of N. E. Wilson:

> My wages, $59 per week, were so small that I began to make pastries, jam and pineapple tarts, coconut tarts, and cheese tarts to take into work to sell to some of the other girls [employees] and to the people who worked in the stores nearby. Then I started making up lunch packets. I'd take orders from the store and prepare the lunches [pastries and cakes] before coming to work in the morning, and then during my lunch break I'd go around delivering the lunch packets. I was making more money doing that than I was from my job, so I quit the store.

She decided to specialize in making rotis, largely because there was less waste: "People can be destructive. They squeeze pastries and ruin them, so you have a lot of loss. But not with roti." In 1994 Uzil sold her rotis to restaurants, mini-marts, and a few individuals in the village. Both her daughters, Yolanda and Abigail, helped out. Every evening Yolanda—20, tall, thin, and pretty—cuts up and cooks the meat, while Abigail, 14, prepares the potatoes, and Uzil makes the roti skins. Starting at 6:00 AM the next morning, Uzil mixes the meat, potatoes, and spices and rolls up the mixture in the skins and then wraps the finished rotis in wax paper. Abigail takes some by bus each morning to the mini-mart across from her school. Yolanda delivers rotis to two restaurants in Holetown. On an average day Uzil makes about 35 rotis, for which she receives three dollars each for the meat and potato and two dollars each for the plain potato. The success of her business has waxed and waned; when a couple of her best customers went out of business, she was hard hit. In 1996, however, she managed to open a snackette in Speightstown. She advertised it with a hand-painted sandwich sign on the curb: "Uzil's Snackette for your great taste in rotis—beef and potato, chicken, lamb and vegetable—and *dhalpuri*" (an East Indian-style flatbread with a filling of seasoned lentils).

For a time, Uzil earned extra cash by picking cotton in her spare time—like Barbara Greaves did. The cotton ground was less than a five-minute walk from her house, so she could easily go there when she had time to pick. Later, she would sit with her sister Pauline and her sister-in-law Daphne, who also picked cotton, and separate the white fibers from the pods while chatting and watching television. Uzil likes to be active, or, as she says, "I don't like to sit. I like to keep moving forward."

Uzil also receives some money each week from her "boyfriend," John, who is the father of her youngest child. John is a self-employed auto body repairman who Uzil has been dating for 12 years. "He helps financially, depending on what he makes," explains Uzil. "I try to be content with whatever he can give me." The fathers of her other two children do not contribute any financial support, and Uzil has not heard from them in years. Uzil saves her money through a meeting turn (an informal credit group described in chapter 6). There are two meeting turns in Josey Hill. The one Uzil organized has eight members, about half of whom are Guyanese. The average "hand," or weekly deposit, is $50; Uzil tries to put in three hands ($150) per week, which entitles her to draw her "turn" once a month. The money she draws each month, about $600, enables her to pay her bills and mortgage on the small house and land she bought a few years ago, which she rents out.

All nine of Uzil's siblings came to Barbados. Seven have stayed in the country, with four living in the Josey Hill area. Uzil had an idea of starting a community center where young people could meet, instead of hanging out on the road, where they could learn crafts and cooking and play games—dominoes, Chinese checkers, and draughts. She planned to volunteer her time to teach needlework, basketry, knitting, and pastry making. But, after discussing the idea with a number of the villagers, says Uzil, "It got back to me that people were saying, 'What is this foreigner wanting to teach us Barbadians? What does she know?' So I dropped the idea. I didn't want to start something and have people getting abusive, calling you all sorts of names."

When asked about the future, Uzil talks about hoping "to become more settled" than she has been. Although she owns the wood frame house her family lives in, it is on rented land. She would like to purchase the land, which would enable her to fix the house's foundation and cement steps leading to the front door. She is reluctant, as a renter, to invest much money in making permanent improvements that she cannot take with her. Ideally, she would like to open her own restaurant or "snackette." The rents for business places, however, are too high at the moment, and there is little prospect of them becoming more affordable in the future. Uzil wants a better life for her children. Even though her youngest child, Michael, is being groomed by his father to follow him into the auto body repair business, Uzil believes it is important that all her children get good educations.

# Chapter 5

# Gender and the Life Cycle

*P*eople in every culture make the same journey through life, although the route may be signposted differently and different meanings are attached to the markers along the way. Gender relations, too, vary from one society to the next, even though people everywhere share the same basic survival and emotional needs. In this chapter we describe in broad strokes the major stages in the lives of men and women in St. Lucy—birth, childhood, adulthood, old age, and death. What is each stage in the life cycle like? Do men and women share the same experiences, and how do they relate to one another?

## Men, Women, and Sex

Although relationships with the opposite gender are eagerly sought by most, many village men seem to regard women with suspicion, claiming they are materialistic and devious.[1] Many women, in turn, believe that men are fixated on sex and fundamentally untrustworthy. These opinions reinforce one another, shaping expectations and behavior. One of our students was surprised, for example, when she was advised by a village friend to try to get more out of her boyfriend when she returned to the US: "You never know how long men are going to be around, so you want to get something out of the relationship," she explained. "I mean, I'm a great girlfriend. I give Stuart [boyfriend] what he wants and I cook for him. All I have to do is ask him for something, and he'll give it to me. I got him to buy me a wardrobe. You should really try to get something out of Jim [the student's boyfriend] while you can."

On the streets casual gender interaction frequently includes sexual banter or taunting (depending on the recipient's point of view). Virtually any woman who is not elderly who walks by a group of men can expect to have her body surveyed, be hissed at, and/or receive sexual offers. Anthropologists Constance Sutton and Susan Makiesky-Barrow, who worked in another part

81

of the island, found that stylized sexual banter between men and women is often enjoyed by both sexes.[2] While it is undoubtedly true that some women enjoy the banter, others merely seem resigned to it as "something men do." Still other women make an effort to avoid such encounters when they can. One young woman we know, for example, waits inside her house on nights she plans to go out until she sees the bus coming. Then she walks quickly to the bus stop to avoid giving the men who hang out nearby the opportunity to make remarks.

Among many working-class village men status comes from the "respect" and reputation for manliness they have among their peers, rather than income. Their manhood, in turn, is achieved largely through sexual conquests and a somewhat utilitarian attitude toward women reflected in Bajan proverbs "Dirty water does cool hot iron" (once a man is aroused, any woman, no matter how undesirable, can satisfy him) and "De new broom sweep cleaner, but de ole broom know de corners" (both new and old sex partners have their advantages).[3] The cross-cultural encounter that has given our female students the most difficulty has been local men's persistent and overt interest in sex. The students often felt bombarded by sexual comments and requests from younger village men, and even from some of the older professionals—including policemen, teachers, and reporters—they met for formal interviews. Likewise, our male students were encouraged by village agemates "to score." The following description from one student's field notes reveals much, not only about his experience but also about younger local men's attitudes toward women:

> The conversation last night among the men was preoccupied with sex. Every man wanted to know how many Bajan women I had scored with. They said they were going to hook me up because if I don't, my Barbados experience will not be complete. They all seemed to regard themselves as great lovers. They told many a creative story of their exploits, such as how they met this lady in a bar and she turned out to be a wild animal. They all told me I should not be shy because I would be surprised what I can get away with. They said if Bajan women think I have money, I will have no problem picking them up. Another recommendation they gave me is to lie and say that I'm a famous actor from the States here on vacation.

A female student described a similar conversation she had with a male Bajan friend:

> Basically, what X told me is that the guys think my host brother is crazy because I am living under the same roof with him and he hasn't "wocked" me yet. . . . When they see white women, the first thing that comes to their minds is sex. When I asked about that, he said that's because white women are more bold than Bajan women. For example, it would be uncommon for a Bajan woman to approach a few Bajan men and say, "Hello. How are you?" So when they see me acting that way it sends them some sort of message. He asked me if I've had the urge to have sex since I've been in Barbados. I told him no and that I have a boy-

friend back home. He tends to get really annoyed when I say I have a boy-friend, because to the Bajan man that means nothing. The common attitude is, "Your boyfriend back home, and you in Barbados now." I told X that he has a one-track mind, and he said, no, that he just wants me to become his "close, personal friend." I asked him why he couldn't just be my friend and what was wrong with talking. He said that the other guys would say that he should be "wocking" me right now. Then he said, "Per-sonally, I think I should be wocking you, too." I explained to him that in America it's common for men and women to be close friends but not in a sexual way.

How much he and his friend's attitudes were influenced by our student's sta-tus as a young, white, foreign woman is difficult to say. The homestay mother that two of our female students stayed with in 2010 had a serious talk with her son before they arrived, informing him that he was to treat them as sisters and not try to have sex with them, and this despite the fact that he had a long-term girlfriend and son. His reported response was, "But Mummy!"

Years ago most village men and women began a serious relationship for-mally. The man asked permission to meet her parents and, on the appointed day, arrived at her home; after a suitable period of conversation and a thor-ough looking over by her parents, he left. If they approved of him, the two were allowed to see each other. Parents kept a close watch on their daughters. Grace Walker, a woman now in her 60s, recalls her father's attitude toward her suitors and the onset of her sexual maturity:

> I had a very good childhood until I got to be a woman. But after I become a woman, my father feel that he don't want me to leave the house. So everybody [young men] that say they like me, he chased them off. My father was very strict. He said I mustn't run around with friends. You know, mustn't run about, going from house to house. No. No. I couldn't do that. I had to stay at home and do what I have to do—wash and cook and keep the house. From home to school and back home, and do what I have to do. Sundays we go to church and then back home, and then back to Sunday School and then back home again. . . . Two young boys write in for me, but he wouldn't permit it.

Anthropologist Sidney Greenfield's research in rural Barbados in the early 1960s found that church and school were the only locations where young men and women could meet.[4] Today, many parents in the parish still keep their daughters reined in, which is one reason so few young women are seen outdoors in the villages at night, unless standing at the bus stop in a group. Opportunities for young men and women to meet in person are quite limited, especially once they leave school. Only a few villages have commu-nity centers, and these are rarely open at night. Before streetlights were intro-duced in St. Lucy, lovers were said to have checked the calendar for full moons and arranged to meet at night in a pasture or cane field. Courting today largely takes place by cell phone, especially texting. Couples make plans to rendezvous at a concert or nightclub in Bridgetown on the weekend.

Those who attend the same church have additional opportunities to meet, since activities for church members are frequent. Church, in some families, provides one of the few socially sanctioned places for young women to mix with men. Local football and cricket matches may also provide opportunities for young men and women to meet.

At night young adults who can afford to do so travel into Bridgetown or the south coast tourist belt to attend concerts, nightclubs, and parties. Local "field parties" are also held to celebrate holidays such as Errol Barrow Day or special events like the return of an immigrant to the community.[5] Here, families and young people mix outdoors, dance to loud music, and eat fried chicken and pudding and souse. Private "house parties" with disc jockeys and sometimes live music are also held in homes or rented halls. There is always a bar and a cover charge to help organizers recoup the cost of food and make a profit; many are fund-raisers for a specific purpose, such as sending someone off the island to school.

Partygoers are disproportionately men, most of whom stand together drinking while watching others dance with the relatively few women present. Some parties are so dominated by men that young women once jokingly referred to them as "male boxes"—an apt pun, since any woman attending is soon boxed in by overly attentive males coaxing her to dance or asking for her telephone number. To encourage the patronage of women, some Bridgetown nightclubs offer women specials like free drinks before a certain hour or no cover charge on a certain night. When dancing, Bajans' uninhibited attitudes toward sex are apparent. Our students used to be startled, and the women intimidated, by the first dancing they witnessed. One student in the mid-1990s described it as "sex with your clothes on, but sex like I've never seen!" Bajan dancing is graphic; without a word or even eye contact, one or more men come up behind a woman to "wuk up," "grind," or "do the dog" to the music's pulsating beat. But cultural practices are continually changing. In 2010, one of our student research assistants wrote:

> If a girl is at a club or a frat party [in the US], she can fully expect to be dancing with her girls one moment, and then have a boy come up behind her and just start grinding with her without saying anything at all, and then, several songs later, to be dancing with a different boy. I would say the main difference in how they dance here [Barbados] is actually just talent. Bajans have incredible control over their hips. They way they "shake their booty" is just so impressive. They tried to teach us, but we really failed.

Sociologist Graham Dann reports that most Bajan men have their first sexual experiences between the ages of 15 and 17, girls slightly younger.[6] Despite the watchfulness of village parents, many young girls end up going out with men several years older. One village girl we knew was referred to by some as a "little force ripe" because of her precocious body and behavior. At age 13 she had a boyfriend who was 20. By dating at such an early age, it is not surprising that many young girls also have sex at an early age.

Although birth control is widely available, the responsibility for its use falls heavily on women; "I don't believe in it [birth control] myself," commented one 17-year-old boy. "Some girls use it nowadays, but it doesn't really concern me." Birth control pills are the most widely used form of contraception, although some village women believe they cause serious side effects: blocked arteries, "damage to your insides," and even birth defects after they are stopped. Condoms are also widely used, although even in the age of AIDS, many young village men prefer not to use them.[7] According to a neighbor who works as a clerk in a mini-mart, "They are ashamed to buy a condom, but they're not ashamed to have sex. Guys come into the store where I work and try to hide them from other customers, and even from me!" But men also resist using condoms for other reasons. Having sex while wearing one was likened by one young man to "washing your foot with a sock on." Condoms are now distributed at many public parties or "fetes" where music with AIDS awareness lyrics is often played. AIDS prevention information is also disseminated in schools, in an attempt to target young people. One concern to AIDS workers is "bashment culture," a set of attitudes and behaviors among many young girls who embrace being sexually active as a way to assert their womanhood. The term bashment refers to fast music that's good for dancing (e.g., a fast calypso is "bashment calypso").

For girls who become pregnant, especially if they are still in school, abortion becomes de facto birth control. Legalized in 1983, it is estimated that 20 percent of pregnancies in Barbados end in abortion, the rate being higher in urban than in rural areas like St. Lucy. Young women claim that it is often their boyfriends who are most in favor of abortion because they do not want the responsibility of parenthood. To many girls, motherhood defines them as women. "Some women don't want the abortion," explained a village friend, "but the men say to them, 'Well, I can't afford to have a child.' So they listen and have one [an abortion]. They love the man so bad that they don't want the friendship to break up." Most women who decide on an abortion go to a doctor, but prior to its legalization some employed their own remedies. One villager remembers trying to terminate her first pregnancy at age 15: "I went to the gully and jumped from a tree, but nothing happened." Other village women drank concoctions like coconut oil and Epsom salts. Many villagers, however, remain strongly opposed to abortion on religious and moral grounds.

Young people's early initiation into sex and lax attitudes toward birth control result in many out-of-wedlock births, although the number of teen pregnancies has gone down in recent years. Nationally, the Child Care Board estimates that 75 percent of Barbadian births are to unmarried women (the figure for the US is 41 percent). Reasons for this high figure are that many young Barbadian women do not understand their own physiology and that few parents explain sex to their children, although school programs fill in some of the information gap. Twenty-two-year-old Marcia Springer remembers being too "scared" to ask her mother a single question about her changing body or sex:

> I could never ask a question. Do you know that, when I first got my
> period, I was over at Shirley's [an aunt] house, and I didn't even know
> what it was? I never told my mother; it was Shirley that told her. Then
> one day my mother said, "Now that you got it [menstruation], you just
> keep away from boys!" That's all she ever said to me about sex.

But by not discussing sex and reproduction, children who are exposed to
adult sexual behavior may imitate their elders' behavior without understanding the consequences. When young girls then get pregnant—and go on to
become parents—they are likely to repeat the cycle.

Peer pressure also plays a role in early pregnancy and out-of-wedlock
births. By having sex with a boyfriend and becoming a mother, many young
girls believe that they are demonstrating their maturity. Motherhood has long
been the defining rite of passage into "womanhood" in Barbados. It is not
uncommon to see very young mothers proudly carrying baby daughters
wearing fancy clothing and jewelry, their hair elaborately adorned with
beads. Having a child while unmarried is not strongly condemned in the villages, unless a woman comes from a very religious home or is still very
young and in school. Her pregnancy will cause comment but will not
severely damage her reputation. (And fatherhood is likely to enhance her
boyfriend's status among his peers.) If she cannot raise her child, there are
always mothers, sisters, aunts, and even grandmothers willing to help or to
assume the responsibility. Such informal adoptions are common in Barbados
and the Caribbean.[8]

# Birth and Marriage

As recently as the 1970s, most expectant mothers in the parish gave birth
at home assisted by a local midwife. As "Nurse Phillips," a 93-year-old
retired midwife says about the village of Pie Corner, "Anybody over 50 years
old is surely one of my babies." Today, however, virtually all women go to the
hospital, and only a few folk beliefs about birth remain. Underlying older folk
beliefs was the "law of sympathy," to use J. G. Frazer's early formulation,
which he believed resulted in two main forms of magic: "imitative magic,"
based on the idea that like produces like, and "contagious magic," based on
the idea that something once in contact with something else continues to
exert an influence.[9] Eating okra (which becomes slimy when cooked), for
example, was believed to help the baby slide out. Eating too much pepper
was to be avoided because it would give a child speckled skin. Some women
still keep their child's umbilical cord. In what was undoubtedly originally an
African practice—although it is found in many parts of the world—the
umbilical cord and placenta were buried near the home, symbolically con-
necting a child to its birthplace (a form of both contagious and imitative
magic). The question "Where you nabel [navel] string bury?" is still sometimes asked by the elderly, meaning, "Where are you from?" Reflecting the

other part of Barbados' cultural heritage, infants are sometimes given silver coins for luck, a custom known as "handseling" in the British Isles.

With the birth of a child several things can happen. The new mother may remain with her parents, or she may move out and establish a household of her own, with or without the child's father. For most women the birth of a child is a good reason for a couple to start living together or to marry; for many men, however, it can be a reason to part. According to research by sociologist Christine Barrow, Bajan men regard attachments to women warily:

> Their general opinion is that women will try to find out their level of earnings, demand more than they can give, accuse them of supporting "outside women" and use "tricks" . . . to satisfy their greed. Women who "pull together with a man to build a home" or remain with him through lean times are said to be rare exceptions.[10]

Many men continue to live in their natal home into their 30s even after they have fathered children of their own. They perform parental duties when necessary, but few take daily responsibility for their children who are looked after by their girlfriends and their mothers.

Economic factors also play a role in most couples' decisions of whether or not to live together. Not everyone can afford to establish a new household. Consequently, many couples continue to live apart after their child's birth, usually maintaining a "visiting" relationship in which the man regularly visits his child and its mother at her parent's house or, if she is older, in her own home. She provides him with domestic labor (cooking, cleaning, and child care) and sex in exchange for a degree of financial support. With the birth of a second child, the man often assumes full responsibility for both his children and moves in with his girlfriend. If she has children by a prior boyfriend, however, he will usually only provide economic support for his biological children. This changes when a consensual union is formalized through marriage; then, the husband is expected to support all children present in the home and officially adopt them. In such cases the husband may demand that his spouse's children by previous unions be sent to live in other households.[11] Many committed couples delay marrying until they can afford to own a house or have a proper wedding ceremony. Bajan weddings are elaborate affairs with a full complement of attendants, rented reception hall, and a lavish feast. For many village couples, marriage ends up being the celebratory capstone to a long relationship and occurs after children have been born.

Religion also shapes a couple's attitude toward marriage. Many church-going couples of even modest means marry because they are good Christians, and Christianity promotes marriage. The following comments of Arlette Holder, a woman in her early 40s, are revealing:

> I had never given marriage much thought, because my mother and none of my sisters are married. But the older I get, the more important it becomes. Looking back on my children's fathers, I'm glad I didn't marry either of them. But I want to lead a Christian life, and the Church teach

Posing for wedding photographs at St. John Parish Church. (Photo by George Gmelch)

that you have to be married or cut out the boyfriends altogether. My boy-friend and I have talked about living together, but I will not unless we get married, which I hope will be soon.

Marriage is thus supported by religion and is a cultural ideal—the "proper" thing to do—even though many people remain unmarried for a variety of reasons.

Household composition in St. Lucy, as in the rest of the country, is often complex. Single-parent, female-headed households are common among poor and working-class villagers. Nearly two out of every three adult Bajan women in the 2000 census headed their own households. Many of these female-headed households are composed of only a mother and her children, but others consist of extended families that span three generations. The norm for middle-class and upwardly mobile villagers, in contrast, is for two-parent, nuclear family households.

Many men, including those who are married or in common-law unions, have "outside women" and father "outside children." In some cases their wives and long-term girlfriends accept the situation. This arrangement resem-bles in some respects the polygynous household structure found in many West African societies and other cultures. In Barbados it reflects a cultural ethos that still measures manhood largely by sexual prowess. Some village men are critical of this attitude, however, as the following remarks of one 26-year-old show:

It's a big thing in certain communities. Mr. Holder thinks he's a dude because he's got ten children from all these different women in the village. My friend Leonard comes up to me yesterday all proud and says, "Hey Malcolm, I got a son. When you gonna get one?" Like I gotta have one to be a man. All most men want from a woman is house tidy when you come home. Food when you want it. Clothes clean. Clothes off.

Of course, women who knowingly pursue sexual relationships with men who are living with or married to another woman share responsibility for these attitudes.

The work of maintaining the household and caring for children falls largely on village women. They are the ones who shop, cook, do the laundry, clean the house, nurture the children, and prepare them for school. Women who do not have male partners in the home control all household finances and decision making; when couples live together, decision making is shared. According to one study, the nature of the couple's union influences their household roles.[12] Couples who are married generally consider the man to be the "head" of household, while one-quarter of the women in common-law unions described themselves as the household head. Patriarchal religious teachings surrounding marriage legitimize male authority.

Village men who live separately from their "girlfriend" or "child-mother" usually contribute money to her household if they wish to maintain the relationship. Men who share a household with their partner and children typically work hard to provide materially for their family. The work profiles of Selwyn and Barbara Greaves, Roosevelt and Judy Griffith, and Siebert and Aileen Allman in chapter 4 attest to this. Many men, however, define their household and familial responsibilities narrowly as merely contributing financial support. Public service announcements aired on television often reveal what Bajan society regards as problem areas; recent ads have encouraged men to talk to their children and spend time with them, in other words, to broaden their familial role to include emotional as well as financial support.

To a large extent even couples who live together lead separate lives. Not only are they apart during the workday, they also do much of their socializing separately. Village women become involved in church activities, visit female relatives, and talk to friends over the telephone. Men spend their free time working in the yard or socializing at the rum shop, a sporting event, or favored spot. "Most husbands and wives in Barbados," asserted one villager, "are not friends. They not really friends. There's not much social life between them." Likewise, when a student of ours referred to a married man and woman she knew as a "couple," she received a surprised reaction and was informed that the word "couple" refers to people who are dating and enjoying each other's company, while "husbands and wives do not."

Many men and women who live together also keep their money and property separate. "I just buy the small things for the house like decorations. He buys the furniture," one woman explained. "I buy the soap for the laundry and the food. He buys the equipment for fixin' up the house. But if you don't have an ambitious man, you have to go ahead and buy the big things yourself." Most couples have separate savings accounts because, in the words of one woman, "men and women spend their money different." Most women also value their independence ("so he doesn't know everything I do") and feel it is important to have their own savings as insurance in case the relationship fails.

Women without a partner are proud of being able to support their children and household without a man, although they must often rely on others for help. When a woman leaves for work, for example, a large part of her parenting and domestic responsibilities falls to other women. "Leaving de child at Granny—dat is my culture," lyrics from the Mighty Gabby's calypso hit "Culture," captures the important role of the grandmother in Bajan society. Sandra Broomes, introduced in chapter 4, has three children by two boyfriends, neither of whom contributes to her household financially. Instead, Sandra relies entirely on her income as a maid and on the help of her aunt. Some women become so used to managing households on their own that with the passage of time they lose interest in marrying or ever living with a man. "I used to think about getting married," commented one 45-year-old woman. "Doesn't everybody? But today I feel different. I'm too old and set in my ways. My friend has his own house, and I'm happy this way. I can run things any way I want."

At the present time, village women want fewer children than in the past. "Times are hard, and to have a lot of children is expensive," explained one 18-year-old. "It used to be that the woman would stay home, keep house and take care of the baby. But now we want jobs; we have education. We want to do the jobs that the men do." In most cases women have also seen their own mother, grandparents, and other relatives struggle to survive and want a different life for themselves. "I want to give my children a good home and a good education," commented Sandra Broomes, "a better life than I had." A majority of Barbadian men now also favor small families, mainly for economic reasons.[13]

Domestic violence is an important societal issue in Barbados. A study by the Caribbean Development Research Services (CADRES) conducted in 2010 found that 27 percent of Barbadian women have experienced some form of domestic violence. (The figure in the United States is usually estimated to be 25 percent.) Despite legislation like the Domestic Violence Protection Order, women's groups working to reduce domestic violence, and the existence of a crisis hotline and shelter for abused women, the prevailing attitude is that domestic violence is "man-and-woman" business and consequently not a concern of others. Separate statistics for St. Lucy are not available, but there is no reason to believe that the parish differs markedly from the rest of the country.

# Childhood and Discipline

In St. Lucy the focus of child rearing in the past was on teaching children to be obedient and respectful. Village children were taught never to speak back to an adult, to say "excuse me" when entering a conversation, to address their elders as Mr. and Mrs., to say "good morning" and "good evening" when passing adults on the street, to offer to carry heavy parcels and run errands for the elderly, and to give them their seat on the bus. Although the older generation regularly complains about today's youth and about the breakdown in social order, these values are still taught by many parents. But children also seem more disconnected from the adult generation. Even younger parents complain about their lack of responsiveness: their tendency to look at you without speaking or "paying respect." In addition, most children are taught early to help around the house. Even four- and five-year-olds may be asked to do small tasks such as water a plant, take their cup to the sink or place empty soda bottles into a crate. By about age eight or nine children are expected to do daily chores. Here a gender division emerges, with girls doing numerous indoor chores such as making beds, folding laundry, ironing, "picking rice" (removing extraneous material), cooking, washing dishes, and minding younger siblings. Boys are more likely to be responsible for outdoor chores: taking out the garbage, weeding, tending animals, and sweeping the yard. Many boys sometimes cook, do dishes, and wash and iron their clothes; the difference is that they usually do not have to do these tasks regularly.

During the school year children get up early to do their chores and prepare for school. After age 11 some begin attending secondary schools outside the parish and must rise as early as 5:00 AM to bathe, iron their uniform, make and eat breakfast, pack a lunch, and catch the bus.[14] If their parent or parents have already left for work, they may also have to help younger brothers and sisters get ready. When primary schoolchildren return from school, most eat a snack and go outside to play. Those in secondary school are more likely to watch television (especially if they have cable), use the computer, or begin their homework, although many boys still go outside to play. As evening approaches, most children disappear indoors; few are allowed back outside after dark. This prohibition was once reinforced with the legend of the "heartman," who was alleged to roam the countryside at night ready to rip out the hearts of any children he found.

With respect to children, the village still functions like an extended family. People tend to watch out for the community's children, going outside to check when they hear a suspicious sound and comforting one another's children when they are injured. Any adult standing near village children who are still playing outside after 6:00 PM is likely to tell them to "go on home." Parents also report on one another's children when they think it is important. One mother we know, for example, did not hesitate to telephone her neighbor to report that she had just seen her neighbor's daughter walk into the bushes with a boy.

All children, but especially boys, are regarded as naturally unruly, as "hard ears" in need of firm discipline and control. "Spare the rod and spoil the child" is a belief shared by many villagers. Even older children threaten younger siblings with "licks" (hits): "You better watch out, girl, and leave me

Uniformed schoolgirls walk to the bus stop. (Photo by Tom Curtin)

be, or you'll have licks." Virtually every adult in St. Lucy can recall the "flog-gings" and "lashings" they received as youngsters. According to one person, "If you sneeze too hard, you got a lash." "I had quite a few floggings by my uncle," remembered a middle-aged man:

> One time I was out on the jetty with my sister and some boys around seven [PM], and my uncle came down, "What are you doing down here at this time of night!" He had a twig behind his back, and we didn't see it. My sister was faster than I was, and she didn't catch any of it, but I got a good one. You just hope that when you get home he didn't tell your mother because you'd get it again.

Teachers also used corporal punishment, administering lashes to chil-dren who were disrespectful or disobedient, who spoke when not spoken to, who lied, who arrived at school late, and who had not done their homework. Being struck several times with a leather strap or wooden switch across the buttocks, back, legs, or the palm of the hand was no laughing matter. One woman remembers hiding to avoid lashes at school:

> When we were going to school, if you were going to be late, you would leave your house and hide in the gully, go home to lunch, and then back to the gully until school was over. We didn't love school as such; it wasn't a place of comfort but more like a correction center.

Attitudes about corporal punishment have changed. More people ques-tion its wisdom, even if they still believe in its effectiveness. Nowadays, lashes are seldom given and when they are, they are given more lightly than in the past. In some schools, lashes can be administered only by the headmaster or head teacher. Many teachers are convinced that lashing is psychologically harmful even if they think that it is effective in getting children to obey and to study. As one primary schoolteacher explained, "When we were young, we got lashes, and we learned. We memorized things, because, if we didn't, we'd know we'd get lashes." Today, many younger and better-educated parents also object to lashing and punish their children by taking privileges away instead. A 27-year-old male agrees with the new attitudes:

> I went through some hard years. Boy, I got a good few licks—like a per-son fighting in a ring. I'd get smashed and slapped. Some people get strong by the more licks they get, but some get to not be bothered by them, and then they go and fight or lick others. Instead of licking, parents should turn off the television: "Okay, you're going to bed early." Or, if the child like sports, they shouldn't let him play a while. I don't believe in licks. I feel that talk should be the way. That changes things, not licks.

Older villagers, however, often complain about the boldness of children and about their lack of respect and blame it on the lack of discipline and proper guidance. "Children are big talkers now," one woman told us. "They'll say, 'You can't tell me what to do; my mother doesn't even tell me what to do.'" According to another, "The young people today are very wicked. They will curse you! Cursing older ones! When I was young, you'd get lashed for sure, for sure. Children today got no culture." Although villagers still watch out for one another's children, gone are the days when they felt free to give any child who was misbehaving a good smack. They are no longer sure the child's parents will back them up.

Growing up in St. Lucy is not all hard work and punishment, nor was it so in the past. Country children, especially boys, have always enjoyed freedom and adventure. Roy Campbell recalled growing up near Rockfield in the 1960s this way:

> What I like about growing up in St. Lucy was the outdoor life. It was the country with wide open spaces, and the sea was near. You could do a lot of running around, and there was nothing that could get you into trouble. You looked forward to the change of seasons. During Easter season, from the beginning of Ash Wednesday, we started flying kites and we'd do that until the crop finished. On Sunday we'd be off to the sea to go fishing. We couldn't afford to buy hooks, so we'd use common pins and a nylon cord. You'd take fish home and roast them in the fire. And when the sea egg season was in you'd get them from the fishermen.[15] They'd give you two or three. Sometimes the sea eggs were in pretty close to shore so you could get them yourself.

If a community is located within easy walking distance of the sea, many of the youths play on the beach or take a sea bath.

Children once made all their own toys: kites from sugarcane stalks, newspaper, and string; scooters and toy trucks from wood and tin cans; cricket bats from pieces of wood; balloons from a pig's bladder; "rollers" from a bike rim rolled along the street with a stick; and rag dolls. Homemade toys can still be found, but most children have manufactured toys that they keep safely indoors. Make-believe games like "father and mother" are common among younger children. Group games like hide-and-go-seek, "sticky" (freeze tag), "camp fight" (capture the flag), marbles, "pick-ups" (jacks), hopscotch, blind man's bluff, "frog in the sea can't catch me" (keep away), Simon says, and skipping rope are still played, but television and computer games, including Nintendo's Wii game system, have now sharply cut into the time children spend together outdoors.

Opinions about when the transition to adulthood occurs vary. Some people regard age 16, because it is the legal age of consent and also the time when most Barbadians leave school, as the age at which adolescents become adults. Others think that adulthood begins at 18: "You adult when the government make you responsible for yourself and you can cast a vote." Still other people say that being an adult is less a matter of age than of how mature a person acts: "A 19-year-old who gets on the bus and laughs or snickers and mixes with little fellows," explained one woman, "is no adult." Independence is another criterion. Children become adults, some Bajans say, when they can "turn their own key."

Economic realities often defer true independence for many years. Only some young adults in St. Lucy find jobs on leaving school and are financially able to move out of their parents' homes; most continue to live at home for a number of years in order to save money to buy a car, land, and a house of their own. Eric O'Neale, profiled in chapter 4, lives with his parents and works at part-time jobs. Other young adults attend a polytechnical school or enroll in a hotel-training or other specialized course hoping to make themselves more marketable. Those with higher career aspirations and some financial help attend the Barbados Community College or the University of the West Indies at Cave Hill. Many from better-off families, or who win scholarships, go abroad to universities in the United States, Britain, Canada, other Commonwealth countries, or Cuba, which offer more advanced training and a broader range of graduate work than is available at home.

# Old Age and Death

Old age in St. Lucy is linked more to fitness than to years. An 80-year-old who is vigorous may not be considered as "old" as someone in his or her early 60s who is in poor health. Most elderly villagers remain active after they retire, raising a few animals and working a small plot of land on which they grow "provisions" such as potatoes, eddoes, and yams. Some men raise and harvest small plots of sugarcane or ground nuts to sell; women often sell homemade baked goods and sweet drinks from their kitchen door. Men with skills such as tailoring, upholstery, and carpentry often continue to work but at a slower pace. George Fitzpatrick, a 72-year-old neighbor, who sewed two pairs of pants a day in his prime, in retirement slowed down to one. Many elderly women are kept busy watching grandchildren while their daughters and sons are at work. The combination of a healthy diet and work means that many rural elderly are not only fit and active but also strong. A 21-year-old joked, "Have you seen the way the old people shove to get on the buses? They strong! That's because they eat a lot of ground provisions instead of hamburgers and stuff." One of our students described the strenuous daily routine of his 70-year-old neighbor:

> Mrs. J., who I see quite often, works long, hard days without complaint. She usually begins to work at 7:00 in the morning and works in the field behind her house until about 11:00 or until "the sun begin to scorch" her. She is either picking crops, weeding the garden, or feeding and tending animals. She hardly ever takes a ten-minute break but, instead, opts to work continuously. She feels that it is her job to do her part "so the Lord will provide." After lunch she heads back to finish her work, and she might be in the fields until four or five in the evening. The night is occupied with fixing dinner and doing household chores. She is usually in bed by 10:00 and sets her alarm to get up by 5:00 the next morning.

"Since I was little," explained an 83-year-old woman, "my momma told me to keep the faith and stay humble and never worry about things that you can't get."

Grandmother and granddaughter. (Photo by Ellen Frankenstein)

Many elderly live in extended households and have daughters and grandchildren around. Those who live on their own usually have children nearby who visit them each day to make sure their needs are met. Older villagers who do not have relatives in the village are looked after by neighbors and visited by church groups, who come to read the Bible and offer companionship and aid. The government also provides basic support and services: small old-age pensions, free medical treatment and bus travel, and reduced rates for water and electricity.

In the past, when storytelling was a part of village life and the outside world was more distant, the elderly were valued for what they had to say. Today, they complain that young people "don't like to listen." "If they were by chance to listen, and they hear an older person talking," observes Marcus O'Neale, "they amazed. They say, 'That happen in your day?' They amazed to hear we once worked for a penny a day. But they embarrassed, too. They don't like to hear how bad things was—about the chiggers and lice."[16] Elderly villagers recount cleaning their teeth with salt and ashes from the kitchen fire, having head lice, walking barefoot to school, and sleeping on flour bag mattresses stuffed with grass. Stories like these do not interest many young people, and even some adults hesitate to tell them. For some, this past is still too recent and painful.

Until the 1960s, when a villager died a wake was held in his or her home for family and close friends who gathered by the corpse to drink rum and cocoa and sing through the night. Before the funeral a viewing was held, after which friends and neighbors accompanied the coffin to the church. In the recent past, the procession was led by the "family car" in which the nearest kin rode, followed by the hearse, and then the "walkers"—neighbors, friends, and more distant kin who walked behind, two abreast, the women dressed in white, the men in black. They were followed by other mourners in cars. Now, the deceased is taken straight to a funeral home and, on the day of internment, transferred to the church.

Funerals are major community events that draw large numbers of mourners and observers, some of whom barely knew the deceased. This is especially true if the departed person was well-known or the death occurred under tragic or questionable circumstances. Attendance is a sign of respect for the dead and his or her family and is facilitated by the daily obituaries and funeral announcements that are read over the radio each morning. Most funerals begin around 4:00 PM and follow a set ritual that starts with the mourners filing past the open casket on their way in. Photographs of the deceased are usually taken; many families later put together an album of the funeral. After about an hour, the coffin is closed and wheeled further into the church for the service, which typically consists of prayers, hymns, an address by the officiating minister, and a eulogy by a friend or family member. Pallbearers then carry the coffin to the cemetery. After the ceremony is over, people retire to the family's home or a rented hall to socialize and eat.

Modern funerals, villagers say, are less somber than in the past. There are fewer ritualized displays of grief; many people now wear colored clothing to the service rather than dress in only black or white; and the atmosphere afterward can seem surprisingly light. The death of a close relative or young person, of course, typically causes great anguish. After the tragic death of an 18-year-old girl in one village, for example, most mourners wept and four young men claimed to have seen "duppies" (spirits) in front of her home.

Beach cricket. (Photo by Darren Fletcher)

# Chapter 6
# Community
## Past and Present

$\mathcal{N}$ot that long ago residents of St. Lucy could obtain almost everything they needed within the village or nearby. Specialists like the midwife, tailor, carpenter, and tinsmith supplied essential goods and services. Families grew most of their own food and purchased the rest from hawkers or the local rum shops or plantation stores which stocked basic supplies like rice, salt fish, and kerosene. Some communities had a corn grinding mill for flour[1] and a community oven. Neighbors shared what they had—peanuts, yams, sweet potatoes, and breadfruit—to be repaid later with a loaf of freshly baked cassava bread, ripe mangos, or a papaya. They also helped one another in other ways: looking after children, clearing brush, moving a chattel house to a new plot of land. People depended on one another and cared: "We was all one big family." St. Lucy's distance from the capital Bridgetown and its relative isolation in the era before paved roads and public transportation reinforced its cohesiveness.

In recent decades, economic development has dramatically altered rural life. Rural life has changed so much that Barbadians who return home after living abroad for many years have difficulty believing the changes that have taken place. To what extent do people in St. Lucy feel that a fundamental transformation in community life has taken place? Are the parish's villages still cohesive communities? And, if not, what do people think about it?

## Modernization and Change

The standard of living for most people in the parish began noticeably to improve in the late 1950s and 1960s, as new employment opportunities

**99**

opened up and new technology and services filtered in. Until that point, few families besides "the great"—local elites such as the plantation manager, schoolmaster, and rector—had more than anyone else. Those who did were villagers with extra ambition and luck who had worked hard and managed to save or else were families with "Panama money"—money earned by relatives who had worked on the Panama Canal and returned home, bought land, and upgraded their homes. Everyone else lived similar and modest lives.

Until the late 1950s most people in St. Lucy cooked outside over wood fires built in "rock kitchens"—simple coral or rock hearths sheltered from wind and rain by low walls and roofs made of branches or galvanized metal. The fires required careful tending and a steady supply of wood, which was cut from the nearest gully. When wood was unavailable, dried coconut husks and cane stalks were used and sometimes cow dung.[2] As meals were prepared, smoke from the outdoor fires curled over the villages like signal fires, coating houses and yards in soot. Afterward, people often buried potatoes and bread-fruit in the embers to roast overnight. Communal meals were not uncommon. One elderly man from River Bay recalled the neighborhood fish fries that took place on the beach when local fishers made a big catch. This no longer happens, he claims, both because of the appeal of television and fewer fish.

Potters in Chalky Mount, St. Andrew fashion charcoal braziers and water jars that were once used island-wide (c.1940). (From Anne Langley, "British West Indian Interlude," *National Geographic* [1941])

The poorest St. Lucy families ate from platters that were little more than cross-sections of wood and from bowls and cups fashioned from the dried gourd-like fruit of the calabash tree. The "calabash" was a common measure: "Put three calabash water to boil the peas," mothers instructed their daughters. Other utensils and containers such as buckets, graters for cassava and potatoes, and "tots" (mugs) were bought from the local tinsmith. In the 1950s mass-produced enamelware plates and utensils began to replace calabashes and tin, and like any new and "expensive" item, enamelware was at first a status symbol. To own enamelware showed not only that a family had the money to buy it but also a degree of refinement, since it probably also meant they no longer had to eat with their hands.

Piped water was one of the earliest public services to change village life. Before it became available, people collected rainwater, used natural springs like those at Spring Garden, River Bay, and Cove Bay, and washed and bathed in natural ponds. In recent years many of these natural springs and ponds have dried up. After the devastating cholera epidemic of 1854, which killed one person in seven on the island and more than a thousand people in St. Lucy, the colonial government worked to extend clean water to the farthest reaches of the island. Eventually, 400 roadside spigots called "stand pipes" (short for "standard pipe") were installed, bringing convenient, piped water to the rural population. Forty-nine were erected in St. Lucy; most were placed near plantations.[3] Even with stand pipes, many villagers still had to carry water home from a considerable distance. Virtually every villager over the age of 75 remembers having to "head" water—that is, balance a heavy bucket on his or her head with only a cloth pad for cushioning and a palm frond or leafy branch on top to keep it from sloshing out. "Carrying water was hard, hard," remembers Arnold Griffith with a grimace. "After getting home from walking through the hills, your head and neck would ache bad, bad. But after a while you become numb to it." Once home, the water would be dumped into a 50 gallon drum for storage. During crop season, plantation mills and sugar factories used so much water that the pressure dropped and the stand pipes often ran dry. Then people took turns walking to the stand pipe to check; when the water came back on, they spread the word and filled every container they had.

Eventually, those who could afford water pipes had them extended to their homes. Valenza Griffith from Coles Cave remembers her father's pride at having piped water put in, "He always used to remind us how he spent all his savings to put water in." When the village stand pipe ran dry, Valenza's mother opened their yard gate and let their neighbors in to fill up. Most people in St. Lucy had piped water by the 1960s. In some areas water mains were not extended to all parts of the village until the 1970s. Having water piped into the yard or house, of course, greatly simplified many household chores and bathing. In the view of one elderly villager, "Young children today living the king's life and the queen's life. Get up, go to the bath, and turn on the shower." Before water was piped to individual homes, however, many adults bathed only in preparation for church, carrying a water bucket and bar of blue soap into a stand of canes or trees at the back of the house. Only a few villages had public bathhouses. Working men typically rinsed off at the stand pipe on their way home from work; children often stripped to wash in the rain. Most women sought some privacy, but they did not feel overly self-conscious if seen bathing. "In the past you would see grown women with their breasts bared bathing at the backs of the houses," remembers Velma O'Neale, "and nobody

One of the dwindling number of standpipes in 2010. (Photo by Sharon Gmelch)

bat an eye. Today men would be peeping at you." When piped water arrived, most people built private bathing sheds and showers in their yards.

Nowadays, virtually all village homes have piped water, 33 percent have solar or some other form of water heater, and 78 percent have indoor toilets.[4] Initially, having piped water, like owning enamelware, was a status symbol, a sign that a family had advanced in the world. In *Growing Up Stupid under the Union Jack,* author Austin Clarke recalls his childhood embarrassment at having to collect water at the stand pipe when other families in his community had "in pipes." Status distinctions within the village were once made on the basis of such differences: "We don't have to bring water," "We don't have to pick up wood," "We have electricity," the children of better-off families would smugly say.

Although stand pipes are still used by some people in the parish (and by many people when there is a problem with the water supply), they are no longer at the heart of village life. Children no longer meet their friends to walk to the stand pipe together. Adults no longer "queue up to catch water," exchanging jokes and news while waiting in line. When elderly villagers are asked what they miss about the past, many immediately mention the "pipe." For, despite the hard work of carrying water and the fights that sometimes broke out when water ran low or someone jumped the queue, the stand pipe to them represents "community" and all that was good about the past.

Laundering is the one household task that has not changed dramatically over the years. Fewer than half (38 percent) of St. Lucy's households have washing machines,[5] and many women continue to wash clothes by hand in a bucket or tub in the yard, vigorously rubbing the fabric over itself and against their wrist or on a wooden "jooking board" (washboard). In the past, people used imported salt meat drums purchased from the local rum shop to create washtubs; they were cut in half and set up in the yard or near a stand pipe. In a few villages, Saturday washing in the "pasture" was an important social event for these women and their older daughters who walked to a nearby pond to wash, spreading the clean clothes on the grass and bushes to dry. Most households also had a "bleach rock," a rock bed on which they spread wet clothing to bleach in the sun. Laundering today is easier, even without a washing machine, because of piped water and commercial cleaning products, which have replaced items like homemade cassava starch. But people now own more clothes and change them more often, creating more laundry.

In the 1950s kerosene stoves began to replace cooking with wood and charcoal. They made cooking easier and cleaner, but, because the stoves lacked ovens, women still baked sweetbread and cassava pone in portable ovens built outside. Most people also continued to roast breadfruit and flying fish over a wood fire, preferring its smoky flavor. In the 1960s, with the introduction of clean burning propane stoves with ovens, cooking began moving indoors. Now, nearly everyone cooks indoors. "Now everything so easy," observes Malcolm Hinds. "You turn the switch, you cook." Although women still prepare most family meals, anyone can easily reheat food.

Electricity reached St. Lucy in the 1960s, bringing with it a host of changes. Before electricity people used candles and "snuff lamps"—glass bottles filled with kerosene and a rag wick—for light. Others used tin lamps made by the local tinsmith or, if they could afford one, a glass chimney lamp with a metal reflector. With electricity, daylight was extended into the night filling "the whole room with light." This gave villagers more time to finish chores before retiring to bed. Streetlights also made socializing outdoors easier. Men, for example, now played *warri*,[6] dominoes, and cards on makeshift tables under the streetlight. Previously, they had assembled at the rum shop and played under an oil lamp or else waited until there was a bright moonlit night. Before streetlights, the only time most people stayed outdoors at night was during a full moon. Then, even children and adults played games together, strengthening community. Today, virtually all parish homes have electric lights.

Electricity dramatically changed the quality of village life in many ways. "After we got electricity, everything went modern," declared one woman. Electricity simplified many household tasks. It made refrigeration possible, and for many people that was as important as light. Previously, few foods could be kept without spoiling in the tropical heat; only the wealthy could afford blocks of imported ice. Most people ate salt fish (dried cod from Newfoundland) and flying fish, which they ate fresh or else dried on the roofs of their homes for later use. Others salted pork and "jerked" it (marinated it with spices) in clay pots made in the village of Chalky Mount. With refrigeration a greater range of foods could be kept. Refrigeration also simplified food preparation. No longer did every meal have to be made from scratch and eaten on the same day; instead, leftovers could be stored in the refrigerator to be reheated as the need arose. Electricity simplified ironing as well. No longer did villagers have to use heavy, cast-iron flatirons, which had to be heated in the coals of the kitchen fire or over the kerosene stove, wiped with a leaf, and then polished with a cloth to remove all traces of soot before use. Few people besides the tailor owned a gas iron, which was fueled by kerosene and lit with methylated spirits. When electric irons arrived, ironing became cleaner, easier, and faster, although it remains a time-consuming household task, since most villagers are fastidious about their dress. While electricity definitely made life easier, some of the innovations it brought weakened community. "Before the refrigerator," says Velma O'Neale, "people always running over to borrow, and I be going over to get something. With the fridge no need to do that."

Electricity also brought entertainment. Television was introduced to Barbados in 1964, and as it slowly began to appear in parish homes it made the mobile movie van obsolete. The movie van was driven into larger villages like Checker Hall and an outdoor screen was set up. Typically, the movies were short documentaries followed by comedies like Abbott and Costello. At the present time, when villagers talk about the importance of different amenities in their lives, they almost always rank television first, although it is rivaled by the computer and the Internet. Neil Rock remembers what happened when his family acquired the first television in their village. "My dad bought a television in 1973. Everyone in the village would come over to watch it at night. It became annoying after a while because the house was always full. But soon everyone bought TVs, and the village scattered, and people stopped coming around to visit. Everyone was busy watching their set." Television has meant that villagers spend more time inside their homes than outside, where they once socialized with neighbors. The evening games and stories that brought people together—adults and children alike—have all but disappeared, as people prefer to watch game shows, *Divorce Court, CSI,* and the Black Entertainment Television (BET) cable network.

Telephones arrived in the parish about the same time as television. The first private household to have one is said to have been that of the parish's representative in Parliament. Before the telephone, when someone needed a doctor, a neighbor or family member had to walk or ride a bike to the Crab Hill police station to summon the police van. When someone died, people walked or pedaled from community to community to pass the news and fetch the undertaker. "Even if the sun was blazing, people need that message, and you got to go," remembers Velma O'Neale. With telephones, emergencies can be handled more easily. They have also made obtaining jobs easier. Successful applicants can be contacted by telephone, whereas before, people in St. Lucy could only be reached by mail, which, villagers claim, could take two weeks. By making communication easy, the telephone also allows friends and family members, including those living overseas, to stay in regular contact. Cell phones and the Internet have greatly increased people's ability to stay in touch, and more will be said in chapter 8 about these developments. By increasing the independence of individual households, however, such technological innovations weaken community.

Prior to nationalization of the bus service in the 1970s, many villages in the parish were quite isolated. The few private bus concessionaires that were in business had few routes and provided infrequent service. Nowadays, the number of government "transport" buses as well as privately-owned minivans, known as "ZRs" or "route taxis," has dramatically increased, and so has their frequency of operation. Moreover, all major roads are paved, which greatly increases the ease with which people can leave the parish to work, attend school, or shop. Many St. Lucyians work in Bridgetown or on the west coast hotel strip. Those who depend on the bus can spend as much as three hours each day on or waiting for buses. This amounts to 15 hours a week, or a month each year spent in transit, similar to the time commuters in North America's more congested cities spend in traffic. The first bus arrives in Josey Hill, the village we often lived in, about a half-hour before dawn and are scheduled for every hour after that. Schoolchildren also use the buses to get to school, creating heavy passenger loads in the morning.

Today, the nearest approximation to the standpipe in creating community is the bus, although this, too, is diminishing in importance as more villagers buy cars.[7] Nevertheless, most villagers in St. Lucy still ride government buses or privately owned minivans to go to work or to shop in town. When we visited two of the parish's main industries in the mid-1990s—the Superchick processing plant and the Wacoal garment assembly plant, each with more than 150 employees—we were struck by the virtual absence of cars in the parking lot (four or five at most).

Riding the bus, like collecting water at the standpipe in the past, is a shared, daily experience with a component of hardship built in. Most rural roads, although paved, are narrow; many follow the cart and footpaths first established in the 17th century. For an outsider, riding a government bus can be a hair-raising experience as it careens around blind corners barely missing approaching cars. For villagers, riding the bus is often an exercise in frustration. When a bus breaks down or a driver calls in sick, the transport board may not arrange for a replacement, leaving people stranded at bus stops all along the route. Occasionally drivers stop to conduct private business, leaving their passengers sitting in the heat. Villagers frequently complain that drivers "make their own schedules." Like the standpipe, however, riding the bus strengthens community bonds. While waiting at the bus stop, people exchange greetings, talk, and catch up on local news. Regular riders watch out for one another's interests, alerting neighbors when the bus is about to come and getting the driver to wait so that a friend can get on. People hold bags and small children for those who must stand, take parcels home for their neighbors, and watch to see that young children get off at their stops. In 2010, with an increase in alternative ways to get around, bus ridership was decreasing.

## Interdependence and Community

Modern technology and services have clearly eliminated the most grueling aspects of daily life and greatly reduced the isolation of rural villages. They have also opened up new forms of entertainment and created opportunities to further education and employment outside the village. Most villagers value these improvements and have no wish to return to the past. The elderly clearly remember the poverty and hardships of their youth. Yet, for every convenience or comfort gained, something is lost. The dilemma of development and "progress" everywhere in the world is that it brings negative consequences along with the good. How have the changes just described affected people's sense of community—their identification with their village and feeling of shared fate?

The village plays a smaller role in most people's lives than it did previously. Although a large majority of St. Lucy's residents were born within the parish and many people are related to each other,[8] villagers live increasingly independent lives. No longer do most people walk to the same plantation in the morning to work, nor do they socialize together at night. At night and on weekends those who can afford to, especially the young, attend parties, concerts, movies, nightclubs, and sporting and religious events elsewhere on the island. When asked whether or not she saw her neighbors much, one woman said, "Used to, but not now. There are people on this street you don't see. Some of them are old and they got pains, but you aren't supposed to stay in all the time, and they do. Children stay in too. Everyone just be watching TV." In some communities, outsiders are moving in, while the offspring of families who have long lived there are moving out in order to be nearer to their work and/or the stimulation of Bridgetown. Many people's friendships and support networks now extend well beyond the confines of the village and parish to include family, friends, coworkers, and church members living in other parts of the island. The village, for a growing number of people, is a community only in a physical sense; it is no longer the focal point of their lives or the primary source of their social support. With cell phones and increased access to the Internet and social networking sites, the need for a nearby support system is being further undermined. Nor do all villagers live at the same standard as their neighbors, and the economic and educational disparities are growing. One of the first comments middle-aged and older villagers make when asked to compare the past to the present is the current lack of "neighborliness." "People here, they don't give you nothing anymore," asserted one woman, "like if you need sugar." Many people claim that villagers are not as friendly or as caring as they were in the past and that they have become materialistic and self-centered. "At one time we live good, but not now," said one man. "People think they're independent now. It used to be that, when the man across the street kill the pig, he would bring over a piece for me and my family, and, when I kill my cow, I do the same thing, but not anymore."

In the past, villagers' isolation from those in other villages and shared poverty and educational level created interdependence and contributed to an egalitarian ethos. "When everybody live together, we learn to share," explained 70-year-old Errol Sobers. "Everybody share. But today things develop. Now, one person feel he more up [is better] than the other." Meryl Cumberbatch, in her 60s, concurs, "When I was young, if you don't have, and I do, then I share with you. But not today. Today is self only!" While most villagers who have paid work are in semiskilled or unskilled jobs, some are white-collar professionals. Educational differences also exist. In the past the "11-plus exam" determined which select few among village children went on to secondary school. The protagonist in George Lamming's semiautobiographical novel *In the Castle of My Skin,* for example, experienced a sense of split identity being both a villager and a high school boy, so unique was the experience. Today, most of the younger generation has completed secondary school and an increasing number is going on for further education or vocational training. In contrast, most elderly villagers have completed at most "seventh standard" (primary school).

As mentioned in chapter 3, some antagonism exists between members of different generations. Many of the elderly accuse present-day youths of being "lazy," "wicked," "unmannerly," and "soft" and talk derisively about the idle young men who "lime" in shady corners. Ralph Cumberbatch, in his 70s, puts it this way:

> The young today have no idea how hard us old folks worked. We worked for nothing. The young today will buy things like stereos for seven hundred dollars. When we were young, we would buy calves or pigs with the small money we had or put it in the bank. The kids today don't think about raising animals. They like the sport life. They like to have fun. The old people don't understand why the young don't put their money in the bank and save it to buy a house or a piece of land.

Many parents, of course, have discouraged their sons and daughters from working the land and have struggled to put them through school so that they can have a "better life." High school graduates can hardly be expected to want to work the land. Colin Jordan, a villager who rose through the ranks to become president of The Barbados Hotel and Tourism Association, explains the shortcomings of today's youth, notably the males, this way:

> It is the women [not the men] who are trying to further their education, trying to move ahead, trying to get a career, trying to get a house. It is the women who do better in school. Our young men are very laid-back; they like to lime [hang out] on the block, and often they get into trouble. Not many of them seem to be trying to make a mark for themselves. Not many of them are seen to be contributing to society. Of course that's a generalization and there are exceptions. . . . There are several reasons people put forward for this state of affairs. One is the struggle of past generations of Barbadians to earn a living. It started with slavery of course, but long after that you had so many Barbadians emigrating to find work and having to work hard in the United States, England, or Canada just to get by. Among them, who sacrificed so much, there is the feeling that their children should not have to work as hard as they did. Secondly, there is also the influence of the US culture on our thinking, with its materialism and emphasis on acquiring wealth and possessions and wanting to do it quickly and often not without the hard work. We Barbadians have been exposed to your consumer society through the media, especially TV shows and the movies. At the same time there has been a breakdown in discipline. This is certainly not limited to Barbados, as I think it's also become common in the United States and elsewhere in the world as well. There's a pretty strongly held view in Barbados that the social movement away from corporal punishment, away from tough punishment, to more talk and negotiation has not worked well. Because of all this we have a lot of young people who have become wayward, undisciplined, and not very ambitious.[9]

Older people are offended by the decline in formal manners and the disrespect they detect. Elders say that youths "look you in the face and don't say nothin' [fail to greet you]." The young, of course, do not know what village life used to be like and are far less critical of the present. They cannot remember the time when life events were everyone's business, when good and bad news was shared by all, and when the experiences of an individual became part of the village's collective consciousness. As a result of their mobility, education, and the influence of modern mass media and technology (e.g., radio, television, videos, the Internet), they are oriented toward the outside world and focused on their own pursuits. What the elderly regard as "neighborliness," the young consider nosiness and interference: "They've already lived their life, and now they want to tell us how to run ours." Many of the young would agree with the views of 20-year-old Shirley Maycock who believes, "Older people like to stick their mouth where it's not wanted. Boy, they stir up trouble."

Crime is another concern of villagers, exaggerated no doubt by the weakening of community bonds. Most people keep their doors locked and their windows closed at night. Many lock their doors whenever they leave the house, even if they remain nearby, and they avoid walking anywhere alone at night. "You used to be able to walk to Speightstown in the middle of the night with no problem, even a girl," remembers an elderly man from Cave Hill. "Now there's rape, murder, and robbery." Our students were surprised at the number of warnings they received about their safety and distressed at having to swelter in the heat when not allowed to keep their bedroom windows open at night. Since first taking students to Barbados in 1983, we have seen a dramatic increase in the precautions that host families take. Although crime—particularly theft and burglary—has risen on the island, especially in more populated tourist areas and there are some gangs in St. Lucy, as elsewhere, Barbados has the third lowest crime rate of the 35 industrialized and developing nations examined by the 2002 International Crime Victimization Survey.[10] People's fears may stem in part from the frequent depiction of crime and violence in the news and television programs. Groups of young men loitering about also increase some people's fears.

Despite many real changes and a definite weakening in the bonds that bind villagers together, there is still evidence of community life in the parish. Many working women, for example, are able to juggle their dual roles as mothers and workers only because of the help they receive from family, neighbors, and friends. Many people still share garden produce (if the monkeys haven't gotten to it first), loan tools, take messages, and perform other small favors for each other. A community party was held in one village during our stay to raise money for a family whose house had burned down. Having said this, it is also true that many goods and services once given free of charge are now more likely to be sold. If a villager butchers an animal, for example, he or she will let others know so that they can place an order, rather than give the meat away for free. Generalized reciprocity is giving way to market exchange.

Several forms of credit still exist in many villages.[11] Many rum shop owners, grocery store proprietors, and local bakers allow their regulars to buy goods on short-term credit. This is especially important at certain times of the year, such as immediately following Christmas, when many villagers are financially pinched. Another community-based form of support is the "meeting turn" or *susu*, an informal rotating credit association.[12] Villagers, seldom more than a dozen, who feel confident of one another's trustworthiness "throw" a specified amount of money each week into a common pool collected by the meeting holder. Each week one member draws the entire sum, until everyone has drawn in turn. If someone has a special need, such as the final payment to make on a refrigerator or funeral expenses, he or she can usually arrange to take their turn early. As a form of compulsory savings and a simple way to acquire an interest-free loan, the meeting turn helps villagers meet their financial commitments and improve their standard of living. Meeting turns also extend beyond the village and parish. One meeting turn in Josey Hill has members in the parishes of Christ Church and St. James. Other villagers belong to work-based groups.

Various community institutions also continue to bind villagers together. Of these, religion is the most important. As a member of a church, a villager belongs not only to a spiritual community but also to a social one. Weekend services, evening Bible study, and prayer meetings are attended regularly by women and children and by a smaller number of devout men. Most congregations also have youth clubs and service groups, like the Salvation Army's League of Mercy, which visits the sick to prepare meals, read the Bible, and clean their homes. Church members also provide one another with needed emotional and financial support, handling funeral arrangements for a distraught family, for example. Religion, of course, also inspires individuals to extend personal acts of Christian charity and generosity. Recall the charitable work of Judy Griffith, described in chapter 4, who visits several elderly people in Josey Hill to run errands, arrange for home repairs, and wash clothes.

The rum shop lies at the other end of the spiritual spectrum yet rivals the church in importance as an institution that binds a certain sector of the community together. Whereas the church is largely a female preserve, the rum shop is strictly a male one. In Barbados there is almost one rum shop for every 300 people.[13] Josey Hill, a fairly typical community, has three. They serve as informal community centers in which men "stand rounds" (take turns buying one another drinks); talk about sports, politics, and women; play dominoes and cards; and pass the time. While men of all ages frequent the rum shop, the regular clientele tends to be middle-aged and working-class. For regulars who have been unable to find steady employment or who have resigned themselves to the impossibility of advancement, the rum shop clientele forms a "fraternity of commiseration."[14] For men who are too old for sports or who are not attracted to other forms of relaxation and entertainment such as picnics, fetes, or church-sponsored events, the rum shop is their primary social outlet.

For many younger villagers, especially men, village and parish-based sports teams are important in creating a sense of community. Any village with a flat piece of land nearby is likely to have a cricket and a soccer team. Typically, as many village teams are created as are needed to accommodate

A village store and rum shop. (Photo by George Gmelch)
Enjoying the beach at Little Bay, St. Lucy. (Photo by George Gmelch)

all the men who want to play. During the cricket season, from May until early December, men's weekends may be filled with cricket play and talk. Large numbers of fans turn out for important village matches.[15] Soccer, which typically lasts from January through April, also contributes to community. Communities near St. Lucy's secondary school and its sports facilities also have basketball teams, which are organized into league play by the Barbados Amateur Basketball Federation. When people watch and root for their home team in games against other villages, they affirm their pride in their community.

Public and religious holidays are also occasions for celebrating community, providing opportunities for families, friends, and courting couples to get together. Picnics are a major form of leisure in the parish, with women spending much of their time preparing food and socializing, while men play dominoes, cards, or sports.[16] St. Lucy's bays and beaches are favored not only by locals but also by people from other parts of the island. Errol Barrow Day, which honors St. Lucy's most prominent son and Barbados' first prime minister after independence, has special importance. It usually spawns village-based field parties at which people gather to enjoy music, dancing, and food. Religious holidays and special church services such as harvest celebrations and children's days are also well attended. Yet, clearly many things have changed and will continue to do so. When we asked Griffith Roosevelt in 2010 how the parish had changed, he described a loss of community, signaled, he felt, by people now driving past their neighbors on the side of the road without offering them a ride. "We're moving fast, but going nowhere," he concluded. "We've gone from village to a sophisticated life."

# Chapter 7

# Religion

$\mathcal{R}$eligion is still a cornerstone of life in St. Lucy. Its physical presence is evident everywhere, from the imposing St. Lucy Parish Church that towers above the cane fields near the entrance to the parish to the modest meeting halls wedged between houses in virtually every village. During the day, radio gospel music spills into the streets. On many weeknights the sounds of tambourines, rhythmic clapping, and exclamations of "Hallelujah" and "Praise the Lord" fill the air. Schoolchildren begin each day with prayer and in the course of their studies learn a repertoire of religious songs. On weekends the roads seem lined with women in brightly colored dresses, elaborate hats, and high heels walking to church—Bibles in hand, well-groomed children in tow. Scattered among them are churchgoing men in neatly pressed shirts and suits. Other people wait at the bus stops or pass by in cars. In this chapter we provide some historical context, but the focus is on contemporary religious practice. What role does religion play in the people's lives in St. Lucy and how does it compare to the rest of Barbados? What changes have taken place in recent years?

## Historical Background

When the British colonized Barbados in 1627, Anglicanism became the colony's official religion. For the next 350 years—until the Church of England was formally disestablished in 1969—the Anglican bishop and clergy were funded by the State from general taxation. Church wardens and a vestry system of local government administered parish affairs and maintained order. Other religions played much lesser roles.[1] When African slaves arrived in Barbados they held on to many indigenous religious beliefs and rituals, although the intermingling of people from different cultures meant that no single African religious system was retained.

113

St. Lucy
Parish Church.
(Photo by
Sharon Gmelch)

The first direct exposure that Barbados' slaves had to Christian beliefs occurred a few decades after their arrival when some Quakers, ignoring the disapproval of other Christians, brought slaves to their meetings. It was not until the late 1700s, however, when Moravian and Methodist missionaries arrived on the island, that modest attempts were made to convert the black population to Christianity. In the early 1800s, the Anglican Church also sent missionaries and schoolmasters—through the Incorporated Society for the Conversion and Religious Instruction and Education of Negro Slaves in the British West India Islands—to Barbados to open charity schools for slave children. Up to that point the native Anglican Church had worked little with slaves. Slave owners were discouraged from providing religious instruction to their slaves on the grounds that it would encourage "notions of equality." This fear seems borne out by the later experience of the Reverend W. M. Harte who performed a marriage ceremony for a slave couple in St. Lucy in the 1840s; afterward they insisted on being addressed as "Mr." and "Mrs." much to the irritation of his white parishioners. Harte's parishioners also objected to what they regarded as his ongoing attempts to "alienate slaves from a sense of their duty."[2]

In their research on Barbadian slave culture, Jerome Handler and Frederick Lange found numerous African religious features including the propitiation and veneration of ancestors; the belief in witchcraft, sorcery, and nature deities; and the concept of great gods, including a creator god. Mortuary practices such as the custom of making food offerings and small animal sacrifices, particularly chickens, at the grave site and "the value attached to locating burial sites close to the houses of the living and interment under the houses" displayed particularly strong African influence.[3] Slaves believed that misfortune was caused primarily by supernatural forces that acted through human agents. According to Jerome Handler, "what was called Obeah evolved into a loosely defined complex involving supernatural practices related to healing and protection and centered on the role of the Obeah practitioner."[4] Although the rituals associated with Obeah were usually aimed at diagnosing and curing illness and other socially positive ends like finding lost property or keeping a husband faithful, they could be used for negative purposes like exacting revenge. Whatever its purpose, Obeah was considered harmful by the British plantocracy, which passed legislation to ban it, thus driving it underground.

By the end of slavery, white attitudes about spreading Christianity to the enslaved population had softened. In 1824 Parliament decided that religious training should be a part of their preparation for emancipation. With the arrival of Bishop William Hart Coleridge from England and the passage of the "Sunday and Marriage Act" in 1826, a concerted effort by Anglicans to convert slaves began. Anglicanism soon became the dominant religion of black Barbadians as well as whites. Its dominant status was not seriously challenged until the late 1800s when Protestant fundamentalists from North America began missionary work on the island.[5] By the 1920s revivalist churches of many stripes were capturing the imaginations and souls of rural villagers. Despite the white iconography of these churches, their work has been characterized as an attempt to form a genuine "people's ministry." Currently, fundamentalist Pentecostal churches rival Anglicanism in rural areas. As yet, African-inspired religions with black iconography such as the Jerusalem Apostolic Spiritual Baptist Church and Rastafarians have few adherents.[6]

# Religion Today

Some African-derived beliefs and practices are still found in Barbados, and especially in rural parishes like St. Lucy. On occasion, people still report seeing "duppies" or spirits. Folk expressions testify to the prominent place duppies have held historically in people's imagination: "duppy-agent" for undertaker and "duppy-pinch" for a bruise of unknown cause.[7] Although most Barbadians would deny believing in the power of Obeah, they acknowledge its continued existence and do not dismiss it entirely. In 2010, a St. Lucy resident told us how a friend and fellow congregant had reacted on hearing that she had thrown out some photographs of a man and woman they both knew were involved in an illicit sexual relationship. Her friend chided her for not taking their photographs to an Obeah man instead so he could place the images back to back and thereby drive the couple apart. During our earlier fieldwork when a young boy in a nearby village died under tragic and seemingly mysterious circumstances, relatives concluded that he had been the victim of "witchcraft and devil worship." Another villager we know attributed the string of bad luck his family was having to Obeah worked by envious neighbors. Obeah has become a folk idiom through which some Barbadians—not only people in St. Lucy—express their fears and anxieties and explain misfortune, madness, illness, and death.

Eighty-one percent of St. Lucy's residents claim some religious affiliation, a figure similar to the US.[8] Most belong to Christian denominations, with Anglicanism having the greatest number of adherents (23 percent), followed by various Pentecostal sects (19 percent), and Seventh Day Adventism (12 percent). Those who claimed a non-Christian affiliation (e.g., Hindu, Muslim) make up just 2 percent of the parish's population. Rastafarians constitute a tiny (.7 percent), yet significant, religious minority in the parish. St. Lucy's religious profile is not that different from the country as a whole. There are, however, many more Adventists and members of the Salvation Army (in percentages) in the parish than elsewhere on the island. While these statistics clearly reveal St. Lucy's religious character, it is important to point out that nearly a fifth of the parish's population claims no religious affiliation at all.

Women, as elsewhere in the Christian world, are more involved in organized religion than are men. At evening prayer meetings, for example, middle-aged and older women predominate: singing, praying, and perspiring in the tropical heat to the accompaniment of piano or organ, tambourines, and guitar. Church is the primary social outlet for many St. Lucy women—the one place they can meet friends, sing and listen to music, and, for a few hours, escape their everyday responsibilities and routines. In Barbados, church is clearly regarded as women's domain. According to a village friend, "Bajan men think you're soft if you go to church. They feel like more a man if they shy away from religious things." Sociologist Graham Dann found that Barbadian men are less likely than women to believe that religion is the most important thing in life or that the church has helped them achieve their goals.[9]

Villagers equate Anglicanism with respectability and elite status. Anglicans are said to be "proper," and Anglicanism is "high church." Remnants of Barbados' class system are still evident in services, in which, as one person characterized it, "The lower class sits with the lower class, and the upper class sits with the upper class." (Before 1969, a system of pew rents helped to maintain class and, to some extent, race-based segregated seating.) The church's historical dominance in Barbados is apparent on holy days like Ash Wednesday, when schoolchildren are bused to Anglican churches for worship regardless of their family's religious affiliation. The appearance of its church buildings also speaks to its past. Most are impressive structures built of solid coral block with bell towers and stained-glass windows.

The church itself is hierarchically organized, and its rituals are formal. Services are led by a robed priest assisted by a sexton, altar boys and girls, and full choir. Centuries-old rituals employing holy water, incense, and bells punctuate the ceremony. One of our students characterized the setting and service as "majestic," although she also thought the congregation looked "bored" in contrast to those in the Pentecostal churches she had attended:

St. Clement's Anglican Church in Lowlands, St. Lucy (top) and a Pentecostal church in Pie Corner. (Photos by George Gmelch and Ellen Frankenstein)

"Other congregations put so much more spirit, rhythm, and joy in their songs." At St. Lucy's Parish Church, however, not every service is staid. Wednesday night meetings and some Sunday services could quite easily be mistaken for Pentecostal with their use of tambourines and exuberant singing. Generally, however, Anglican services (and burials) are comparatively subdued. Most services consist of hymns accompanied by organ and choir, readings from the Bible and Book of Common Prayer, communion (the symbolic and communal partaking of the Body and Blood of Christ), and a sermon, which typically stresses the importance of leading a righteous life and discusses a current social issue such as decaying moral values and drugs. "I feel the Lord should be worshiped in solitude and seriousness," explained Randolph Broomes, defending the solemnity of Anglican services. "The singing and raving of the others [Pentecostals]—it's like a festival, like Crop Over. Shouldn't there be a distinction between worship and festivity?"

## Pentecostalism

After Anglicanism, Pentecostalism has the greatest number of adherents in the parish. The churches are democratic in style and organization and their services are lively, intense affairs. One village friend, who used to be Anglican but recently joined a fledgling Pentecostal sect, explained her decision: "The [Anglican] priest used to tell us what to do, and I'd just listen. This is the first church where I really feel that I can approach God on my own. That he cares about me." At Pentecostal services all members of the congregation are free to participate. Many services begin with an open prayer session, during which congregants call on the Lord and shout his name each in his or her own fashion. Loud, joyous gospel singing is also a central feature of the service, as people, with arms outstretched, sway, clap, and harmonize to the accompaniment of tambourines, guitar, and drums. A letter to the editor in the daily newspaper, the *Advocate*, bemoaning the corrupting influence of dub music on Barbadian culture, accused some congregations of having gone too far in the direction of entertainment—doing everything from "jump and wave to 'roll yah bam-bam,' 'lift ya leg up,' 'bump,' 'boogie,' and 'jam it'" in their services.[10]

Enthusiastic worship expresses the Pentecostal's commitment to the Lord and gives full reign to the Holy Spirit. One of our students, Johanna, described the effect a Pentecostal service had on her:

> I had to force myself not to cry at one point because I have never had such a gratifying spiritual experience in a church. These people knew where it came from. The words they spoke and sang came from deep down inside their souls and burst out in utter joy. If these people don't truly believe with every ounce of conviction that God is their Lord and Savior, then I don't know where on earth to find people that do. I found myself singing the choruses and clapping along with them, although I

tried not to make too much of a spectacle of myself. There were already a lot of people looking at me, including a little girl in the pew in front who stared at me literally for a full hour. She analyzed every move I made, watching my mouth when I sang, my hands tapping on the bench, and even got down on the floor to look at my legs underneath the bench.

A significant doctrinal difference from other Christian churches is the Pentecostals' belief that "holiness," or a sinless state, can be attained by all who exert self-control. Adult baptism and sanctification means that even women with children born outside of marriage are not excluded from full church membership and that their status as unwed mothers does not carry a lasting stigma. Women involved in a current sexual union, whether living with their boyfriend or not, can hope eventually to be sanctified by regularizing the union through marriage.

Pentecostals believe in the power of the Holy Spirit to enter and cleanse them and to help them resist the devil. Spiritual healing is a critical component of worship. During services people with physical ailments are called forward to "let the Lord minister" to them. Amid the congregation's calls of "Oh, God!" and "Oh, dear Jesus help them," each person is "anointed" with the Holy Spirit by an elder or the pastor, who vigorously rubs olive oil on their forehead, arms, and neck while entreating the devil to leave them. Many of those treated walk away crying, later testifying to feeling much better. God also reveals himself to worshipers through dreams and revelations, and the Holy Spirit sometimes manifests himself at services when congregants experience glossolalia.[11] During periods of intense praying, as people begin to chant, raise their arms, and dance, some slip into a trance-like state and speak in tongues. "You have to be inspired," explained one man. "You just feel these words that you can't put into a natural language. . . . It's a direct prayer." If the congregant has received the gift of interpretation, a message from the Holy Spirit may also be imparted to the rest of the congregation.

Pentecostals believe in a literal interpretation of the Bible, such as the Genesis creation account in which the universe was fashioned in six days. Mark 16:17 is the scriptural foundation for glossolalia: "And these signs shall follow them that believe; in my name shall they cast out devils; they shall speak in new tongues." The church stresses the importance of knowing the Scriptures, and part of being properly dressed for Sunday service is having your Bible in hand. One congregation begins its morning devotions by "breaking the Bible," that is, allowing the Bible to fall open and the Lord to inspire the verse selection for the day. Sermons typically consist of reading the Scripture and then elaborating on its meaning. Members are reminded to "study the word of God" so that they will know it by heart and be better able to resist the temptation and sin—movies and parties, drinking and smoking, gambling and cheating, adultery, and even other churches—that surrounds them. At one service the pastor cautioned people to be wary of the "enemy," denominations as diverse as Seventh Day Adventists, Jehovah's Witnesses, and the Tie Heads (members of the Jerusalem Apostolic Spiritual Baptist

Church). He warned them not to speak to such people: "Just get them out of your house as fast as you can and tell them never to come back!"

In some churches the young are called forward to join hands while the congregation prays for them. Many of those called forward are visibly moved by the experience and join in, crying out, "Touch me Lord!" and "I feel Jesus!" At least once a week all members are invited to give public "testimony" to what God has done for them. At the close of Sunday service, after the offering is taken, visitors and new members are introduced, community announcements are made, and the benediction is given, the congregation files out, members greeting one another with further exclamations of "God bless you" and "Praise the Lord." Pentecostal services emphasize emotional release and community.

# Seventh Day Adventists

Seventh Day Adventism is also a significant part of St. Lucy's religious landscape; it has the third largest number of adherents in the parish. Saturday is the Adventists' Sabbath because it is believed to be the day God rested from Creation. From sundown on Friday until sundown on Saturday the devout refrain from all work and secular distractions: they do not cook, watch television, or operate electrical appliances. It is a holy day, devoted to the Lord. Adventists believe in denial and moderation. Members are discouraged from eating meat (especially pork) and shun alcohol and caffeine. They are not supposed to smoke, wear jewelry or makeup, or go to movies. Many parents censor television and videos for violence and other bad influences. Some believe that birthdays should not be celebrated with gifts since they mark a child's entry into a world of sin. Like other fundamentalists, Adventists believe in a literal interpretation of the Bible. They look forward to the Second Coming of Christ and to the Last Judgment, which most believe to be imminent. The church stresses the need to forgive the sins of others, for only then can people expect forgiveness for themselves. By forgiving others and not sinning themselves, Adventists can achieve perfection and "enter God's kingdom."

Adventists spend several hours at church each week. Services are typically more restrained than those of Pentecostals but livelier than Anglican services. They usually begin with a hymn, followed by a welcome to visitors. Then the microphone changes hands many times as congregants make announcements and lead hymns. Many people have their own hymnals, but some churches also project the lyrics on a screen in front. Many congregations hold a Sabbath school, during which the congregation—divided into age groups or classes—studies a weekly lesson (e.g., "What is friendship and evangelism?"). This is followed by the "divine service" for the entire congregation, which consists of hymns, prayers, Scripture reading, and the minister's sermon punctuated by comments and exclamations from the congregation: "Amen," "Yeah!," and "Alright." During the service there is a fair amount of moving about. Afterward, many people linger in their seats or congregate outside to visit with friends and neighbors. Some congregations share a communal lunch before conducting a second, afternoon service. The youth service is typically more casual and, at one church, consists of hymn singing and religious quiz games, followed by a discussion of a religious topic.

Like Pentecostals who send "missionaries" out into the community, Adventists emphasize the recruitment of new members. Above the altar in the Adventist church in the village of Grape Hall are the words "Tell the whole world, Jesus and the Family." "Bible workers" regularly go to people's homes to discuss Adventist doctrine and distribute pamphlets such as "The Prophecies of Daniel and the Revelation." At least once a year a major "crusade" is held from a large tent. These open-air services are held for several weeks "to give the people in the area an idea of what we believe in," explained one man. Attracted by the music and activity, local people and passersby, no matter how casually dressed, are invited into the tent, where they are given literature on Adventism and told about the church. At the end of the crusade a graduation ceremony is held, and new members are baptized and their names "read into the church."

# Rastafarianism

Although Rastafarianism has a tiny following in the parish, its members are highly visible and have been the subject of considerable local comment, especially in certain communities. Rastafarianism is a black-inspired Christian religion and has been important in heightening black Barbadians' awareness of the African part of their heritage. It was inspired by the teachings of Marcus Garvey, the Jamaican-born founder of the Universal Negro Improvement Association, who in the 1920s and 1930s advocated self-reliance for blacks and a "back to Africa" consciousness. Garvey denounced the colonial mentality that had taught blacks in the Caribbean, United States, and other parts of the world to be contemptuous of their African heritage. Redemption was equated with repatriation to Africa. His prophecy that a black king would be crowned, signaling deliverance, appeared fulfilled in 1930, when Ras Tafari was installed as Emperor Haile Selassie I of Ethiopia. In the following years, as Rastafari beliefs and religious culture developed, the movement was spread by Jamaican activists among the poor of that country and then expanded throughout the Caribbean and into parts of Kenya and Ethiopia and urban areas of the United States, England, Canada, Australia, and New Zealand.

Rastafarianism was introduced to Barbados in the early 1970s; interest in it is said to have been heightened after the Jamaican band Third World visited the island. When we first lived in St. Lucy in the mid-1980s, most villagers actually knew very little about Rastafarians, and their opinions of them varied. They were admired by a small minority for their knowledge of plants and herbs, their healthy vegetarian lifestyle, and their rejection of the materialism and the false values of "Babylon" (outside world). But for most middle-aged and older villagers, Rastafarians were and still are considered to be little more than lazy dropouts and borderline criminals. A colony of about 30 male Rastafarians who once lived in caves south of Cove Bay near two St. Lucy villages created local resentment. Its members were accused of stealing clothing from people's clotheslines and of pilfering fruit and vegetables from their gardens. Local antipathy in the area was so strong that one resident—it was rumored—placed poison in his cucumbers and succeeded in poisoning two Rastafarians. A few villagers told us they stopped planting kitchen gardens in order to eliminate a food source for the "Rastas." Local experiences coincided with press reports of crimes committed in other parts of the country by "dreadlocks," men wearing "dreads" (long, uncombed tresses), who most likely had adopted the outward appearance of Rastafarians but not the religion of Rastafari.

Rastafarianism's African iconography and emphasis on the righteousness of black people is an interpretation of numerous biblical references, especially in the books of Isaiah, Romans, Corinthians, and Numbers. Its teachings appeal primarily to men; it is the only religion in Barbados to have a higher male than female membership. Female adherents clearly occupy a subordinate role. They can only be called to Rastafari through a male and must seek men's guidance in spiritual matters. They also observe numerous behavioral restrictions, some of which are found in other religions. When menstruating, for example, they cannot prepare meals for men, nor can they approach a male ritual gathering. They must also keep their heads covered at all times in contrast to men's flowing dreadlocks. Rastafari's central symbol—the majestic, powerful lion—is clearly linked to men and not to women.

# Secularization

Despite the ubiquity of religious activity in St. Lucy, a fifth of villagers claim no religious affiliation. Older people claim that religion is losing ground. In their day, every child went to Sunday school: "You wake up on Sunday mornings," remembers 80-year-old Marcus O'Neale about his childhood, "and you *know* you had to go to Sunday school. You wasn't asked if you wanted to go. You got up and get ready!" Sunday schoolteachers sometimes came to the homes of families whose parents were not practicing Christians in order to bathe their children and bring them to church. They even provided them with clothing if they did not have something suitable. Today, villagers say that fewer children are going to Sunday school or accompanying their parents to worship services. Some people think this reflects a general breakdown in parental discipline; now that parents no longer routinely "lash" their children, elders claim, children no longer fear authority and are no longer as obedient. Threats of otherworldly punishment no longer work either. "Years ago if a child didn't go to Sunday school," explained Marcus O'Neale, "you'd tell it, 'You going to hell. The devil will burn you in the fire. The fire going to burn you up.' Things like that. Children don't believe that now-a-day."

Some middle-aged and younger adults also express disillusionment with religion. Some villagers attribute this to a failure in church leadership. "They are backing away from the truth, the actual Christianity of the church," claimed Theo Thornhill, who went on to explain:

> Church is actually something like a business today. . . . It's not like years ago where you find church as an encouragement to push you on further in life, to give you something to hold onto, to relax your mind when you got a problem.
>
> Years ago you find religious people getting groups [of people together] sitting down together on the lawn or under the streetlight preaching religion, preaching it. But nowadays every pastor want to build a church to teach religion. And every pastor that has a church have an office in it, and the office has a secretary, and a treasurer controls the money. . . . Twenty-five years ago if you see a pastor on the road walking, you would stop and say, "You know something, Pastor? I really got to talk to you." And he'd say, "Okay, I listen now." Today you say, "Pastor, I got a problem. I got to talk to you." He'll say, "Okay, call my secretary, and she'll make an appointment for you to see me. Right now, I'm in a hurry."

This perception is true of some clergy, but it is also contradicted by the behavior of others who devote hours each week and sacrifice much of their personal lives to counseling their parishioners. One Pentecostal pastor we

Congregants leave a Sunday service in the middle of Checker Hall, St. Lucy, while a neighbor looks on from his porch. (Photo by Sharon Gmelch)

know, for example, spends many hours on the telephone each day and regularly receives early-morning and late-night visits from members of his congregation who come to seek his advice, all in addition to his preaching duties and a full-time civil service job.

For many people, religion is no longer the sole solace or source of information they turn to for guidance. One study found that when Barbadians were asked who they turned to for advice on a variety of issues—including concerns such as death, the future, and marriage which normally fall within the religious domain—only 10 percent mentioned their minister (another 15 percent reported praying).[12] Friends were much more likely to be consulted. While older villagers may read the Psalms to find spiritual comfort and advise one another to "Trust in the Lord," younger people often seek advice and suggestions from colleagues and friends. Barbadians today are also better educated and generally better informed. The mass media, new forms of recreation, and better transportation also make the local church less vital as a social institution. "Back in the '50s," recalls 82-year-old Pastor Emerson Yearwood with sadness, "you would meet people flocking to Sunday schools learning the Scriptures. . . . [It was] a subject like math or English. You would never see a cricket team on the field or a football [soccer] team on the field on a Sunday. People used to like going to the churches." In the past even nonmembers often walked to church on Sundays to listen outside. "Used to be everybody strewn around the churches to see what was going on," remembers Marcus O'Neale, "even if you wasn't a member of that church. They [sermons] carried more meaning. It [religion] was more sacred than today." Such observations are supported by research, which indicates that it is young, single, and better-educated Barbadians, as well as those with higher incomes, who are the least interested in organized religion. Despite the decline in the number of people who claim a religious affiliation, a large majority of Bajans nevertheless feel that they possess "spiritual well-being."

## Chapter 8

# The Global Village

*B*arbados, like all places, is continually changing. Some changes are due to internal events and decisions; others are caused by Barbados' contact with and dependence on the outside world. "We're no longer an island," journalist Charmaine Gill once opined. "Through telecommunications we belong to the world. We're part of the global village." The term "global village" was coined by philosopher Marshall McLuhan in the 1950s to refer to the single, homogeneous world culture he believed the electronic media was creating, and in some respects his prophecy seems to have come true. On a daily basis, television and the Internet bring world events and popular culture directly into the homes of all Barbadians. Events and decisions made thousands of miles away in North America, Europe, and beyond also have a profound effect on the island. After September 11, 2001, for example, fewer Americans travelled abroad, reducing the revenue Barbados earned from tourism. Tourism itself creates change, impacting not only the island's economy but also its environment and culture. Change also comes when Bajans travel abroad, which many now do; whether to work, further their education, visit relatives, or become tourists themselves. When they return, they often bring back new ideas and perspectives. In this chapter we look at St Lucyians' connections to the outside world and at how tourism, the electronic media, and travel and emigration are affecting village and all Barbadian life. We end with some thoughts about the influence and impact of American culture in this process.

## Tourism

While tourism is not new to Barbados it has attained a scale and importance of transformative proportions. Barbados was once known as the "sanatorium of the West Indies," the place foreigners went to recover their health

Staying in touch with the world outside the island. (Photo by George Gmelch)

in the island's warm air and salubrious sea breezes. These early visitors stayed in small guest houses or private homes. In 1751 Lawrence Washington, who was suffering from tuberculosis, arrived in Bridgetown with his younger half-brother George. They rented a house then on the outskirts of city, and stayed for nearly seven weeks hoping for his cure.[1] (Today the Washington House at Bush Hill is a heritage tourist attraction.)

By the early 1900s no fewer than 11 steamships made regular calls to Barbados, and tourism had become a "notable feature" of the economy.[2] The number of tourists who arrived, however, was small. They tended to be wealthy and to stay for substantial periods of time since transportation was expensive and the ocean voyage from England and Europe was long. Although a few large hotels existed, most tourists stayed at small, exclusive "colony" or "club" resorts made up of individual bungalows, which fostered an intimate friendliness between visitors and local staff. In the late 1950s this changed as the era of mass tourism took off.[3] The jetliner made travel faster and easier. Postwar affluence and the adoption of paid holidays for most North American and European workers gave many people guaranteed time off and the money to travel. Travel agencies and tour operators sprang up to package and promote foreign vacations. They popularized the idea of winter vacations in "exotic" tropical locales and helped bring Caribbean holidays within the price range of many middle-income people. Today, well over a million tourists arrive in Barbados each year; roughly half are "stay-over" visitors who spend on average a week on the island; the rest arrive aboard cruise ships and stay less than a day.[4]

Tourism, as noted in chapter 3, now touches nearly everyone on the island and directly employs more than 10 percent of the workforce. Residents of St. Lucy work as maids, security guards, waitresses and barmen, receptionists, and gardeners. Others, like taxi drivers, work in related tourism services or are self-employed as water sport operators or beach vendors. Still other

Sharon Gmelch visits George Washington House and Museum, now a heritage tourism site in Bridgetown. (Photo by George Gmelch)

people sell locally grown vegetables and fruit to hotels and restaurants. The rest of the population experiences the indirect effects of tourism on Barbados' infrastructure and services, environment, and social climate.

Some of the effects of tourism are good. By creating consumers for art and entertainment, for example, tourism has encouraged the development of local music, dance, theater, visual arts, and crafts. Due to tourism demand, the quantity and quality of live entertainment available in Barbados is high, particularly considering the island's small population. This mainly benefits younger St. Lucyians who are more inclined to visit nightclubs and hotels for entertainment. Tourism has also created a major cultural festival known as "Crop Over" that the entire population enjoys. It is based on the end-of-harvest celebration that plantation workers once enjoyed; it included decorating the carts that brought in the last load of sugarcane and holding a party in the mill yard. In 1974 this tradition was commodified as "Crop Over" and turned into a national festival to promote tourism during the slack summer season. It was later reoriented to the domestic market.[5] Crop Over retains some traditional elements like the decorated carts and the crowning of a King and Queen of the Crop—the man and woman who have cut the most sugarcane—but its main features are elaborate costumes and commercially sponsored floats and music performances and competitions in calypso tents. The influence of Trinidad's carnival is evident. Crop Over now entices many Barbadians living abroad to come back home to celebrate.

Tourism's impact on the environment is markedly less positive. Much of the south and west coastline of Barbados is now so crowded with hotels and condominiums and tourist-oriented businesses such as restaurants, boutiques, and gift shops that it is difficult for residents to catch a glimpse of the sea. Coastal property has been priced beyond the reach of most locals. Beaches are being eroded by hotels having built too close to the high tide line. At high tide, the waves strike hotel seawalls, preventing the deposition of sand particles that would normally drop out of the water as it runs up the beach. The government has established setback requirements for coastal construction, but these are often ignored. Water pollution from hotel waste water and laundry detergents is seriously damaging the island's reefs. Although it poses no health risk, the large amount of phosphates and nitrates remaining in treated water stresses living corals, and the particulate matter retards their growth by blocking sunlight. Over time the corals die, and the reef begins to break down. Without a reef barrier to absorb wave energy, there is nothing to prevent further beach erosion. Healthy, growing corals generate the material—sand—necessary to replenish beaches. Because corals are nurseries for many fisheries, their deterioration also threatens another resource, namely, reef fish.[6] Only the steep cliffs, the heavy surf, and the strong undertow along St. Lucy's coastline have saved it from the tourist development and environmental degradation found along the tourist belt on the west and south coasts of the island.

These are impacts few visitors see or understand. From their perspective tourism is benign. A visit to Barbados simply represents a trip away from

Tourists relax at a resort pool. (Photo by George Gmelch)
Cruise ships dock at Barbados' deep water harbor outside Bridgetown. (Photo courtesy of Barbados Tourism Board)

home for the purpose of rest or recreation. To most tourists, Barbados is usually the tropical paradise with a friendly population that the tourism industry advertises. Behind their reserved exteriors, most Bajan tourism workers are friendly and tolerant people who typically excuse tourist misbehavior with an indulgent, "They're just here to have fun." Yet, tourism does place a social burden on the host population. Tourists depend on local people to fulfill their needs by serving food, cleaning rooms, and providing transportation, entertainment, and a stress-free environment. Despite their sometimes boorish behavior, tourists also expect to be treated well by local people no matter how they act, while local people are expected to be cheerful and courteous no matter how they feel.

The fact that most of the tourists who go to Barbados are white and most Barbadians are black can color the interaction between host and guest. Racism—or expectations of it based on the country's colonial history and many black Bajans' personal experiences as emigrants living in England, the United States, and Canada—sometimes arises in interactions between tourists and locals. Some hotel employees, for example, render indifferent service. As one hotel manager explained, "Too many of my people . . . equate service with servitude." Richard Haynes, as leader of the opposition in Barbados' parliamentary system of government, once warned his countrymen to consider the damage racial confrontation would inflict on the country, "I urge you to reflect on the damage which even a 10 to 15 percent decline in tourism expenditure will do to the Barbados economy. . . . National pride, yes. Racism, no."[7] "Treat them well and they'll come back," television public service announcements once advised local people in an educational effort. Workshops for teachers are organized so that they can introduce tourism into Barbados' school curriculum, teaching students to be aware of their demeanor and of the need to change their deportment in order to match the expectations of visitors. The fact that adults as well as students have to be told how to act indicates something of the unnatural strain tourism places on the population.

When tourists display their ignorance of Barbados, residents are understandably annoyed and offended. "Tourists often tell me 'I'd never heard of Barbados before I came here,'" one St. Lucy resident complained. "Dey don' have de slightest idea wha Barbados is. Dey ask me about de size, wha type of people live on de island, our language. Man, why dey come?" complained one beach vendor. "Dey tink it [Barbados] sometin' like de wilderness of Africa. Dey expect tah see de people runnin' round wid a cloth about de waist," said another. "People are surprised when I speak," the owner of a small restaurant reported. "They say, 'My, but you speak well.'" "Their ignorance is sometimes profound," noted a former hotel manager:

> They'd come and ask where they can get stamps. I'd tell them, "There's a little shop around the corner that sells stamps." They'd come back, "Well, they don't sell American stamps. We want to post a letter to the States." I'm telling you, it's absolutely amazing. Any five-year-old in the Caribbean would know that, and they don't because to them the USA is

the whole world. . . .? Some of these people have saved up a long time to come to the Caribbean, and, when they get here, they figure everybody here has to be more ignorant than they are. They're just the tops, and aren't we glad they came!

Some Bajans who have prolonged contact with tourists can benefit financially. Hotel workers and vendors who get to know a particular tourist well over a period of days or weeks may receive a substantial tip or gift at the end. In some instances friendships develop that are maintained over the years through correspondence and return visits. One St. Lucyian was able to set himself up in the water-ski business because of the financial help he received from a foreign woman friend. A young St. Lucy woman who had looked after an American couple's children during their two-week vacation returned with them to the States to work for a while as a live-in babysitter.

The most intimate and noticeable tourist–local relationships are those between female tourists and "beach boys." Most beach boys are young and muscular and prowl the beaches in revealing swimsuits. Some wear dreadlocks to enhance their exotic appeal. While some are homosexual or bisexual and cater to gay tourists, the dominant beach boy–tourist relationship is heterosexual. Some Bajans believe that any foreign woman who arrives on the island without a male companion has come for more than tourism's conventional "three Ss"—sun, sand, and sea. While some women undoubtedly do have sex in mind when they arrive in Barbados, other women fall into romantic relationships with local men, which they believe are genuine and unique. Fantasy notions of "the Other" clearly play a part in beach boy–tourist interactions; many white women regard black men as more "natural" and virile. Being a tourist is also a liminal experience or "time out" during which a person's behavior seems not to really count; she need never return to Barbados, and no one at home need ever know what she has done.

"Romance tourism," as anthropologists Deborah Pruitt and Suzanne LaFont note in a study of beach boys in Jamaica, is not just a gender inversion of the "sex tourism" found in developing countries like Thailand or the Philippines, in which male tourists travel explicitly to avail themselves of the paid services of local prostitutes, most of whom have been tricked or forced into prostitution. Relationships between beach boys and female tourists are voluntary and "constructed through a discourse of romance and long-term relationship" with money seldom directly changing hands.[8] Unlike the local Filipina or Thai woman, the Barbadian beach boy in many respects has the upper hand. He is the person who is on familiar ground, while the tourist is in a foreign land.[9] He is familiar with such relationships, while she may not be. Ironically, in addition to being her personal guide and sex partner the beach boy often acts as a single woman's male protector while she is on the island. Ultimately, however, it is the female tourist who controls the relationship since she pays the bills, can break it off, and will leave the island to return home. Both may be emotionally vulnerable, but it is the beach boy who is financially dependent and who must show deference and appreciation in order to maintain the relationship.

For the local beach boys, some of whom live in St. Lucy, relationships with white female tourists provide intimacy and sex with a foreigner, short-term comforts (e.g., dinner, drinks, a nice room), and enhanced status among their peers—as self-styled nicknames like "Dr. Love" suggest—and sometimes, financial help or help with emigration. Most local people view beach boys as disreputables. Yet, they also seem to hold a pragmatic attitude toward this special tourist–local relationship. "The people that are being approached are not innocent," claimed one villager. "They're both getting what they want [sex]. It's like trying a different type of food." According to a young woman we know: "The guys get a good time out of it. It's good for them. The only time it's a problem is when they [female tourists] mess with my guy." Being a beach boy is a young man's occupation, and those who engage in it move on to more respectable work by their 30s.

Other kinds of tourist–local encounters are undoubtedly more in keeping with the Tourism Board's assertion that "social interaction between people of diverse origins and cultural backgrounds [brings] positive benefits."[10] We have both listened to tourists and local people share information about their personal lives and their countries' customs, economy, and politics. A young hotel worker from St. Lucy, for example, struck up a conversation one afternoon with a Venezuelan couple at the hotel pool. As they clung to the side, he practiced his Spanish with them, and they asked him to explain Bajan dialect. Together they talked about the need for people to learn other languages so they can better understand one another's cultures. The Mighty Gabby, Barbados' best known calypsonian, frequently talked to tourists during his early career as a singer on tour boats: "They'd talk about things I had no experience of—fascinating things, like countries, the size of them, the fastness of them, the kind of things that you could do there. . . . I was a young man having all this information fed to me. . . . I was fascinated, and I wanted to go see for myself."[11] One tourist behavior of which Bajans disapprove is the wearing of beach clothing in public. Locals interpret this as disrespect. "They walk around in these skimpy bathing suits. . . . Even in supermarkets you see men walking around without shirts and the ladies in only their swimwear," commented one woman with distaste. "A Bajan would be arrested if they were caught walking around with the lack of clothing that tourists walk around in." Local people are far from prudish; they just think that businesses and the streets of town are not the proper place. Some store owners have put up signs informing tourists: "No bare backs" and "No scantily dressed persons allowed in the store."

Tourism is often credited or blamed with transferring outside values and behaviors to the societies tourists visit. Many tourists are living manifestations of the affluence St. Lucy's residents and other Barbadians so frequently see on TV. Tourists staying at the best hotels wear expensive clothing and jewelry, and some seem to flash their money and the latest electronic gadgets and sports equipment. "The locals see what the tourists have and how they're living, and they want it," explained one hotel worker. "They don't see the 50 weeks of work behind it. They think it's easy." "There's a feeling out there among the younger guys," elaborated a professor at the University of the West Indies,

> that there's a lot of money to be had and that "We want part of it, and we want it now." Serious steady work is not fast enough for them and doesn't pay well enough. So there's a tendency to hustle and perhaps cut corners for it [money]. There's a thin line between hustling and cutting corners and doing illegal things. . . . I think [tourism] has had that kind of impact, although it's hard to separate this from the impact of television, which has changed expectations—expectations that are unrealistic given the resource base of this country.

Not all tourists are wealthy, of course. Some, including college students on spring break, take advantage of package tours and stay at inexpensive south coast hotels. But Barbados is known for luxury, especially along the west coast and portions of the south coast. Here luxury hotels, resorts, gated condominiums, and golf, polo, and yachting developments like Port St. Charles in nearby Speightstown all contribute to local people's sense of relative deprivation. Even those who do not work in tourism have heard stories about how much hotel rooms can cost. "Do you know at Sandy Lane that some people pay as much as $2,000 US a day!" exclaimed a police superintendent during an interview about tourism and crime in the 1990s. Hotel workers watch tourists purchase drinks and food at inflated prices and then waste much of it. For most villagers going to a restaurant is still a bit of an extravagance, but times are changing.

More people today are engaging in activities that were once strictly the domain of foreign tourists, including eating out, going to a nightclub, taking a vacation in a hotel, and even visiting eschewed "heritage sites" like St. Nicholas Abbey, a restored plantation in nearby St. Peter. (Most Barbadians have shown little interest in preserving historical sites that have associations with the former plantocracy and slavery or have little cultural meaning to them, including Amerindian archaeological sites.)[12] Attitudes toward working in tourism are also changing. According to Bernice Critchlow-Earle, director of the Barbados Hospitality Institute, the reason is "people can earn more from tourism today [2010]. It's the sector that has the most jobs, although some jobs are still associated with servitude issues—waiting and junior cooks, for example."

The degree of contact St. Lucyians have with tourists varies, of course. Those who work in the industry have daily contact, while most people's exposure is limited to brief encounters and observations they make on the streets or in the stores in town. Few tourists stay in St. Lucy as there are no hotels and only one small guest house. In the 1960s a resort with an Olympic-size swimming pool was built at North Point, but poor management, lack of a good beach, and its isolation from the tourist belt led to its closing. Exposed to salt spray and strong winds for many years, it is now a ruin. Some tourists do visit the parish to enjoy its natural beauty, such as scenic Cove Bay with its view of Pico Teneriffe, a craggy rock spire, or to explore the Animal Flower Cave, a wave-eroded underground cavern that opens beneath the cliffs onto the sea. Some island bus tours wind their way through the parish, but typically the passengers only leave the bus to glimpse the sights and take a few photographs and are soon back on board. Off the beaten path, some villages in the parish are never visited by even the most intrepid traveler. However, the new housing and commercial development, with a 200-unit hotel, to be built at Pickerings, mentioned earlier, will likely increase the contact between St. Lucyians and tourists in the future.

# Electronic Media

Wireless radio arrived in Barbados in the 1930s with Radio Distribution, which relayed British Broadcasting Corporation (BBC) programs from the UK and short-wave stations from the US and Canada to the island. But many people were poor then, especially in St. Lucy, and did not have the receivers needed to get the transmission. In 1963 Barbados launched its own radio service, the CBC's Radio Barbados. At that time—on the eve of independence—there were an estimated 25,000 radio receivers on the island but an even larger audience since neighbors often listened together. A year later, CBC launched a single television channel, TV8. Within months there were 4,000 television sets on the island; five years later the number had more than tripled.[13] Television was wildly popular, although at first it was a rare commodity in St. Lucy. Most people in the parish did not acquire television sets until the 1970s. By 2000, however, nearly every household had at least one TV (and one or more radios).[14] Many people also owned DVD players.

With television, world news and foreign lifestyles and tastes, particularly from the United States—once largely gleaned from the letters emigrants' wrote and from returnees' tales—are beamed directly into people's homes.[15] Most villagers are avid television viewers. In many homes the set is constantly on and the sound seldom turned down. While it is still common to see neighbors talking outside in the early evening, more people are inside watching television. Although TV8 offers some locally produced programs, and the government recently launched an educational television (and radio) service, American shows dominate the programming that Bajans watch and prefer. Game shows, sports, and programs like *Divorce Court, CSI,* and *Dancing with the Stars* were especially popular in 2010, as was the Black Entertainment Television (BET) network. So many people were still watching the nightly broadcast of "Days" (*Days of Our Lives*), the long-running American soap opera, that telephoning someone between 6:00 and 7:00 PM remained virtually taboo. One friend reported calling her doctor and being told to phone back after the program. An elderly woman we know becomes so absorbed in the drama that she yells at the program's villains, frets about the safety of her favorite character—"She just got to be careful 'cause I don't trust he. I don't

Tourists visit Animal Flower Cave in St. Lucy (top); scenic Pico Teneriffe on St. Lucy's Atlantic coast. (Photos by Sharon Gmelch)

trust he a'tall, a'tall, a'tall"—and commiserates by phone with a friend following each episode. Once darkness falls most villages seem eerily deserted, with disembodied dialogue drifting into the streets through open windows radiating a flickering blue glow.

Some Barbadians worry about American cultural penetration. "Man, we're the 51st state!" exclaimed one man who had lived in the States.

> I came back home because I wanted my children to grow up in an unspoiled environment, but now Barbados is the same as the States. My kids want to wear American clothes, eat American food, do American things, play American games. They're even watching American football and baseball on TV.

In the opinion of Sandra May Shorey, formerly of the Barbados National Trust, television programming should be controlled:

> Television should be tempered with more Barbadian and Caribbean-influenced programs. It's obviously easier to get *Days of Our Lives* and *Dallas* than something from Trinidad or Jamaica. Those countries produce very little, and what they have produced might not yet be of a standard high enough for the tastes of Barbadian viewers. But we don't really make an effort to get anything else. . . . We've never made an effort to develop programs, to explore our culture, because there's this ready-made culture, and we can just buy it.

Because commercial sponsors buy advertising time on programs they know are popular, the money to develop local programming remains limited. Nor can the Barbados government afford to support expensive program development. "We haven't got the money to do good programming—the gloss and the glitter. The government can't afford it," explained a St. Lucy educator. "So how can we retain our culture? How can we compete with the rest of the world?"

Despite the enjoyment that television brings, it is blamed for a variety of social ills. Communities and families, people say, are no longer as close. "People don't visit one another's place like b'fore—that gone," observed an elderly neighbor. Instead of being outside with their friends, many children stay indoors to watch television, play computer games, or search the web. Recent research conducted with secondary school students aged 14 to 17 found that they watched an average of 22 hours of television per week, a figure similar to US teens.[16] When asked what they liked about their favorite programs, they cited the humor of programs like *Everybody Loves Raymond* and *The Simpsons;* the thrill of programs like *Fear Factor, X-men,* and *WWE SmackDown;* and the emotional warmth of family programs like *Gilmore Girls.* The single most popular network was the US-based BET.

Bajans sometimes describe themselves as "quick to want and to acquire." "It's impossible to see the equivalent of *Dynasty* and *Knots Landing* [TV shows popular in the US in the 1980s] every night of the week, month after month, without assuming that you, the viewer, are also entitled to this standard of life," the late columnist and author John Wickham explained to us. Anxious to "improve" their lives, many people feel it is important to keep current with what is shown on TV. Many women watch television not only to view their favorite programs but also to track the latest fashions. Some young women in St. Lucy flatly refuse to leave their homes to attend a party or concert unless they can dress in the latest style. Men are not immune. In the mid-1990s teenagers and young adults walked around the villages wearing Nike sweatbands and sport shoes, baggy name-brand jeans, and T-shirts emblazoned with American sports team logos. In 2010, many boys and young men wore the very low-slung pants with exposed boxer shorts popularized by American rap subculture. The young son of a maid and a security guard we know begged his parents to buy him an expensive pair of Nike shoes—the equivalent of a week's combined wages—so he would feel comfortable at school. They gave in, reasoning that their modest income should not prevent him from being "happy." Ubiquitous advertising on TV, of course, is based on creating dissatisfaction that can be remedied if the viewer purchases and uses the ad's product—that is, happiness is linked to the product.

Some Bajans, like many Americans, believe that television and films contribute to violence and crime. The film *Colors,* which graphically portrayed the activities of a Los Angeles gang, was singled out as having spawned a number of mimic gangs in Barbados after its release in 1988. St. Lucy's first reported gang, which called itself CBC (the same acronym as the television network), made its appearance a year later in 1989. Its members confined themselves mainly to breaking bottles in the streets, minor theft, making noise, and hassling passersby; nonetheless their behavior shocked many residents. Expressing the views of many at the time, a resident of the village of Broomefield wrote the local newspaper, "Well, we know that they have drugs all over Barbados. . . . But I never thought we would have lawless young people in St. Lucy walking about making other people miserable. You only hear about that kind of thing in Bridgetown."[17] Many gang names in the early 1990s suggested media influence. In Bridgetown and neighboring areas the major gangs then were CNN, Vietnam, Beirut, and Q-8 (after Kuwait); in St. Lucy, as mentioned, CBC. Two were names of television networks, while three were countries or cities in which televised wars and violence had recently taken place. In 2010, gang names included Black Mobs, Outlawz, and Dog Pound and no longer had an overt media connection.

Although the research findings are mixed, some studies suggest when violence is rewarded on TV there is a greater tendency for children and adolescents to imitate it. The sheer frequency of violent acts and images on television normalizes violence and desensitizes children to real people's suffering. Both violent and high-action programs arouse their viewers, which can contribute to violent behavior in aggression-prone individuals. In a US study, which followed children over a 22-year period, from third grade through adulthood, Rowell Huesmann and fellow researchers found that heavy television viewing was more predictive of later aggression than any other factor, including poverty, grades, single-parent homes, or exposure to real violence.[18] When we asked Barbadian police about the connection between television and crime and youth gang activity, they emphasized the more direct influences of unemployment and drugs instead.[19]

Some people in the parish worry about the moral tone of much television programming, not only the violence but also the glorification of material wealth, greed, corruption, casual sex, and power striving at any cost. Pornography, available on satellite TV, was a particular concern to some parents in the 1990s. "It sickens me," said one father. "You wouldn't believe what you can see—I was talking to my friends about it this morning—it's gone past pornography. And who's to stop the children from seeing it? We're creating a sick society." Now, with the Internet, pornography is more readily available than ever before.

Television has a good side, of course, and this is the side that most villagers see. It provides inexpensive entertainment and can also be educational. Locally produced public service announcements, aired throughout the day, promote proper parenting, environmental awareness, HIV/AIDS prevention and treatment, and good citizenship. Documentaries, international news, and some talk shows increase Bajans' awareness of social issues outside the country, although with an American bias. "Before Anita Hill," one professional woman told us in the 1990s, "there was no concept of sexual harassment in Barbados. There was no name for it. I know I got no sympathy when I complained [five years earlier], so I dropped it." (Anita Hill was the African-American law professor who accused Supreme Court nominee Clarence Thomas during his widely watched confirmation hearings in 1991 of sexual harassment when she had worked for him.)[20] Bajans' current interest in diet and fitness likewise is attributed by many to the influence of American TV.

Two of the most significant changes to have occurred in Barbados in recent years are the widespread use of the Internet and cell phones that, among other things, have greatly increased people's communication with each other. At the time of the 2000 census, just 13 percent of St. Lucy households had a computer and only half those had Internet access.[21] The figures for both parish and nation are much higher today. In 2010, half the country's entire population used the Internet.[22] Although we do not have a specific figure for St. Lucy, all the families we visited in 2010 had computers and Internet connections, with at least one family member regularly surfing the web and using e-mail and Facebook. In the 1990s we first learned of a serious computer virus from a teenage girl in Checker Hall who e-mailed George to warn him; the first person to invite him to become a friend on Facebook, in 2008, was also living in St. Lucy.

One recent study discovered that Bajan adults use the Internet primarily for e-mail (49 percent) and research (36 percent), followed by online shopping and news (5 percent each) and general web browsing and music downloading (just over 2 percent each).[23] The study of secondary school students mentioned earlier found that their favorite Internet activities were chatting with family, friends, and non-Barbadian e-pals living overseas, followed closely by searching for music, lyrics, and information about their favorite recording artists. Other popular uses were e-mail, shopping online and playing games, and conducting research. Boys were twice as interested in gaming and online shopping as were girls, while girls were more interested in online chatting and searching for music and lyrics. What these secondary students liked most about the Internet was the information it provided and the feeling it gave them of participating in the world beyond the local community.[24] Three-quarters of their online friends lived outside Barbados, about half in the US. They spent an average of 11 hours online per week in addition to their 22 hours of television viewing.[25]

Facebook, founded in 2004, quickly became popular in Barbados. Virtually every person we asked or visited in St. Lucy in 2010 had at least one member of their household using it; nationally, there were over 100,000 Facebook users.[26] When we visited the O'Neales in Round Rock one afternoon, their son Eric was not at home so we left our e-mail addresses; the very next morning we both had a "friend request" from him on Facebook. "Everybody on it," asserted Ermine Greaves, a 58-year-old friend in Checker Hall. She only looks at her Facebook account every few days and doesn't post much on it since "everybody see it and it a small island," but she values having an account because it allows her to keep in touch with distant family and friends. One friend living on the island of St. Lucia, whom she had not heard from in ten years, recently found her through Facebook, as have several adult nieces and nephews living in the States whom she hasn't seen since they were very young. Her household has wireless Internet service that is used by many family members when they visit. Her grandson, who lives next door, drops by each day to help her manage her online farm—Facebook's Farm Town game. Ironically, while many people in St. Lucy have given up real farming because of the cost and effort of keeping chickens or black-bellied sheep or the difficulty of growing a garden in the face of constant damage by monkeys, some have taken up operating virtual ones.

Not all villagers of Ermine's generation feel as comfortable with the Internet as she does. Roosevelt Griffith, profiled in chapter 4, uses it indirectly. Curious and mechanically inclined, Griff is interested in energy and in making his household more self-sufficient. With plans obtained online, he has built a small, wind-generated electricity plant, and when we visited in 2010 he was working on a system to convert his pig waste into biofuel. His granddaughter does the Internet research, which he then implements.

Shopping is another common Internet activity. Just over half the adults who were interviewed for one study of online shopping had used the Internet to buy a service or goods.[27] The vast majority were from retailers in the States, yet another example of America's cultural hegemony and market influence in the region.

The government actively promotes the use of computers in schools and community centers and waives import duties on such items.[28] Although in

2010 only one of Barbados' eight national libraries provided public Internet access, elsewhere wireless Internet access is becoming common, including business offices, coffee shops, restaurants, and hotels in tourist areas—and at a handful of dedicated Internet cafes.

The Internet has transformed the way Bajans communicate with each other. Besides e-mail and Facebook, in 2010 many people in St. Lucy, and other parishes, plug a USB device called a "Magic Jack" into their computers, which, for a nominal yearly fee, allows them to make and receive free telephone calls to and from the United States and Canada. Other people Skype relatives and friends abroad. The Internet thus allows Bajans to contact a range of people unimagined a decade ago—they now speak to, text, and, with Skype, see each other.

At the time of the 2000 census, about a third of St. Lucy's households had telephone landlines and another 7 percent had cell phones, but when we returned in 2010 it seemed as if everyone had switched to cell phones. In fact, it was difficult to contact many of the people we knew because they had abandoned their landlines and thus were no longer listed in the telephone book. We often resorted to Facebook to find them. Cell phones allow Barbadians to keep in frequent contact with each other. They also provide entertainment. As anthropologists Heather Horst and David Miller found in Jamaica, cell phones can also alleviate loneliness.

> Whenever men are hanging around, what they seek is an answer to the ubiquitous question "Wa gwaan?" They crave simply for something to be going on, for there to be a happening. . . . But, if there isn't anything and one is fed up playing dominoes or kicking a ball around, then at least one or two individuals can be on the cell phone, playing games, sending text messages or just scrolling through names, looking for someone who might have enough credit on their phone for a chat.[29]

Many St. Lucy parents now give cell phones to their children, some as young as six and seven years old, for security and for the convenience of being able to contact them at any time. According to Jeff Broomes, a secondary school principal, parents in Barbados no longer trust other people to look after their children in the same way they used to; rather than relying on the principal to contact them should something go wrong at school, for example, they want direct contact with their children. But many parents also give in to pressure; cell phones are trendy and every child wants one. So many schoolchildren at all age levels in Barbados had cell phones in 2007 that the government banned their use in schools.[30]

# Emigration and Travel

Emigration has a long history on the island, prompted both by poverty at home and opportunities abroad, and was one of the earliest outside influences to affect the average Bajan. Most early emigrants travelled to other islands in the Caribbean and to South America. From the mid-1800s to the early 1900s an estimated 50,000 people left Barbados to work as seasonal agricultural laborers in British Guiana (Guyana) and Trinidad.[31] During the construction of the Panama Canal as many as 60,000 people, including many from St. Lucy, left to work as "pick and shovel men" for ten cents an hour.[32] Other Bajans emigrated to England, Canada, and the United States, fleeing the kind of poverty the Reverend F. Godson described in the parish in 1916:

> In Crab Hill and neighboring villages I came in contact with the worst poverty and destitution I ever saw up to then—except perhaps in one village in St. Kitts. It was a specially [sic] dry year, even for that area; there was little work on the plantations around and very little money; the people's own gardens were bare; and the price of imported foodstuffs, together with sugar, were soaring. So I met with hunger, rapes, dilapidated shacks, idling, and praedial larceny on an exceptional scale.[33]

Emigration tides waxed and waned over the years. In 1924, for example, emigration to the United States virtually stopped when national quotas on the number of immigrants allowed in were set; the entire British West Indies was limited to 200 people, and only five from Barbados.[34] By the 1930s most emigration outlets within the Caribbean had also closed. "There was nothing coming in terms of food. We ate sweet potatoes morning, noon, and night," remembers one villager. "It was a very hard time." Opportunities for emigration did not open up again until World War II, when Britain, Canada, and the US needed workers to help in war industries and alleviate manpower shortages in agriculture. Some Barbadians also travelled to Britain as volunteers in the armed forces. After the war, large-scale emigration began once more. Many people, like Siebert Allman (chapter 4), went to Britain on the Sponsored Workers Scheme. British companies and government agencies including the London Transport Executive and the British Hotel and Restaurant Association sent recruiters to Barbados, and people from all over the island traveled to Bridgetown to be interviewed. If they measured up, as most did, they were assigned a job, trained, and transported to England. Many women went to Britain to become nurses or to work in light industry in cities like Manchester, Liverpool, and Birmingham. The Barbados government even provided some people with travel loans. Between 1955 and 1961, 19,000 Barbadians left for Britain; nearly 4,500 were "assisted migrants."[35]

In the 1960s the emigration tide shifted to Canada and the United States, which had eased their immigration restrictions, at the same time that Britain was closing its doors. Although American and Canadian policies favored skilled workers and professionals, some unskilled workers managed to obtain "labor certification" to become domestic workers and seasonal agricultural laborers. Our landlord in Josey Hill went to the United States six times during the 1960s to pick fruit in the Northeast. Another neighbor cut sugarcane in Florida for five years. A friend from Pie Corner went to Canada for training in instructional technology. Emigration continues today. Household surveys in five St. Lucy villages in 1994 and 1996 found that a quarter of the households then had one or more children living abroad. Families we know have adult children who have studied filmmaking in Cuba, clinical psychology in the US, art in the UK, and international law in Europe. Many return to Barbados bringing their expertise with them. The former principal of St. Lucy's Secondary School and current principal of Alexandra Secondary in nearby Speightstown was student body president at Union College in upstate New York.

For those at home, the influence of emigration is felt as soon as people leave. When parents go, young children often move in with granny or an aunt. Most emigrants send back "remittances," money to help support family members in Barbados or to save for their return. Men living on their own sometimes send back half their pay to their mothers or wives. Roosevelt Griffith, profiled in chapter 4, managed to save a large part of his income and returned home to build a wall house. In 2004 remittances to Barbados amounted to US$200 million or 4.3 percent of the country's GDP; they were the country's third largest source of foreign exchange, after the money earned from tourism and the sale of domestic exports.[36] Some people in St. Lucy still receive containers of clothes and other goods from abroad each Christmas. An older villager remembers the time when even a carton of hand-me-downs or secondhand clothes was valued: "No matter how old, from America, it look new." Barbadians abroad also help family members when they emigrate. Indeed, many people belong to "transnational families" whose members, although scattered in countries around the world, continue to share the normal family functions of economic support, decision making, and nurturing from a distance.[37]

Most Bajans who emigrate intend to stay only a few years and then return. "On the way over to England," remembers Roy Campbell, who grew up in the village of Rockfield, "my thinking was that I'd be away no more than five years. I had a goal of saving a certain amount of money and then coming back to Barbados and getting a little house." A good indication of most Bajans' strong attachment to home and of their intention to return is the fact that they have one of the lowest naturalization rates of any foreign-born immigrant group in the United States.[38] When Bajans do return home, they often become agents of change. Most return with substantial capital from their savings and the sale of their overseas assets (e.g., house, car), which they invest in housing at home. In St. Lucy the most substantial wall houses have been built by returnees, the earliest with "Panama money." Returnee housing is almost invariably large and of high quality, setting a standard to which others in the parish aspire. Early returnees also introduced material innovations. Those who came back from Panama, for example, are credited with introducing better household sanitation and window screens. North American returnees once brought back wall-to-wall carpeting. Today, however, because of the pervasive influence of television, film, and the Internet, there is relatively little new in the way of material objects that returnees can introduce that villagers are not already familiar with.

New homes of well-off return migrants. (Photos by George Gmelch)

Returnees continue to be an important source of information, nevertheless. In the words of Valenza Griffith, who lived in England:

> When I was a child the people that came back from overseas were accepted back into the community [Coles Cave, St. Lucy]. We were eager to learn things from them—what the houses were like, what the education was like, do they write like us. . . . Today people know a lot more about America and England than they did in my time. But some people still asked me some weird questions [when I returned in 1973], like if you get false teeth for free in England or if they really bury three and four people in the same grave or if people's toes drop off in England from the cold.[39]

In an earlier survey of Barbadian returnees, one of us found that nearly half of those who took jobs at home believed that they had been able to introduce changes at their workplace based on knowledge they had acquired abroad.[40] An American-trained certified public accountant, for example, introduced the electronic processing of financial accounts to a Bridgetown firm. A nurse trained in England introduced new techniques for monitoring babies before birth. In some fields major innovations can be attributed to the influence of return migrants. A movement to deinstitutionalize child care in Barbados came from returnees working in the Ministry of Social Services who had become familiar with new approaches while working in Canada. While most of these changes have taken place outside the parish, they still have an indirect effect on many villagers' lives.

Some returnees, of course, have a direct impact on the parish. A former rector of the St. Lucy Parish Church instituted policies he learned in England that expanded his parishioners' participation in church services. Siebert and Aileen Allman ran a small general store in the village of Sutherland for several years. Another St. Lucy couple shipped three buses home from England and set up a minibus service. Although such enterprises typically do not employ many people, they do provide needed services and contribute to the smooth running of the parish economy and the convenience of its residents. Anthropologists Constance Sutton and Susan Makiesky believe that, in the village they studied, return migrants had a greater influence on people's racial and political consciousness than did either better-educated middle-class Barbadians or student radicals.[41]

The influence that returnees have at the local level, however, is much less than it could be. Many returnees encounter jealousy and resistance to their ideas. A civil servant who also had worked in England believes his colleagues at home ignored his ideas "because . . . they feel threatened. They don't want to admit that maybe you have the answer, especially when you've only been on the job half as long." A teacher recalls the way her colleagues would "push up their faces" (grimace skeptically) at her suggestions. Another frustrated returnee explains, "We [returnees] have the same ideas as North Americans who live here. The difference is that people will listen to what the foreigner has to say but not to their own kind. They'll say, 'Who the hell is he to tell us what to do? He's only Barbadian like us.'"

Nowadays, many more Bajans travel abroad for business, education, and pleasure. In 2009, over 11,000 people were issued nonimmigrant visas to enter the US for these reasons.[42] Other popular destinations include Canada and England and, to a lesser extent, South America and other Caribbean islands. Several parish friends have been on cruises to other islands in the Caribbean. One returned from a cruise with new ideas for remodeling his house; he removed most of a ceiling to create a vaulted great room with a gallery above. Aileen Allman, profiled in chapter 4, has joined her daughter, who works abroad, on several vacations to Africa and Europe. One young woman from St. Lucy travels regularly to New York and Miami to shop for clothes: "Here you might have to pay $30 [US] for a pair of shorts and they not even brand. . . . I love to travel and I only travel where I can shop. I won't go nowhere I can't." Many people take shopping lists from family and friends along and return with suitcases and boxes packed with clothing, fabric, linens, and small appliances purchased at a fraction of what they cost at home; others ship loaded barrels home. School groups from St. Lucy also travel, most recently, to visit Puerto Rico, Venezuela, and Disney World in Florida.

Despite all this travel, many people in the parish have never left the island and some seldom leave St. Lucy. While fund-raisers help defray the costs of school trips, for example, many parish children still cannot afford to go. This difference captures a very real feature of the parish—the growing disparity in its residents' lives. It was not so long ago that most people worked on the same plantations, lived in the same modest houses, and shared very similar lives. Today, St. Lucy's residents earn different incomes, have had different opportunities and experiences, and consequently, have much less in common. Their closest ties are as likely to lie outside the parish as within it.

# Final Thoughts

$\mathcal{T}$he modern phenomenon of globalization is actually a continuation of a much older reality. Barbados and other Caribbean societies have a long history of involvement in the world system, as anthropologist Sidney Mintz and other social scientists have pointed out.[1] Their cultures emerged out of one of the earliest colonial encounters with the West that involved the exploitation of the region for newly desired staples such as sugar, the decimation of aboriginal populations, and the introduction of new populations from Africa, Europe, and Asia. After slave emancipation, globalization was further fostered by the widespread emigration of Caribbean people to Europe and North America. Today telecommunications play a key role.

Despite Barbados' long-term involvement in the outside world, the focal point of most people's daily lives, until comparatively recently, was their local community. People were connected to their village or neighborhood and to one another by kinship, friendship, economic cooperation, and the homogeneity of their experiences and beliefs. Today many of these ties remain, but it is also true that "community" is becoming increasingly detached from place; the village is no longer the focal point of life for most people. More than ever before, people belong to "relational communities" that are geographically dispersed and include people living outside the village and parish, in other parts of the island and in other countries in the Caribbean, North America, and Europe. As families have become transnational, Barbadian culture has become increasingly "deterritorialized."[2]

The Caribbean today is less a part of the Third World than the First World's first annex.[3] In 2010, Barbados was for the first time categorized as "highly developed" according to the criteria of the United Nations Development Program's human development index. With this increasing affluence—despite periodic setbacks like those caused by economic restructuring in 1991 and shifts in international tourism—more of St. Lucy's residents are directly participating in the world economy and other cultures: buying imported consumer goods, watching foreign television, surfing the Internet, communicating across national boundaries through e-mail and Facebook, and traveling off the island for advancement and pleasure. Barbados' beautiful environment and comfortable standard of living attract hundreds of thousands of foreign tourists each year who create job opportunities and spawn new desires as well as new problems. Similarly, the island's political stability, legal system based on English common law, disciplined workforce, high literacy rate, advanced telecommunications, as well as favorable tax laws lure international business.

Does this growing international orientation on the part of Barbadians combined with US cultural penetration threaten Bajan culture? When villagers are asked to describe their "culture," most people are hard put to think of anything to say. There is little they regard as uniquely Bajan except foods—flying fish and coucou[4] (which the younger generation now seldom prepares)—and traditions such as Land Ship[5] and Crop Over. It is fairly common to hear Barbadians claim that "Barbados has no culture." The suspicion that Bajans may be "mimic men," versions of someone else rather than truly themselves, is a recurring theme in the former colonies of the Caribbean.[6] It is an unfair, although understandable, characterization given the island's heritage of colonization, enslavement, and the destruction and transformation of traditional African lifeways. Barbadians, like other Caribbean peoples, created their own Creole culture—a mix of European colonial culture and their African past.[7] Black Barbadians became "Barbadians," they did not remain Africans, nor were they ever imitation Britons despite the appellation of "Little England" commonly used by western foreigners.

The issue of cultural identity in Barbados took on special meaning in the late 1960s with the island's independence and the end of its economic and emotional dependency on Great Britain—"the mother country." These events coincided with a new shift in emigration to North America, the development of mass tourism, which brought many more North Americans, including Canadians, to the island, and the introduction of television (which today is dominated by American content). As we have seen throughout this book, the signs of US cultural penetration are everywhere. America's cultural hegemony came at a bad time—so close on the heels of independence. Just when Barbadians were free to examine the roles their African and British heritages had played in creating their Creole culture and identity and to forge stronger regional ties with other countries in the Caribbean, they were overwhelmed by America. Moreover, the Internet has greatly facilitated the diffusion of American culture.

Although Caribbean countries were colonized by diverse European powers, their shared historical experience unifies the region.[8] These Caribbean nations share broad social frameworks resulting from the plantation system, enslavement and the African past, and the process of creolization. A common curriculum emphasizing Caribbean history, geography, and literature prepares students for higher education and has replaced the old European-based curricula. It has introduced new, unifying concepts—oppression, colonization, colonialism, slave mentality—and a more critical analysis of the past.

Regional church, tourism, university, sports, and development organizations and associations are also beginning to unite neighboring islands.[9] Carifesta, a regional creative arts festival periodically organized and hosted by different Caribbean countries, celebrates the creativity and popular traditions of the region through art displays, drama, dance, and music. Held in Barbados in 1981, it is credited with strengthening Bajans' awareness of their shared heritage with other Caribbean nations. The National Cultural Foundation, which was founded by an act of Parliament in 1983, thereafter organized festivals, workshops, and lectures that reinforced this regional awareness as well as instilled an awareness of Barbados' unique history and traditions.[10] Today, the annual Crop Over festival, an event that Bajans take great pride in and that is similar in many respects to Carnival in Trinidad and other islands, serves as a symbolic affirmation of country's "Afro-Caribbean" identity.

On a daily basis in the villages and in many urban neighborhoods, African influences are expressed through the use of Bajan dialect, African-derived proverbs and folk beliefs, traditional foods, herbal remedies, dance, and attitudes toward death and the afterlife.[11] It is rare, however, for people in St. Lucy to connect such everyday practices to Africa. Indeed, many villagers still harbor negative stereotypes about the continent that is more likely to conjure up images of poverty, famine, and war than cultural pride. None of the adults from our neighborhood, for example, were interested in joining the many people from Bridgetown who gathered at Farley Hill in the adjacent parish of St. Peter to celebrate Nelson Mandela's release from prison in 1990. The African-inspired art, clothing, hairstyles, and personal names and the intellectual interest in Africa found in some urban circles are still unusual in the parish. Most villagers, indeed most Bajans, are much more oriented to North America and, to a lesser extent, other Commonwealth nations, than to Africa.

This orientation will remain strong, given the economic dominance of the United States, the pervasiveness of its media, the appeal of its consumer goods, and the many personal contacts Bajans have with the country through work, study, and travel. Barbados' small size, its limited economic resources, and modest political clout also mean that its relationship with the outside world is asymmetrical. Although cultural flows are never unidirectional as Barbadian recording artist Rihanna's global success indicates, the future many Barbadians foresee for their island is one that is increasingly Americanized. "Come back in 20 years and you will see that we have become the latest outpost of American civilization," a local teacher asserted with resignation. "The St. Lucy that I grew up in is finished." Clearly, the St. Lucy of his youth is gone, but it is unlikely that Barbadians will ever lose all sense of their own Afro-Euro Caribbean culture and identity. While cultures are constantly changing, they are surprisingly resilient at their core.

# Appendix A
# Students and Barbadians
## Lessons from the Field

*O*n this book we have occasionally included the experiences and observations of our field school students—who lived and conducted research in Barbadian villages over a 20-year period—to support points we make about life in St. Lucy. Here we look at the students' own experiences in terms of what they learned about culture and about themselves by living in a Barbadian household and community for ten weeks.

First, a word about field schools. The primary aim of a field school is to teach anthropology students how to do field research; how to develop a research "problem" or set of questions, design an appropriate methodology, record data in field notes, and, near the end of the term, analyze that data and write up a research paper. Good field schools represent experiential learning and cultural immersion at their best. We became acquainted with cultural anthropology field schools many years ago while in graduate school. George spent a summer in a mountain village in the state of Tlaxcala, Mexico; Sharon spent a summer in a fishing village on the southwest coast of Ireland. Both were NSF-funded field schools designed to prepare graduate students for their dissertation fieldwork. Our experiences were challenging, with bouts of illness, loneliness, and culture shock. But they were also exhilarating—real-life adventures—and unquestionably, the most memorable and valuable part of our graduate training. Once we began our teaching careers, it was natural that we would want to provide students with a similar experiential opportunity.

## Rural Life

Most of the students we took to Barbados attended Union College in upstate New York and grew up in suburbs or cities and had never lived in the countryside. For them, a significant part of their field school experience was living in a rural village among people who are close to the land. Each morning, before dawn, they were awakened by the sounds of animals in the yard. Many of the families they lived with grew crops and raised a few animals. The students quickly began to learn about the behavior of chickens, pigs, sheep, and cows. Some witnessed animals giving birth and being slaughtered. They experienced the satisfaction families got from consuming food they had grown or raised themselves. One student described her initial surprise at an everyday occurrence:

> I was in Mrs. S.'s kitchen and she was making sugar cakes. The recipe calls for a lime, and, when she didn't have any in the kitchen, she just walked into the yard and pulled a few off the nearest tree. It was nothing to her, but I was amazed, and I thought how in that situation I would have had to drive to the supermarket.

The students also lived close to nature as some shared their bedrooms with a green lizard or two and/or mice, cockroaches, and frogs. They were struck by the darkness of the night sky and the brightness of the stars with no city lights to diminish their intensity. A student from Long Island described it as "like living in a planetarium."

The social world of the village was also unlike anything most students knew. In doing a household survey, for example, they discovered that everybody seemed to know everybody else and that many families were related to other households in the village. Not only that, but they knew one another in more than one context. Relationships were not single stranded, as they often are in the suburbs and cities the students had come from; instead, people were tied to one another in multiple ways. Few students had known a place of such intimacy before, in which relationships were so embedded with different meanings and a shared history. Some students reflected on and compared the warmth, friendliness, and frequent sharing of food and other resources they witnessed in the villages with the impersonality, individualism, and detachment of urban and suburban life at home. But they also learned some of the drawbacks to living in small communities: the lack of anonymity being one. People were keenly interested in the affairs of their neighbors. As the students became integrated into the community, they discovered that they, too, could become the object of local gossip. One year several female students learned, to their dismay, that stories were going around that they were either mistresses to their host fathers or sleeping with their host brothers. The gossip hurt, for they had worked hard to gain acceptance, valued the friendships they had made, and naturally were concerned about the damage to their reputations that such rumors might cause. Even though the students spent only ten weeks in their villages and many would never return, they still cared a great deal about what people thought of them.

But the first adjustment students had to make was to the tropical climate. The sun in Barbados is intense, especially in the middle of the day, and especially for students raised in New England, as many of our students were. The saying "only mad dogs and Englishmen go out in the midday sun" is an apt warning. For the first few weeks the students were debilitated by the heat, from which there is little respite since village homes are not air-conditioned. Inevitably, the skin of some of the women students broke out, causing them more misery and self-consciousness about their appearance.

The students also had to adjust to the slow pace of village life; the diversions and entertainment that they were accustomed to at home were largely absent. It seemed to most like there was little to do apart from their research. In the early weeks, many felt desperate to escape their community, but we didn't permit it except on designated days. Our reason for doing this was to force students to seek companionship and recreation within their communities and build friendships. They learned to be resourceful and also spent a good deal of time just "liming," socializing with people in the village, a practice that resulted in a good deal of informal education about Bajan culture. By midway through the term most students had adapted so well to village life that they no longer reported being bored or felt a strong need to get away. Some no longer left their village on their day off.

# Materialism

While living in rural Barbados, many students arrived at a new awareness of their own comparative wealth and materialism. One of the strongest initial impressions many students had of their villages was that people were poor—most of their houses were small, their diets were limited, and they lacked some of the amenities and conveniences the students were accustomed to. Even little things sometimes reminded students of the difference in wealth, as Betsy recounted after her first week in the field:

> At home [Vermont] when I go into a convenience store and buy a soda, I don't think twice about handing the clerk a twenty-dollar bill. But here when you hand a man in the rum shop a twenty-dollar bill [equal to ten US dollars] he often asks if you have something smaller. It makes me self-conscious of how wealthy I appear, and of how little money the rum shop man makes in a day.

The initial response of the students to such incidents and to the lower standard of living they saw around them was to feel embarrassed and even guilty that they had so much in comparison. Such feelings were short-lived, however, for, as the students got to know the families and their communities better, they no longer saw poverty; even the houses no longer seemed so small. They discovered that most people not only managed quite well on what they had but were quite content as well. In fact, most students eventually came to believe that the villagers were, on the whole, more satisfied with their lives than most Americans were. Whether or not this was true, it is an important perception for students whose ideas about happiness have been shaped by an ethos that measures success and satisfaction by material gain. About his host family Dan said:

> I ate off the same plate and drank from the same cup every night. We only had an old fridge, an old stove, and an old TV, and a few dishes and pots and pans. But that was plenty. Mrs. T. never felt like she needed any more. And after awhile, I never felt like I needed any more either.

Many students claimed that after Barbados they became less materialistic. When they returned home, they were surprised at how many possessions they had. Some went through their drawers and closets and gave the Goodwill and Salvation Army the things they didn't really need. Some reported that when they returned to campus they didn't bring nearly as many things with them as they had before. Most also said they would no longer take luxuries that they were accustomed to on campus and at home, such as hot showers, for granted. Amy said:

> When I came back I saw how out of control the students here are. It's just crazy. They want so much; they talk about how much money they need to make, as if these things are necessities and you'll never be happy without them. Maybe I was like that too, but now I know I don't need those things. Sure I'd like a great car, but I don't need it.

When alumni of the program were asked in a survey—conducted years after their return from Barbados—how their attitudes had been changed by having lived and done fieldwork in a Bajan village, most said they were less materialistic today than their friends who have not had a similar experience. One compared her attitudes with those of acquaintances who had served in the Peace Corps.

# Gender

Female students quickly learned that gender relations are quite different in Barbados. Indeed, the most difficult adjustment for many was learning how to deal with the frequent and aggressive advances of Bajan men, as noted in chapter 5. At the end of her first week in the field Jenny described a common plight of female students:

> When I walk through the village, the guys who hang out at the rum shop yell comments. I have never heard men say some of the things they tell me here. My friend Andrew tells me that most of the comments are actually compliments. Yet, I still feel weird. . . . I am merely an object that they would like to conquer. I hate that feeling, so I am trying to get to know these guys. I figure that if they know me as a person and a friend, they will stop with the demeaning comments. Maybe it's a cultural thing they do to all women.

Many Barbadian men feel it is their right as males to accost women in public places with hissing, appreciative remarks, and offers of sexual services. This sexual bantering is ignored by most Barbadian women, but students like Jenny were not sure what to make of it. They did not know whether it was being directed at them because local men thought white girls were "loose" or whether Barbadian men behaved that way toward all women. Anxious to be accepted and not wanting to be rude or culturally insensitive, most female students tolerated the remarks the best they could while searching for a strategy to politely discourage them. Most found that, as people got to know them by name, the verbal harassment subsided. But they still had to get accustomed to other sexual behavior. For example, when invited to their first neighborhood parties most students in the early years were shocked at the sexually explicit dancing, in which movements imitate intercourse. (In more recent years, dancing in the US has become much more sexually explicit and more similar to the Bajan style.) One female student wrote, after having been to several such fêtes:

> I was watching everyone dance when I realized that even the way we dance says a lot about culture. We are so conservative at home. Inhibited. In the US one's body is a personal, private thing, and when it is invaded we get angry. We might give a boyfriend some degree of control over our bodies, but no one else. Bajans aren't nearly as possessive about their bodies. Men and women can freely move from one dance partner to the next without asking and then grind the other person.

Students discovered that, to an even greater degree than in the United States, women in Barbados are regarded by most men as both subordinates and sexual objects. Masculinity is based in large part on men's sexual conquest of women and also on their ability to give them pleasure. Being sexually active, a good sex partner, and becoming a father all enhance young men's status among male peers.

# Race

Virtually everyone in the villages in which the students lived was black, while all but two of the nearly 100 students we took to Barbados over the years were white. (One student was African American and the other was a Japanese exchange student.) Before going to Barbados, many students had little contact with African Americans, and they had never experienced racial prejudice themselves. During their first few weeks in the field, most were acutely aware of their own "race," of being white while everyone around them was dark. Students were often called "white boy" and "white girl" by people in the village until they got to know people personally. Village children sometimes asked if they could touch the students' skin or hair; others marveled at the blue veins that showed through the students' white skin. Those with freckles were sometimes asked if they had a skin disease. One student's homestay mother asked how she managed to drink from a glass with such a "big nose." During the second week one student wrote, characteristically:

> I have never been in a situation before where I was a minority purely due to the color of my skin and treated differently because of it. When I approach people I am very conscious of having white skin. Before, I never thought of myself as having color.

A few students became hypersensitive to race during the early weeks of their stay. When they left their villages, they were often the only white person on the bus. Often they were stared at (sometimes because other passengers worried that they had gotten on the wrong bus as it headed into the countryside of St. Lucy). They noticed that as the bus filled up, the seats next to them were often the last to be taken. Some students reacted to this with feelings of shame or guilt. Here is the extreme reaction one student had to a disturbing encounter with a local woman during her first week in Barbados when she took a bus to a remote area:

> The woman glared at me as if she was seeing the evil white woman who has been responsible for the oppression of her people. I felt like I had chained, maimed, and enslaved every black person who had ever lived. The feelings were so strange. . . . Somehow I felt responsible for the entire history of the relationship between blacks and whites. I carried this woman's face with me for the rest of the day. When I got on the bus to go back to my village I felt very alone and very unwanted, like the mere presence of my color was making a lot of people very uneasy.

But concerns about race, even the awareness of race, diminished rapidly as the students made friends and became integrated into their villages. In fact, by the end of the term most said they were "rarely" aware of being white. Several students described incidents in which they had become so unaware of skin color that they were shocked when someone made a remark or did something to remind them that they were different. Sara was startled when, after shaking the hand of a woman in her village, she remarked that she had never touched the hand of a white person before. Several students reported being surprised when they walked by a mirror and got a glimpse of their white skin. Betsy wrote that, although she knew she wasn't black, she no longer felt white.

What was the outcome of all this? Did students develop a better understanding of what it means to be a minority? Did these experiences translate into their having more empathy at home? We think so. Most of the students we questioned about the impact of their experiences mentioned a heightened empathy for African Americans and, for some, other minorities as well. Several said that when they first returned home they wanted to go up to African Americans and have a conversation. "But I kept having to remind myself," said one student, "that most blacks in America are not West Indians, and they wouldn't understand where I am coming from."

# Social Class

American students, particularly compared to their European counterparts, have little understanding of social class. Even after several weeks in Barbados most students were still fairly oblivious to class and status distinctions in their villages. The American suburbs in which our students grew up are fairly homogeneous in social composition and housing; most homes fall in the same general price range. In contrast, Barbadian villages, as described in chapter 1, exhibit a spectrum of housing, from the large two-story masonry homes of return migrants to the tiny board houses of people who eke out a living from a small plot of sugarcane and a kitchen garden.

It was largely from comments that their host families made about other people that our students became aware of status distinctions within the village. They also learned about class and status by making mistakes, from violating norms concerning relationships between different categories of people. Kristen learned that there are different standards of behavior for the more affluent families after she walked home through the village carrying a bundle on her head: "Mrs. C. told me never to do that again, that only poor people carry things on their heads, and that my doing it reflected badly on her family."

The experience of one student is worth recounting in some detail. Johanna met 24-year-old Joseph on the street outside the primary school in her village. They began talking while watching the children play, and at the end of the conversation they arranged to meet the following week in front of the village store. Joseph had grown up in the parish but had become interested in Rastafarianism while smoking ganja (marijuana), listening to Bob Marley's "Redemption Song," and particularly after visiting a Rasta colony where the brethren explained their religion to him. After becoming a Rasta, Joseph left his parents' home, gave away all his belongings, and moved to "Creation"—some secluded caves where he now lived with four other orthodox Rastas. When Johanna's seven-year-old host sister returned from school later that day, she told Johanna that the children at school had been upset when they saw her talking to Joseph and had said, "Oh no, that man is going to take Johanna into the mountains and kill her!" Her teacher also told her to warn Johanna not to talk to Rastas. Despite the warnings, Johanna met Joseph the following week and left the village with him to visit Creation. There she visited the tiny community and learned how they collected and grew their own food and cooked it in calabash pots as most of St. Lucy's families once had. While in Creation, Joseph and the other orthodox Rastas did not wear clothes. Nor did they drink alcohol or smoke, except for sacramental ganja.

Johanna visited Joseph a number of times and was accepted by the Rastas as a "daughter" and "woman of consciousness." But, as the days went by, she noticed that people in her village were becoming less friendly. "What was once a hearty greeting from across the road has become a malicious stare," she recorded in her journal. A group of young village men who had verbally harassed her at the beginning of her stay but who stopped once they had gotten to know her had begun to treat her as a sexual object again. One day, as she passed the local rum shop, a loud voice called her "the devil's child." On another day an elderly woman mocked her as she walked by, asking, "You goin' to the cave to have a time [sex]?"

When Johanna's host mother learned of her visits, she called her into her room and shut the door. "Have you been up with the Rastas?" she asked. "The way she reacted frightened me . . . looking so desperate and disappointed," Johanna reported. "I don't think I ever realized the stigma attached to Rastas until this moment." Her host mother then told her that people in the village were talking, saying she was smoking marijuana and bathing naked. "I don't want my house and my children connected with these things," she informed her. "I know you only have a little time left in Barbados, but I have to live here for the rest of my life." As Johanna wrote in her journal:

> The gravity of what I was doing was suddenly apparent to me. She was kind enough to have me stay in her house, and now I was jeopardizing her reputation and the reputations of her children. We talked about it. How the fact that I was a woman alone made it ten times more despicable than if I were a male or with a group of people. "See those people sittin' around the shops?" she said. "They'll all be sayin', 'That Johanna is a drug addict.'" Indeed, they did.

Reflecting on her experience Johanna wrote, "I have discovered the power of a societal norm: nice girls don't talk to Rastas. When girls who were formerly nice talk to Rastas, they cease to be known as nice. Exceptions, none." (Johanna was allowed to finish her stay with her host family, but her fieldwork in the village was never as good as it had been before she began hanging out with the Rastas.)

As in many field situations, the first villagers to offer the students their friendship were sometimes marginal members of the community. This created special problems when a student was a guest in the home of a higher-status village family. Then host parents became particularly upset when they discovered their student was seeing a disreputable man or woman (e.g., beach bum, drug user, or sexually permissive woman). In the early years of the field program, some female students dated local guys they met on the beach. These "beach bums," as they were locally known, were generally considered to be disreputable hustlers. The female students who entered into these relationships, which sometimes were romantic, were oblivious to what the local reaction would be and to how little privacy there was in a village. One student said she wrongly assumed that people would look favorably on her going out with a local man because it would show that she wasn't prejudiced and that she found blacks just as desirable as whites.

# New Perspectives on North America

In learning about Barbadian society, students inevitably made comparisons with American culture. Especially in the early stages of fieldwork, students typically thought about Barbadian customs in terms of how similar or different they were from those at home. They were often assisted in making such comparisons by local people who knew a lot about the United States from various media (particularly television, films, and the Internet), from tourists visiting Barbados, and from their own travel (see chapter 8). Students quickly discovered, however, that the villagers' perceptions about the United States were often at odds with their own. Many people, for example, believed that all the students were wealthy, owned nice cars, vacationed in exotic places, and so on. Early in the term, students often found themselves defending the United States from criticism. For example, one student described getting very annoyed when a guest at his host family's dinner table criticized the United States and talked about all the chemicals (hormones and antibiotics) that adulterated American chicken. He knew this to be true but said, "I couldn't take it anymore and fought back. I felt like an idiot afterward, defending American chicken."

Over time the students felt less compelled to defend their own society. Indeed, many became quite critical of the United States, or at least aspects of it. Why? What made them question their own society after a few months in Barbados? Part of the answer is found in their growing appreciation for Barbadian life and their identification with local people. They came to see many things from the perspective of their village friends. Another factor is the students' exposure to North American tourists. When they went to the beach or town on their free day, they encountered tourists and were sometimes disappointed or embarrassed by what they saw and heard—tourists entering shops and walking the street in skimpy beach attire or their loud and intrusive voices. "When we'd be walking in town where there were lots of tourists," said Anne, "we'd make comments like, 'Don't they know that Bajans are conservative dressers? No Bajan would ever wear her bathing suit or short shorts in town, and especially in a store.'" In the words of another student, Pearl:

> When we'd see them [American tourists], we'd be like, "I hate them."
> We'd sort of be kidding but the truth was, we really didn't like them. I
> didn't like the fact that most tourists just take Barbados for granted and
> treat it as some kind of Disneyland. They think Barbados is here for their
> own pleasure. I hated seeing Bajans having to cater to tourists just
> because they need their money.

From a variety of sources students learned about the negative impacts of tourism (as discussed in chapter 8). Viewing tourism as part of a broader "Americanization" of the region, many students became critical not only of tourists but of the United States' presence abroad generally. To their dismay, they were usually regarded by Barbadians as tourists themselves. Whenever they left their villages, they become just another white face in a predominately black society. Even when they were in their home villages—where most local people know that their reason for coming to Barbados was for education rather than recreation—they were still thought of as tourists, largely because they were short-term visitors, and they were there in winter, the prime tourist season.

## Fieldwork and Education

Students learned about more than just cultural differences from their experience of living and doing anthropology in a Caribbean village. Most returned from Barbados with a more positive attitude toward education. This stemmed in part from seeing the high value that villagers placed on formal education, which is the chief means of upward mobility in Barbados. They learned that they were accorded respect and adult status largely because they were working toward a university degree. And as the weeks passed, most students also became deeply involved in their own research and were surprised at how much satisfaction they got from doing something they previously had

Students Pearl Jurist-Schoen and Chelsea Tussing with the O'Neale family. (Photo by George Gmelch)

regarded as "work." A number of the students have told us that they didn't see education as an end in itself, as something to be enjoyed for the sake of learning and intellectual stimulation, until their fieldwork in Barbados. One student wrote about her changed attitude after returning from the field:

> I feel isolated from many of my old friends on campus, and I no longer feel guilty missing social events. . . . I appreciate my education more and I do much more work for my own understanding and enjoyment rather than just for the exam or grades. I find myself on a daily basis growing agitated with those who don't appreciate what is being offered to them here. Several of my classmates blow off class and use other people's notes. A lot of what I feel is from seeing how important education was to my Bajan friends, compared to the lax attitude of my friends here.

In the field, students spent a good part of each day talking to people, often directing conversations toward topics they were investigating. To succeed at their studies they had to be inquisitive, learn to probe sensitively in order to dig deeper into the person's knowledge or memory of particular events or aspects of culture, and to concentrate, that is, to really *listen* to what they were being told, and later, to recall it so that they could record it in field notes. Most students became proficient at maintaining lengthy conversations with adults and at asking pertinent questions. These are interpersonal skills they brought back with them and will make use of in many aspects of their own lives.

While the students spent a term discovering and making sense of the differences between their own culture and that of the Barbadians around them, most ended up concluding that beneath the differences, beneath the veneer of custom, Barbadians and Americans are not all that different, that there is a shared "human nature." In the words of one student, who is now an anthropologist:

> If I had to sum up my whole trip in one experience it would be this. It was late at night, a full moon, and I sat in a pasture with a local Rastafarian. After hours of talking, about everything from love to politics, the two of us came to an interesting conclusion. Although we lived a thousand miles away from each other, and that our skin color, hair style, and many personal practices were quite different, at heart we were the same people.

While this may seem naively romantic to some and mere commonsense to others, it is not a notion that many college students who have not lived abroad share. For the students, living in a Barbadian village meant not only getting to know another culture but also looking in a mirror and catching a glimpse of themselves—of who they are as Americans and as human beings.

# Appendix B

## Village Occupations by Economic Sector

| Occupation | N | Occupation | N[a] |
|---|---|---|---|
| **Agriculture[b]** | | **Manufacturing** | |
| Farmers | 24 | Machine operator | 7 |
| Cotton pickers | 5 | Factory (misc.) | 3 |
| Vegetable sellers/hawkers | 3 | Mechanic/"engineer" | 2 |
| Cane cutters | 1 | TOTAL | 12 |
| TOTAL | 33 | | |
| **Tourism (hotels)** | | **General Services** | |
| Maid | 11 | Shopkeeper | 9 |
| Waiter/waitress | 3 | Store clerk/cashier | 9 |
| Gardener | 2 | Bank teller | 9 |
| Cook | 1 | Baker | 7 |
| Security guard | 1 | Hairdresser | 7 |
| Other | 6 | Butcher | 4 |
| TOTAL | 24 | Seamstress/tailor | 3 |
| **Government** | | Secretary | 2 |
| Police | 8 | Auto mechanic | 1 |
| Nurse | 7 | Barman | 1 |
| Schoolteacher | 6 | Bus driver (private) | 1 |
| Civil servant | 6 | Data entry | 1 |
| Postal service | 4 | Pharmacist | 1 |
| Road worker | 3 | Store manager | 1 |
| Telephone | 3 | Taxi driver | 1 |
| Military | 2 | Other | 3 |
| Social worker | 2 | TOTAL | 60 |
| Bus driver/conductor | 1 | **Construction** | |
| Customs officer | 1 | Carpenter | 13 |
| Engineer | 1 | Mason | 9 |
| TOTAL | 44 | Electrician | 2 |
| | | Plumber | 1 |
| | | Other | 6 |
| | | TOTAL | 31 |

[a] $N = 196$

[b] The absence of any fishers in this table is due to the fact that none of the surveyed villages is a fishing community; only two of St. Lucy's approximately 30 communities are fishing villages.

# Endnotes

## Chapter One

[1] The 2000 census—the latest for which figures were available at the time this edition was being written in 2011—counted 268,792 people with an estimated undercount of 16,172 (Barbados Statistical Service). With an area of 166 square miles, Barbados then had a population density of just over 1,700 persons per square mile. The parish of St. Lucy has a population density of 256 per square kilometer, the second lowest density of the 11 parishes on the island.

[2] The population of St. Lucy in 2000 was 9,328. Ninety-nine percent were classified as "black" or "mixed"; in addition, there were 47 white individuals and 38 East Indians (Barbados Statistical Service, 33).

[3] Ibid., 61. The 1990 census had found that 85 percent of St. Lucy's population had been born in the parish; in 2000, the figure was 72 percent.

[4] With the exception of one African-American student and one Japanese foreign-exchange student, all the students in our anthropology program over the years were white (and predominantly middle-class) Americans.

[5] See Beckles, *The History of Barbados*; and Watson, *The Civilized Island, Barbados*. The census of 1712 reported 1,208 whites and 2,742 blacks living in St. Lucy. According to P. Jackman, most of the poor whites lived in the eastern part of the parish, near Pie Corner.

[6] According to the 2000 census, 44 percent of the total adult Barbadian population owned at least one motor vehicle (Barbados Statistical Service, 277).

[7] In 2010, the St. Lucy post office listed 108 districts with separate postal codes within the parish, but these do not reflect separate communities. The Arawak Cement plant, for example, has its own code; the adjacent village of Checker Hall has five.

[8] All names of villagers are pseudonyms except for those profiled in chapter 4.

[9] Barbados Statistical Service, 212, 214.

[10] Ibid., pp. 218, 220.

## Chapter Two

[1] Henry Powell, an English ship captain who sailed to Guiana just weeks after he delivered the first group of English settlers to Barbados, is said to have taken 30 Amerindians on board in Guiana and brought them back to Barbados. They arrived as freemen but were later enslaved. There are also early accounts of Amerindians from St. Vincent, located 92 miles away, sailing to Barbados on their own in long, dug-out canoes. Richard Ligon notes, however, that the Indians constituted only a slight fraction of the total Barbadian population.

[2] Handler, "Amerindians and Their Contributions," 195–97.

[3] Ibid., 204.

[4] See Beckles, *The History of Barbados*, 13–14.

[5] Ibid., 21.

[6] Eighty percent of Barbados indigenous flora was eventually lost to sugarcane. McManamon, "Hidden Data," 2.

[7] By 1670 the bulk of white servants coming to the West Indies chose to go to Jamaica and the Leeward Islands instead, where opportunities to own land someday were greater. See Beckles, *The History of Barbados*, 31.

[8] Handler, *The Unappropriated People*, 73.

[9] Williams, *Capitalism and Slavery*, 54.

[10] Mill, Book 3.

[11] Beckles, *The History of Barbados*, 43.

[12] Ibid.

[13] Voyages Database. The Caribbean received nearly one-half of all Africans brought to the Americas in the 350-year span of the organized transatlantic slave trade (Knight, 111).

[14] Thornton, 97.

[15] T. Phillips.

[16] Parry et al., 89.

[17] Behrendt et al.

[18] T. Phillips.

[19] Galenson, 39.

[20] Voyages Database.

[21] Edwards, 32.

[22] Quoted in Beckles, *Afro-Caribbean Women . . .* , 19.

[23] Handler and Lange.

[24] Later in the slave period many plantations also had a small infirmary, or "sick house," descriptions of which range from a "horrible unhealthy hole" to one planter's exaggerated claim in 1823 that "there is a good hospital on almost every estate" (Handler and Lange, 98).

[25] Quoted in Handler and Lange, 77.

[26] Ibid.

[27] Dickson, *Mitigation of Slavery*.

[28] Handler and Lange, 68.

[29] Quoted in Beckles, *Afro-Caribbean Women . . .* , 15.

[30] Beckles, *The History of Barbados*, 61.

[31] Quoted in H. Watson, 91.

[32] Ibid.

[33] Ibid., 33.

[34] For a thorough and comparative study of "marronage" see Handler, "Escaping Slavery in a Caribbean Plantation Society."

[35] Quoted in Beckles, *Afro-Caribbean Women . . .* , 64.

[36] Handler, *The Unappropriated People*, 16.

[37] See Handler, "Slave Revolts and Conspiracies . . . in 17th Barbados."

[38] See Handler, "Freedmen and Slaves in the Barbados Militia."

[39] H. Watson, 28–29.

[40] Beckles, *The History of Barbados*, 56.

[41] See http://www.nationalarchives.gov.uk/education/lesson52.htm (last accessed 2/8/11).

[42] Ibid.

[43] Quoted in H. Watson, 84.

[44] Handler and Lange, 33, 214. See also Handler and Frisbie.

# Chapter Three

[1] Hagelberg, 87.

[2] Howard, 36.

[3] Handler, "Small Scale Sugar Cane Farming in Barbados."

[4] Handler, *The Unappropriated People*, 117.

[5] Quoted in Carmichael, *Barbados: Thirty Years of Independence*, 26.

[6] Barbados Ministry of Tourism; the exact figures were: stay overs 526,541 and cruise 539,092.

[7] "Managing the Open Economy in a Time of Crisis," Address by Dr. DeLisle Worrel, Governor of the Central Bank of Barbados, BIBA Investment Conference on 28 October 2010. http://www.centralbank.org.bb/WEBCBB.nsf/vwNews/ DE7816140C976F74042577D8006DA538?OpenDocument (last accessed 2/2/11).

[8] Doxey, 120.

[9] Director Bernice Critchlow-Earle, personal communication, 2010.

[10] Holder, 210.

[11] These occupational data were obtained from household censuses ($N = 212$) that were randomly administered in four St. Lucy villages by the students in our field program in 1994. In each household the interviewee was asked to list all occupations of every adult living in the household who was no longer in school. We did a similar occupational survey in Josey Hill in 1992. The percentages of different occupations produced in that survey are in line with those gathered by the students in 1994, suggesting a degree of reliability.

[12] Freeman, *High Tech and High Heels . . .* , 87.

[13] According to Freeman (*High Tech*), Barbados is more accurately described as a "near-shore" location. This term distinguishes it from "onshore" operations in the US and more distant "offshore" locations like China or India.

[14] Freeman, *High Tech and High Heels . . .*

[15] Freeman, "Designing Women," 184.

[16] Freeman, *High Tech and High Heels . . .* , 253.

[17] See Wilson, *Crab Antics*; and Horowitz.

[18] Stanford.

[19] French, 44–45.

[20] Levy and Lerch.

[21] See "Barbados Country Profile," p. 48, in *The Global Gender Gap 2008 Report*. https://members.weforum.org/pdf/gendergap/report2008.pdf (last accessed 12/2/11).

[22] http://hdr.undp.org/en/statistics (last accessed 2/22/11).

# Chapter Four

[1] In 1996, a mere 175 acres of cotton were reaped compared to 750 acres the year before.

[2] Freeman, "Designing Women," 283.

[3] A company representative claimed that the only eyestrain employees suffer is due to their failure to get or wear prescription glasses.

# Chapter Five

[1] This discussion deals only with heterosexual relationships. Little is said openly about homosexuality in Barbados, and in the villages most homosexuals remain closeted. Nor are bisexual, transgendered, and intersexed individuals and relationships openly discussed.

[2] Sutton and Makiesky-Barrow, "Social Inequality and Sexual Status in Barbados," 492.

[3] Hoefer and Wilder, 256–57.

[4] Greenfield.

[5] Errol Barrow, a native of St. Lucy, became Barbados' prime minister in 1961 and led the country to independence in 1966. He served until 1976 and was reelected in 1986 but died a little more than a year later. He is now one of Barbados' national heroes; his birthday, on January 21, was declared a national holiday in 1989.

[6] Dann, *The Barbadian Male*, 43–44.

[7] As of 2007, there were 2,078 known cases of AIDS in Barbados and 3,408 people with HIV; 1,379 people had died. www.hivsurveillance2009.org/docs/session_ix/pres3.ppt (last accessed 2/21/11).

[8] Senior, 189.

[9] Frazer.

[10] Barrow, "Male Images of Women," 58.

[11] Powell.

[12] Ibid.

[13] Dann, *The Barbadian Male*, 150.

[14] At age 11 all children take the Common Entrance Examination. Their score determines which secondary schools they will be allowed to enter. Girls, who are believed to mature earlier and therefore have an academic advantage over boys, must score ten points higher on the exams. Older schools like Harrisons, Queens, Combermere, and Lodge are recognized as being superior to schools like St. Lucy Secondary and are usually selected by parents as the top choices for their children. This system separates the academically talented and privileged children—those raised in middle-class and more affluent homes—and reproduces inequality, since some schools end up with student bodies made up entirely of children with top test scores, while others primarily have children scoring at the bottom. (The prestige of the secondary school a child attends also carries great weight later in life.) Many village friends now become separated, since they travel to different parts of the island to attend secondary school—the school they attend (and its prestige) clearly evident from their uniforms.

[15] Sea eggs are the edible sex organs of the white sea urchin (*Tripneustes ventricosus*). It was a popular food until the sea urchin population declined in the 1970s. Folklore maintains that sea eggs enhance virility and fertility.

[16] The chigger (*Tunga penetrans*) is a tropical skin-burrowing flea, very common in Barbados (and elsewhere in the Caribbean) during the period of slavery and well into modern times. The female burrows into a person's skin, usually between the toes or under the toenail, and remains there while her eggs develop. Causing intense itching, the developing eggs eventually break through the skin, leaving a sore that can become gangrenous and that can also be a pathway for tetanus and other infections (Fraser et al.).

# Chapter Six

[1] Most corn mills were privately owned. Villagers typically ground 5 to 8 gallons of corn at a time, repaying the owner for use of the mill with a pint or two of flour. The owner also got what flour remained in the mill at the end of the day, which was unusually fine.

[2] Many people also cooked in pottery charcoal braziers or in cast iron "coal pots" (tightly lidded pots). Portable ovens sometimes were made out of wooden boxes lined with tin or aluminum sheeting. These contained two or three shelves and were typically heated by a coal pot at the base.

[3] Information from Vestry Minutes, 3 September 1885; cited in P. Jackman, 27.

[4] 2000 Population and Housing Census, vol. 1, 237.

[5] Ibid.

[6] *Warri* is an African pit and pebble game still played by some villagers, using a board with two rows of six cuplike depressions and 48 horse-nicker seeds or pebbles for counters. After World War II Barbadians returning from the United States popularized dominoes, which replaced warri as the game of choice.

[7] According to the 2000 census, 37 percent of St. Lucy households own a car (compared to 44 percent nationally). Judging by traffic on the roads in 2010, this number had certainly increased in the intervening ten years.

[8] A random household survey conducted in five St. Lucy villages by our students in 1996 asked how many households in the village the interviewee's household was related to; results ranged from zero to 20 households, with an average of five. One-quarter of those interviewed, however, reported not being related to any other household in the village.

9 G. Gmelch, *Behind the Smile*, 193.

10 www.oas.org/dsp/documents/victimization_surveys/Barbados/2002_international_comparisons.pdf.

11 A source of external credit that still plays an important role in the economic strategies of some poor households is the traveling Indian salesman, long referred to as the "coolie man." Once or twice a week these salesmen—who are based in Bridgetown but originally emigrated to Barbados from Trinidad, Guyana, India, and Bangladesh—drive into St. Lucy's villages to sell clothing, fabric, and kitchen supplies. They also take special requests for large items such as mattresses and televisions. Despite the existence of public transportation and delivery services, which makes the stores of Speightstown and Bridgetown accessible, poorer villagers continue to buy from these salesmen who offer convenience and easy credit. Most allow their customers to pay for goods in small weekly installments, usually ten dollars but sometimes as little as two. Despite the pejorative label, most villagers speak positively of the coolie man. Currently, at least three itinerant salesmen visit St. Lucy's villages.

12 Similar rotating credit associations are found in Africa, Asia, and among immigrant populations in the United States and Britain as well as in other parts of the Caribbean. In Trinidad and St. Lucia, for example, they are known by the Yoruba name *susu*. In Jamaica they are known as "partners" and in Guyana and Antigua as "box-hands."

13 See Stoute and Ifill.

14 Ibid.

15 The Barbados Cricket League organizes village cricket throughout the island, grouping village "clubs" into divisions, which in turn are grouped into zones and a "Super League." Teams representing companies and government agencies can also participate.

16 See Corbin.

# Chapter Seven

1 Within the propertied classes, Jews and Quakers constituted important minorities during the 17th and 18th centuries. Many of the white indentured laborers and servants who were brought to the island were Roman Catholics, but it was not until the military garrison asked for a Catholic chaplain in 1839 that a Catholic mission was established in Barbados.

2 Schomburgk, *History of Barbados*, 122.

3 Handler and Lange, *Plantation Slavery in Barbados*, 214.

4 Handler, "Slave Medicine and Obeah in Barbados, ca. 1650–1834," 57. See also Bilby and Handler, "Obeah: Healing and Protection in West Indian Slave Life."

5 The Christian Mission (Pennyites) began proselytizing in 1891, followed by the Church of God, Pilgrim Holiness, Salvation Army Society, and others.

6 The former is also referred to as the Sons of God Apostolic Spiritual Baptist Church. Its members are commonly known as Spiritual Baptists, or "Tie-heads," for the cloth head wraps they wear. This is Barbados' only indigenous religion. It was founded in 1957 by Granville Williams. During a 16-year stay in Trinidad, he was exposed to the Spiritual Baptists, a revitalization movement with African roots. After experiencing his own revelation, he returned to Barbados to preach. The church now has an estimated seven thousand members, including a small number of St. Lucy residents.

7 Collymore, *Barbadian Dialect*, 35.

8 Barbados Statistical Service.

9 Dann, *The Quality of Life in Barbados*, 180–84.

10 *Advocate*, 7 February 1996.

11 Glossolalia refers to the patterned vocalizations church members make when they slip into a trancelike state. These vocalizations are very similar cross-culturally due to the regular, rhythmical tightening and relaxation of the muscles of the vocal apparatus that occurs while in trance. They also share a characteristic intonation pattern.

12 Dann, *The Quality of Life in Barbados*, 180.

# Chapter Eight

[1] Lawrence went alone to Bermuda afterward, staying several months before returning home to Mt. Vernon where he died of acute "consumption" in July 1752. It was in Barbados that George Washington contracted and survived smallpox, gaining future immunity to the disease.

[2] Cave, Shepherd and Co., 17.

[3] In 1956 Barbados passed the Hotel Aids Act that permitted the importation of duty-free construction materials and gave tax relief to the tourism industry, encouraging its growth.

[4] In 2006, there were 526,541 "stay-over" and 539,092 cruise ship tourists in Barbados.

[5] See Drayton.

[6] Wayne Hunte, personal interview, 1992.

[7] Speech to Barbadian hoteliers in 1989.

[8] Pruitt and LaFont, 432.

[9] Karch and Dann.

[10] Richard Haynes, speech to Barbadian hoteliers, 1989.

[11] Quoted in Gmelch, *Double Passage*, 184.

[12] Fitzpatrick.

[13] F. Jackman.

[14] Barbados Statistical Service, 252, 250. In 2000, 91 percent of parish households had radio, 88 percent had TV and 60 percent had VCRs; countrywide, the figures were 89, 93, and 68 percent, respectively. That same year, 12 percent of St. Lucy homes subscribed to DirecTV, compared to 22 percent countrywide.

[15] When a multichannel cable television subscription was added in 1987, the scope of what people watched widened to include programming from Canada, Europe, the Caribbean, and Latin America as well as the US. In 1996, American satellite television provider DirecTV entered the market. Combined, these providers make television available to Bajans 24 hours a day.

[16] Evelyn. A 2009 Nielson study found the typical American teenager spent 104 hours and 24 minutes per month watching television and 11 hours and 32 minutes online per month. http://www.physorg.com/news165213203.html.

[17] Boyce.

[18] Huesmann et al.

[19] Barbados is one of several drug transshipment sites in the Caribbean—although a minor one compared to the Grenadines and Antigua—with couriers taking premium marijuana and crack to North America via airlines, yachts, and cruise and container ships. Drugs are often landed on isolated beaches along St. Lucy's coast, but most crime and gang activity in Barbados is found in Bridgetown and the more urban parishes of St. Michael, Christ Church, and St. James, where the demand for and availability of drugs and opportunities for theft and burglary are greatest, due in large part to the number of tourists.

[20] The incident increased awareness of gender discrimination and gave many women who may have otherwise kept silent about their experiences of sexual harassment the courage to stand up for themselves by reporting it or confronting the person harassing them.

[21] The national averages were then about double: 22 and 14 percent, respectively, of Barbados' 83,026 households (Barbados Statistical Service, 256, 258).

[22] Internet World Statistics, www.internetworldstats.com/caribbean (last accessed 6/11/10).

[23] Fraser and Henry.

[24] They also reported liking the Internet because it enhanced their education, relieved stress and boredom, and, for some, provided the opportunity to participate in otherwise disapproved behavior (e.g., viewing pornography).

[25] Evelyn, 104, 163. The percentages do not add up to 100 because of rounding.

[26] As of August 31, 2010, Barbados has 100,920 Facebook users.
http://www.internetworldstats.com/car/bb.htm (last accessed 2/24/11).

[27] Fraser and Henry.

[28] In 2000 the government introduced the EduTech (Education Sector Enhancement) program, which was a major initiative to revamp instruction by introducing more learner-centered ped-

agogies and placing computers in Barbados' schools, with Internet access at the secondary level. Laptops were also made available to many students.

[29] Horst and Miller. 127.

[30] A government circular dated 30 January 2007 announced that "students are not permitted to bring cell phones, pagers or other communication devices to school." www.barbados.gov.bb (last accessed 6/15/10).

[31] Marshall, "The History of Caribbean Migrations," 6–7.

[32] Richardson (*Panama Money in Barbados, 1900–1920*) reports that 60,000 Barbadians emigrated to Panama between 1904 and 1914. Lowenthal places the figure at 45,000 between 1880 and 1914. The West India Royal Commission reported that the total population of Barbados had declined by 20,000 between 1896 and 1921 (West India Royal Commission, 243).

[33] West India Royal Commission, 11.

[34] The US Immigration Act of 1917 imposed a literacy test and a gradation system that placed West Indians at the bottom of the list of those allowed in.

[35] See Gmelch, *Double Passage*; and Chamberlain.

[36] Stanford.

[37] Wiltshire, *The Caribbean Transnational Family*.

[38] In 1977, 2,756 Barbadians were admitted into the United States, but by 1989 only 805, or 29 percent, had become naturalized US citizens.

[39] Quoted in Gmelch, *Double Passage*, 125.

[40] Gmelch, "Work, Innovation and Investment."

[41] Sutton and Makiesky-Barrow, "Migration and West Indian Racial and Political Consciousness."

[42] See http://travel.state.gov/visa/statistics/invstats/invstats_4582.html (last accessed 7/14/10.)

# Final Thoughts

[1] See Mintz, "So-called World System"; and Mintz and Price.

[2] See Olwig.

[3] Besson, 27.

[4] Coucou, served with flying fish, is considered Barbados' national dish. It is an African-derived dish made of corn flour paste and okra.

[5] Landship societies have waxed and waned in popularity for more than a hundred years. They are "friendly societies" in which members contribute annual fees in return for sickness and death benefits. Landship members wear naval regalia, parade, and dance, their movements imitating a ship and its crew at sea. Their dances also show African influence (see Fraser et al.)

[6] The term "mimic men" comes from V. S. Naipaul's novel about Trinidad. See D. Miller's discussion of modernity and identity.

[7] Barbadians have a self-satisfied, smug reputation within the Caribbean (see Wickham, "The Thing about Barbados"; and Hearne). For a discussion of the development of Bajan Creole culture, see Welch.

[8] See Mintz, *Sweetness and Power*; and Mintz and Price.

[9] Barbados has become more involved in the regional economy and polity, developing ties with its neighbors in the Leeward and Windward Islands. In 1973 it joined with several other Caribbean countries to found the Caribbean Community (CARICOM). Today CARICOM is composed of 14 English-speaking countries and Surinam. Barbados is also a member of the Association of Caribbean States (ACS), a group of 25 nations in the Caribbean Basin, whose goal is to form a trade bloc.

[10] See, for example, Granville.

[11] See Collymore; and Handler and Jacoby.

# Bibliography

Allen, S. *New Minorities and Old Conflicts.* New York: Random House, 1971.

Alleyne, W., and H. Fraser. *The Barbados-Carolina Connection.* Basingstoke: Macmillan Caribbean, 1988.

Archer, E. D. "Effects of the Tourist Industry in Barbados, West Indies." Ph.D. diss., University of Texas, Austin, 1980.

Austin, D. "Culture and Ideology in the English-Speaking Caribbean: A View from Jamaica." *American Ethnologist* 19, no. 2 (1983): 223–40.

Austin-Broos, D. J. "Pentecostals and Rastafarians: Cultural, Political and Gender Relations of Two Religious Movements." *Social and Economic Studies* 36, no. 4 (1987): 1–19.

Barbados Improvement Association. *The Tourist Guide to Barbados.* Bridgetown: Barbados Improvement Association, 1913.

Barbados Ministry of Tourism. *Annual Tourism Statistical Digest.* Bridgetown: Barbados Ministry of Tourism, 2006.

Barbados Statistical Service. *2000 Population and Housing Census.* vol.1. Bridgetown: Barbados Statistical Service, 2002.

Barrow, C. "Anthropology, the Family and Women in the Caribbean." In *Gender in Caribbean Development,* edited by P. Mohammed and C. Shepherd, 156–69. Mona: University of the West Indies, 1988.

———. "Finding the Support: A Study of Strategies for Survival." *Social and Economic Studies* 35, no 2 (1986): 131–76.

———. "Male Images of Women in Barbados." *Social and Economic Studies* 35, no. 3 (1986): 51–64.

———. "Migration from a Barbados Village: Effects on Family Life." *New Community* 5 no. 4 (1977): 381–91.

———. "Ownership and Control of Resources in Barbados: 1834 to the Present." *Social and Economic Studies* 32, no. 3 (1983): 83–120.

———. "Reputation and Ranking in a Barbadian Locality." *Social and Economic Studies* 25, no. 2 (1976): 106–29.

Basch, L. "The Politics of Caribbeanization: Vincentians and Grenadians in New York." In *Caribbean Life in New York City,* edited by C. Sutton and E. Chaney, 160–81. New York: Center for Migration Studies, 1987.

Basch, L., N. G. Schiller, and C. Szanton Blanc, eds. *Nations Unbound: Transnational Projects, Global Predicaments, and Deterritorialized Nation-States.* New York: Gordon and Breach, 1994.

Beckles, H. *Afro-Caribbean Women and Resistance to Slavery in Barbados.* London: Karnak House, 1989.

——. *The History of Barbados,* 2nd ed. Cambridge: Cambridge University Press, 2007.

——. *Natural Rebels: A Social History of Enslaved Black Women in Barbados.* New Brunswick, NJ: Rutgers University Press, 1989.

——. *White Servitude and Black Slavery in Barbados, 1627–1715.* Knoxville: University of Tennessee Press, 1989.

Beckles, H., and V. Shepherd. *Caribbean Slave Society and Economy.* New York: New Press 1991.

Behrendt, S., D. Eltis, and D. Richardson. "The Costs of Coercion: African Agency in the Pre-modern Atlantic World." *Economic History Review* 54, no. 3 (2001): 454–76.

Besson, J. "RAI News (Summary of Sidney Mintz's 1994 Huxley Memorial Lecture)." *Anthropology Today* 2, no. 2 (1995): 27.

Besson, J., and J. Momsen, eds. *Land and Development in the Caribbean.* London: Berlin, 1987.

Best, G. "Proud to be a Barbadian." *The Nation,* September 11, 1992.

Bilby, K. M., and J. S. Handler. "Obeah: Healing and Protection in West Indian Slave Life." *Journal of Caribbean History* 38 (2004): 153–83.

Bolles, A. L. " 'Goin' Abroad': Working Class Jamaican Women and Migration." In *Female Immigrants to the United States: Caribbean, Latin American and African Experiences,* edited by D. Mortimer and R. Bryce-Laporte, 56–85. Occasional Papers no. 2. Washington, DC: Smithsonian Institution, RITES, 1981.

Boyce. "Gang Trouble Reported in St. Lucy." *The Nation,* October 10, 1989.

Brinkerhoff, J. *Digital Diaspora: Identity and Transnational Engagement.* Cambridge: Cambridge University Press, 2009.

Brooks, D. *Race and Labour in London Transport.* London: Oxford University Press, 1975.

Brown, A., and R. Sanatan. *Talking with Whom? A Report on the State of the Media in the Caribbean.* Seminar report. University of the West Indies, Cave Hill, 1987.

Bryce-Laporte, R. S. "New York City and the New Caribbean Immigration: A Contextual Statement." *International Migration Review* 13 no. 2 (1979): 214–34.

Bryce-Laporte, R. S., and D. Mortimer, eds. *Caribbean Immigration to the United States.* Occasional Papers no. 1. Washington, DC: Smithsonian Institution, RIIES, 1976.

Bullen, R. P. "Barbados and the Archaeology of the Caribbean." *Journal of the Barbados Museum and Historical Society* 32 (1966): 16–19.

Bush, B. *Slave Women in Caribbean Society: 1650–1838.* Bloomington: Indiana University Press, 1990.

Campbell, P. F. "Barbados Vestries, 1627–1700, pt. 2." *Journal of the Barbados Museum and Historical Society* 37, no. 2 (1984): 174.

——. *The Church in Barbados in the Seventeenth Century.* Bridgetown: Barbados Museum and Historical Society, 1982.

Carmichael, T. A., ed. *Barbados: Thirty Years of Independence.* Kingston, Jamaica: Ian Randle Publishers, 1997.

Carnegie, C. V. "Strategic Flexibility in the West Indies: A Social Psychology of Caribbean Migration." *Caribbean Review* 2, no. 1 (1982): 10–13, 54.

Cave, Shepherd, and Company. *Barbados (Illustrated): Historical, Descriptive and Commercial.* Bridgetown: Cave, Shepherd and Company, 1911.

Chamberlain, M. "Family and Identity: Barbadian Migrants to Britain." In *Migration and Identity*, edited by R. Benmayer and A. Skotnes, 119–36. London: Oxford University Press, 1994.

Chandler, A. A. "The Expansion of Barbados." *Journal of the Barbados Museum and Historical Society* 13 (1946): 106–16.

Chaney, E. "The Context of Caribbean Migration." In *Caribbean Life in New York City*, edited by C. Sutton and E. Chaney, 3–14. New York: Center for Migration Studies, 1987.

Clarke, A. *Growing Up Stupid under the Union Jack.* Toronto: McClelland and Stewart, 1980.

Clarke, E. T. "Mental Illness among Barbadians in Barbados and England." Ph.D. diss., University of Surrey, 1981.

Coleridge, H. N. *Six Months in the West Indies.* New York: Negro Universities Press, 1970 [1836].

Collymore, F. *Barbadian Dialect.* Bridgetown: Barbados National Trust, 1955.

Corbin, B. "Picnics in Barbados." In *Everyday Life in Barbados: A Sociological Perspective*, edited by G. Dann, 103–23. Leiden: Royal Institute of Linguistics and Anthropology, 1979.

Cross, M. *Urbanization and Urban Growth in the Caribbean.* Cambridge: Cambridge University Press, 1979.

Cumper, G. E. "Working Class Emigration from Barbados to the U.K." *Social and Economic Studies* 6, no. 1 (1957): 76–83.

Cutsinger, L. "Informal Marketing in Barbados, West Indies." Ph.D. diss., Department of Anthropology, Washington State University, 1990.

Dann, G. *The Barbadian Male: Sexual Attitudes and Practices.* London: Macmillan Caribbean, 1987.

———. *Everyday Life in Barbados: A Sociological Perspective.* Leiden: Royal Institute of Linguistics and Anthropology, 1979.

———. *The Quality of Life in Barbados.* London: Macmillan, 1984.

Davison, R. B. *Black British: Immigrants to England.* London: Oxford University Press, 1966.

———. *West Indian Migrants: Social and Economic Effects of Migration from the West Indies.* London: Oxford University Press, 1962.

Deere, C. D., et al. *In the Shadows of the Sun: Caribbean Development Alternatives and U.S. Policy.* Boulder, CO: Westview Press, 1990.

Dickson, W. *Letters on Slavery.* London: J. Phillips, 1979. http://www.yale.edu/glc/archive/1162.htm (last accessed 2/8/11).

———. *Mitigation of Slavery.* Westport, CT: Negro Universities Press, 1970 [1814].

Dominguez, V. *From Neighbor to Stranger: The Dilemma of Caribbean Peoples in the United States.* New Haven, CT: Yale University Press, 1975.

Doxey, G. V. ed. *The Tourism Industry in Barbados.* Ontario: Dusco Graphics, 1971.

Drayton, K. "Art, Culture, and National Heritage." In *Barbados: 30 Years of Independence*, edited by T. Carmichael, 197–237. Kingston, Jamaica: Ian Randle Pub, 1996.

Drewett, P. L. "Archaeological Survey of Barbados. First Interim Report." *Journal Barbados Museum Historical Society* 38, no. 1 (1987): 44–80.

———. "Archaeological Survey of Barbados. Second Interim Report." *Journal Barbados Museum Historical Society* 38, no. 2 (1988): 196–204.

———. "Archaeological Survey of Barbados. Third Interim Report." *Journal Barbados Museum Historical Society* 38, no. 3 (1989): 338–52.

————. *Prehistoric Barbados.* London: Institute of Archaeology, University College London and Barbados Museum and Historical Society, 1991.

Dunn, R. *Sugar and Slaves: The Rise of the Planter Class in the English West Indies, 1624–1713.* Chapel Hill: University of North Carolina Press, 1972.

Ebanks, G. E., P. M. George, and C. Nobbe. "Fertility and Number of Partnerships in Barbados." *Population Studies* 28, no. 3 (1974): 449–61.

————. "Patterns of Sex-Union Formation in Barbados." *Canadian Review of Sociology and Anthropology* 11, no. 3 (1974): 230–46.

Editorial. "Parish Boundaries." *Journal of the Barbados Museum and Historical Society* 38, no. 2 (1988): 131–36.

Edwards, P., ed. *Equiano's Travels: His Autobiography: The Interesting Narrative of the Life of Olaudah Equiano or Gustavus Vassa, the African.* Long Grove, IL: Waveland Press, 2006.

Ellis, P., ed. *Women in the Caribbean.* Kingston: Kingston Publishers, 1986.

Eriksen, T. H. "Liming in Trinidad: The Art of Doing Nothing." *Folk* 32 (1990): 23–43.

Evelyn, V. "Adolescent Interface with Television and the Internet: Subjective Responses to Objective Possibilities." PhD Dissertation, Dept. of Sociology, Cave Hill: University of the West Indies, 2008.

Family Welfare Association. *The West Indian Comes to England.* London: Routledge and Kegan Paul, 1960.

Fisher, L. E. *Colonial Madness: Mental Health in the Barbadian Social Order.* New Brunswick, NJ: Rutgers University Press, 1989.

Fitzpatrick, M. "Examining the Disparity between Tourist Development and Cultural Resource Preservation: A Barbados Example." Paper presented at the Western Social Science Association Meetings, San Diego, CA, 2000.

Foner, N. *Jamaica Farewell: Jamaican Migrants in London.* Berkeley: University of California Press, 1978.

————. "West Indians in New York City and London: A Comparative Analysis." *International Migration Review* 13, no. 2 (1979): 284–97.

Forde, G. A. *Folk Beliefs of Barbados.* Barbados: National Cultural Foundation, 1988.

Franck, H. A. *Roaming through the West Indies.* New York: Century, 1920.

Fraser, H., et al. *A–Z of Barbadian Heritage.* Kingston: Heinemann Publishers (Caribbean), 1990.

Fraser, H., and R. Hughes. *Historic Houses of Barbados.* Bridgetown: Barbados National Trust, 1982.

Fraser, S., and L. Henry. "An Exploratory Study of Residential Internet Shopping in Barbados." *Journal of Eastern Caribbean Studies* 32, no. 1 (2007): 1–20.

Frazer, J. G. *The Golden Bough: A Study in Magic and Religion: A New Abridgement from the Second and Third Editions.* Edited by R. Fraser. New York: Oxford University Press, 2009.

Freeman, C. "Designing Women: Corporate Discipline and Barbados's Off-Shore Pink-Collar Sector." *Cultural Anthropology* 8, no. 2 (1993): 169–86.

————. *High Tech and High Heels in the Global Economy: Women, Work, and Pink-Collar Identities in the Caribbean.* Durham, NC: Duke University Press, 2000.

French, J. "Colonial Policy towards Women after the 1938 Uprising: The Case of Jamaica." *Caribbean Quarterly* 34, no. 3–4 (1986): 38–76.

Galenson, D. *Traders, Planters, and Slaves.* Cambridge: Cambridge University Press, 1986.

Gill, M. "Women, Work and Development: Barbados, 1946–1970." In *Women, Work and Development* (Women in the Caribbean Project, vol. 6), edited by M. Gill and J. Massiah. Cave Hill, Barbados: Institute of Social and Economic Research, University of the West Indies, 1984.

Gmelch, G. "Barbados Odyssey: Some Migrants Fulfill Their Dreams by Returning Home." *Natural History* 94, no.10 (1985): 34–38.

———. *Behind the Smile: The Working Lives of Caribbean Tourism*, 2nd ed. Bloomington: University of Indiana Press, 2012.

———. *Double Passage: The Lives of Caribbean Migrants Abroad and Back Home.* Ann Arbor: University of Michigan Press, 1992.

———. "Learning Culture: The Education of American Students in Caribbean Villages." *Human Organization* 51, no. 3 (1992): 245–52.

———. "Return Migration." *Annual Review of Anthropology* 9 (1980): 135–59.

———. "Work, Innovation, and Investment: The Impact of Return Migrants in Barbados." *Human Organization* 46, no. 2 (1987): 131–40.

Gmelch, G., and S. B. Gmelch. "Barbados's Amerindian Past." *Anthropology Today* 12, no. 1 (1996): 11–15.

———. "Ethnographic Field Schools: What Students Do and Learn." *Anthropology and Education Quarterly* 30, no. 2 (1999): 220–27.

———. "Gender and Migration: The Readjustment of Women Migrants in Barbados, Ireland and Newfoundland." *Human Organization* 54, no. 4 (1995): 470–73.

Gmelch, S. B. (ed.). *Tourists and Tourism*, 2nd ed. Long Grove, IL: Waveland Press, 2010.

Gonzalez, N. S. "Family Organization in Five Types of Migratory Wage Labor." *American Anthropologist* 63, no. 6 (1961): 1264–80.

Goodall, E. A. 1977. *Sketches of Amerindian Tribes, 1841–1843.* London: British Museum Publications.

Gooding, E. *The Plant Communities of Barbados.* Barbados: Ministry of Education, 1974.

Graburn, N. "Tourism: The Sacred Journey." In *Hosts and Guests: The Anthropology of Tourism*, edited by V. Smith, 17–31. Oxford: Blackwell, 1978.

Granville. "Be Fully Aware of Our Past." *Advocate*, January 31, 1996, 15.

Great Britain. *West India Royal Commission Report.* Command Paper, 6607. London: His Majesty's Stationary Office, 1945.

Greenfield, S. *English Rustics in Black Skin: A Study of Modern Family in a Pre-Industrialized Society.* New Haven, CT: Yale University Press, 1966. Reprint, Bridgetown: Barbados Museum and Historical Society, 2011.

Greenwood, R., and S. Hamber. *Arawaks to Africans.* London: Macmillan, 1979.

Griffith, D. C. "Women, Remittances, and Reproduction." *American Ethnologist* 12 no. 4 (1985): 676–90.

Griffith, W. "CARICOM Countries and the Caribbean Basin Initiative." *Latin American Perspectives* 17, no. 1:63 (1990): 33–54.

Griswold, W. *Cultures and Societies in a Changing World.* Thousand Oaks, CA: Pine Forge Press, 1994.

Hackenberger, S. "An Abstract of Archaeological Investigations by the Barbados Museum, 1986." *Journal of Barbados Museum Historical Society* 38, no. 2 (1988): 155–62.

———. 1987. *Archaeological Investigations, Barbados, West Indies.* MS, Barbados Museum.

Hagelberg, G. B. "Sugar in the Caribbean." In *Caribbean Contours*, edited by S. Mintz and S. Price, 85–126. Baltimore, MD: Johns Hopkins University Press, 1985.

Handler, J. S. "The Amerindian Slave Population of Barbados in the Seventeenth and Early Eighteenth Century." *Caribbean Studies* 8, no. 4 (1969): 38–64.

———. "Amerindians and Their Contributions to Barbadian Life." *Journal of the Barbados Museum and Historical Society* 35 (1977): 189–210.

———. "An Archaeological Investigation of the Domestic Life of Plantation Slaves in Barbados." *Journal of the Barbados Museum and Historical Society* 34, no. 2 (1972): 64–72.

————. "Aspects of Amerindian Ethnography in Seventeenth Century Barbados." *Caribbean Studies* 9, no. 4 (1970): 50–72.

————. "Disease and Medical Disabilities of Enslaved Barbadians from the Seventeenth Century to Around 1838: Part 1." *Journal of Caribbean History* 40 (2006): 22–23.

————. "Escaping Slavery in a Caribbean Plantation Society: Marroonage in Barbados, 1650s–1830s." *Nieuwe West-Indische Gids—New West Indian Guide* 71 (1997): 183–225.

————. "Freedmen and Slaves in the Barbados Militia." *Journal of Caribbean History.* 19, no. 1 (1984): 1–25.

————. "Plantation Slave Settlements in Barbados, 1650s–1834." In *The Shadow of the Plantation: Caribbean History and Legacy*, edited by A Thompson. Kingston, Jamaica: Ian Randle, 2002.

————. "Slave Medicine and Obeah in Barbados, ca. 1650–1834." *Nieuwe West-Indische Gids—New West Indian Guide* 74 (2000): 57–56.

————. "Slave Names and Naming in Barbados, 1650–1830." *William and Mary Quarterly* 53 (1996): 685–728.

————. "Slave Revolts and Conspiracies in Seventeenth-Century Barbados." *New West Indian Guide* 56, no. 1–2 (1982): 5–42.

————. "Small Scale Sugar Cane Farming in Barbados." *Ethnology* 5, no. 3 (1966): 264–83.

————. *The Unappropriated People: Freedmen in the Slave Society of Barbados*, 1974. Reprint, Bridgetown: University of the West Indies, 2009.

Handler, J. S., and S. Bergman. "Vernacular Houses and Domestic Material Culture on Barbadian Sugar Plantations, 1650–1838." *Journal of Caribbean History* 43 (2009): 1–36.

Handler, J. S., and K. M. Bilby. "On the Early Use and Origin of the Term Obeah in Barbados and the Anglophone Caribbean." *Slavery and Abolition* 22 (2001): 87–100.

Handler, J. S., and R. S. Coruccini. "Weaning among West Indian Slaves: Historical and Bioanthropological Evidence from Barbados." *William and Mary Quarterly* 43 (1986): 111–17.

Handler, J. S., and C. Frisbie. "Aspects of Slave Life in Barbados: Music and Its Cultural Content." *Caribbean Studies* 9 (1972): 5–46.

Handler, J. S., and J. A. Jacoby. "Slave Medicine and Plant Use in Barbados." *Journal of the Barbados Museum and Historical Society* 41 (1993): 74–98.

Handler, J. S., and F. Lange. *Plantation Slavery in Barbados: An Archaeological and Historical Investigation.* Cambridge: Harvard University Press, 1978.

Harlow, V. T. *A History of Barbados, 1625–1685.* Oxford: Clarendon Press, 1926.

Harper, R. *Colour in Britain.* London: British Broadcasting Corporation, 1965.

Harrison, D., ed. *Tourism and the Less Developed Countries.* London: Belhaven Press, 1992.

Hatch, A. "The Salvation Army and the Red Light District." *Bajan*, July 1978, 31–32.

Hearne, J. "What the Barbadian Means to Me." In *Caribbean Essays: An Anthology*, edited by A. Salkey. London: Evans Brothers Ltd, 1973.

Hernandez-Alverez, J. *Return Migration to Puerto Rico.* Berkeley: California Institute of International Studies, 1968.

Heuman, G. *Out of the House of Bondage: Runaways, Resistance, and Maroonage in Africa and the New World.* London: Frank Cass, 1986.

Higman, B. W. *A Concise History of the Caribbean.* Cambridge: Cambridge University Press, 2001.

————. *Slave Population and Economy in Jamaica, 1807–1834.* Cambridge: Cambridge University Press, 1976.

————. *Slave Populations of the British Caribbean, 1807–1834.* Baltimore, MD: Johns Hopkins University Press, 1984.

Hill, D. R. "The Impact of Migration on the Metropolitan and Folk Society of Carriacou, Grenada." *Anthropological Papers of the American Museum of Natural History* 54, no. 2 (1977).

Hoefer, H., and R. Wilder, eds. *Barbados.* Singapore: APA Productions, 1986.

Holder, J. F., ed. *Caribbean Tourism: Policies and Impacts: Selected Speeches and Papers.* Barbados: Caribbean Tourism Research and Development Centre, 1979.

Holder, J. F., and C. Wilson, eds. *Caribbean Tourism: Profits and Performance through 1980.* Port of Spain: Key Caribbean Publications, 1976.

Holmes, C. *John Bull's Island: Immigration and British Society, 1871–1971.* London: Macmillan, 1988.

Hope, R. K. *Economic Development in the Caribbean.* New York: Praeger, 1982.

Horowitz, M. M. *Morne-Paysan: Peasant Village in Martinique.* Long Grove, IL: Waveland Press, 1992.

Horst, H., and D. Miller. *The Cell Phone: An Anthropology of Communication.* Oxford: Berg, 2006.

Howard, M. C. *The Economic Development of Barbados.* Cave Hill, Barbados: University of the West Indies, 2006.

Hoyos, F. A. *Barbados: A History from Amerindians to Independence.* London: Macmillan, 1978.

Huesmann, L. R., et al. "Longitudinal Relations between Children's Exposure to TV Violence and Their Aggressive and Violent Behavior in Young Adulthood: 1977–1992." *Developmental Psychology* 39, no. 2 (2003): 201–21.

Hughes, G. *The Natural History of Barbados.* New York: Arno Press, 1972[1750].

Hutt, M. B. *Exploring Historic Barbados.* Nova Scotia: Layne, 1981.

Jackman, F. "Notes on the History of the Electronic Media in Barbados, 1933–1993." *Journal of the Barbados Museum Historical Society* 42 (1994–95): 150–59.

Jackman, I. "Barbadian Games of Yesterday." In *Everyday Life in Barbados: A Sociological Perspective,* edited by G. Dann. Leiden: Royal Institute of Linguistics and Anthropology, 1979.

Jackman, P. *St. Lucy under the Lens: A Socio-economic and Political View from 1680–1900.* Caribbean Studies bachelor's thesis, University of the West Indies, Cave Hill, 1993.

Karch, C. "The Transformation and Consolidation of the Corporate Plantation Economy in Barbados, 1860–1877." Ph.D. diss., Rutgers University, 1979.

Karch, C., and G. Dann. "Close Encounters of the Third Kind." *Human Relations* 34 (1981): 249–69.

King, M. "St. Lucy Project to Push Growth in North." *The Nation,* June 1, 2010.

Klein, H. S. *Slavery in the Americas: A Comparative Study of Virginia and Cuba.* Chicago: University of Chicago Press, 1967.

Knight, F. *The Caribbean: The Genesis of a Fragmented Nationalism,* 2nd ed. New York: Oxford University Press, 1990.

Lamming, G. *In the Castle of My Skin.* Ann Arbor: University of Michigan Press, 1991[1953].

Langley, A. R. "British West Indian Interlude." *National Geographic* 79, no. 1 (1941): 1–46.

Lazarus-Black, M. "Why Women Take Men to Magistrate's Court: Caribbean Kinship Ideology and Law." *Ethnology* 30, no. 2 (1991): 119–33.

Lea, J. *Tourism and Development in the Third World.* New York: Routledge, 1988.

Lent, J. *Mass Communications in the Caribbean.* Ames: Iowa State University Press, 1990.

Levitt, P. *The Transnational Villagers.* Berkeley: University of California Press, 2001.

Levy, C. *Emancipation, Sugar, and Federalism: Barbados and the West Indies, 1833–1876.* Gainesville: University Press of Florida, 1980.

Levy, C., and P. B. Lerch. "Tourism as a Factor in Development: Implications for Gender and Work in Barbados." *Gender and Society* 5, no. 1 (1991): 67–85.

Lewis, W. *Soul Rebels: The Rastafari.* Long Grove, IL: Waveland Press, 1993.

Ligon, R. A. *A True and Exact History of the Island of Barbados.* London: Frank Cass and Company, 1970[1657].

Lowenthal, D. *West Indian Societies.* New York: Oxford University Press, 1972.

Lowenthal, D., and L. Comitas. *Consequences of Class and Color.* New York: Doubleday, 1973.

Lynch, L. *The Barbados Book.* London: Andre Deutsch, 1972.

MacCannell, D. *The Tourist: A New Theory of the Leisure Class.* New York: Schocken Books, 1976.

Maggiolo, C. "Champagne Taste on a Mauby Pocket: The Socio-environmental History of Mauby in Barbados." B.A. Honors Thesis, Anthropology, College of William and Mary.

Makiesky-Barrow, S. "Class, Culture and Politics in a Barbadian Community." Ph.D. diss., Brandeis University, 1976.

Mandle, J., and J. Mandle. *Caribbean Hoops.* New York: Gordon and Breach, 1994.

Marshall, D. "The History of Caribbean Migrations: The Case of the West Indies." *Caribbean Review* 11, no. 1 (1982): 6–9, 52.

———. "Migration as an Agent of Change in Caribbean Island Ecosystems." *International Social Science Journal* 34, no. 3 (1982): 451–67.

Marshall, P. "Black Immigrant Women in *Brown Girl, Brownstones.*" In *Caribbean Life in New York City*, edited by C. Sutton and E. Chaney, 87–91. New York: Center for Migration Research, 1987.

———. *Brown Girl, Brownstones.* New York: Random House, 1959.

Marshall, T. "Post-emancipation Adjustments in Barbados, 1838–1876." In *Emancipation I*, edited by A. Thompson, 8–108. Barbados: National Cultural Foundation, 1986.

Marshall, W. *Emancipation II: Aspects of the Post-Slavery Experience in Barbados.* Barbados: National Cultural Foundation, 1987.

———. "The Termination of Apprenticeship in Barbados and the Windward Islands: An Essay in Colonial Administration and Politics." *Journal of Caribbean History* 2 (1971): 1–45.

Massiah, J. *Women and the Family.* Cave Hill: Institute of Social and Economic Research, University of the West Indies, 1982.

———. *Women as Heads of Households in the Caribbean: Family Structure and Feminine Status.* Colchester: UNESCO, 1983.

McCullough, D. *The Path between the Seas.* New York: Simon and Schuster, 1977.

McManamon, F. P. "Hidden Data: Learning about Ecosystems from Archeological Sites." *Federal Archeology* 8, no. 1 (1995): 2.

Midgett, D. K. "West Indian Ethnicity in Great Britain." In *Migration and Development*, edited by H. I. Safa and B. DuToit, 57–81. The Hague: Mouton, 1980.

———. "West Indian Migration and Adaptation in St. Lucia and London." Ph.D. diss., Department of Anthropology, University of Illinois at Urbana-Champaign, 1977.

Mill, J. S. *The Principles of Political Economy.* New York: Oxford University Press, 2008[1848].

Miller, D. *Modernity: An Ethnographic Approach: Dualism and Mass Consumption in Trinidad.* Oxford: Berg, 1994.

Mintz, S. *Caribbean Transformations.* Chicago: Aldine Publishing Co., 1974.

———. "The So-Called World System: Local Initiative and Local Response." *Dialectical Anthropology* 2, no. 4 (1977): 253–70.

———. *Sweetness and Power: The Place of Sugar in Modern History.* New York: Penguin Books, 1985.

———. *Three Ancient Colonies: Caribbean Themes and Variations.* Cambridge, MA: Harvard University Press, 2010.

Mintz, S., and S. Price. *Caribbean Contours.* Baltimore, MD: Johns Hopkins University Press, 1985.

Moxly, Rev. J. H. Sutton. *An Account of a West Indian Sanatorium and a Guide to Barbados.* London: Low, Marston, Searle, and Rivington, 1886.

Musgrove, P. "The Economic Crisis and Its Impact on Health and Health Care in Latin America and the Caribbean." *International Journal of Health Services* 17, no. 3 (1987): 411–41.

Naipaul, V. S. *Mimic Men.* New York: Macmillan, 1967.

Nurse, L. *Residential Subdivision of Barbados: 1965–1977.* Cave Hill: Institute of Social and Economic Research, University of the West Indies, 1983.

Olwig, K. F. *Global Culture, Island Identity: Continuity and Change in the Afro-Caribbean Community of Nevis.* New York: Harwood Academic Publishers, 1993.

Parry, J., P. Sherlock, and A. Maingot. *A Short History of the West Indies*, 4th ed. New York: St. Martin's Press, 1987[1956].

Pastor, R. *Migration and Development in the Caribbean.* Boulder, CO: Westview Press, 1985.

Patterson, O. "West-Indian Immigrants Returning Home." *Race* 101, no. 1 (1968): 69–77.

Patterson, S. *Dark Strangers: A Study of West Indians in London.* Harmondsworth: Penguin, 1965.

———. *Immigration and Race Relations in Britain, 1960–1967.* London: Oxford University Press, 1969.

Peach, C. *West Indian Migration to Britain: A Social Geography.* London: Oxford University Press, 1968.

Phillips, E. "The Development of the Tourist Industry in Barbados, 1956–1980." In *The Economy of Barbados.* Bridgetown: Central Bank of Barbados, 1981.

Phillips, T. *A Journal of a Voyage Made in the Hannibal of London, Ann. 1693, 1694, From England, to Cape's Monseradoe, in Africa, And thence along the Coast of Guiney to Whidaw, the Island of St. Thomas, An so forward to Barbadoes.* London: Walthoe, 1848. (Google ebook, digitized March 4, 2010.)

Philpott, S. B. *West Indian Migration: The Montserrat Case.* New York: Humanities Press, 1973.

Portes, A., and R. Rumbaut. *Immigrant America: A Portrait.* Berkeley: University of California Press, 1990.

Postma, J. *The Atlantic Slave Trade.* Westport, CT: Greenwood Press, 2003.

Powell, D. "Caribbean Women and Their Response to Familial Experiences." *Social and Economic Studies* 35, no. 2 (1986): 83–130.

Price, N. *Behind the Planter's Back: Lower Class Responses to Marginality in Bequia Island, St. Vincent.* London: Macmillan Caribbean, 1988.

Prior, M. "Matrifocality, Power, and Gender Relations in Jamaica." In *Gender in Cross-Cultural Perspective*, edited by C. Brettell and C. Sargent, 310–17. Englewood Cliffs, NJ: Prentice-Hall, 1993.

Pruitt, D., and S. La Font. "For Love and Money: Romance and Tourism in Jamaica." *Annals of Tourism Research* 22, no. 2 (1995): 422–40.

Rediker, M. *The Slave Ship: A Human History.* New York: Viking, 2007.

Richardson, B. C. *Caribbean Migrants: Environment and Human Survival in St. Kitts and Nevis.* Knoxville: University of Tennessee Press, 1983.

———. *Panama Money in Barbados, 1900–1920.* Knoxville: University of Tennessee Press, 1985.

Rubenstein, H. *Coping with Poverty: Adaptive Strategies in a Caribbean Village.* Boulder, CO: Westview, 1986.

———. "Remittances and Rural Underdevelopment in the English-Speaking Caribbean." *Human Organization* 42, no. 4 (1983): 295–306.

Schomburgk, R. H. *The History of Barbados.* London: Frank Cass and Company Ltd., 1971[1848].

Senior, O. *Working Miracles: Women's Lives in the English-Speaking Caribbean.* Bloomington: Indiana University Press, 1991.

Shepherd, V., B. Brereton, and B. Bailey. 1995. *Engendering History: Caribbean Women in Historical Perspective.* New York: St. Martin's Press, 1995.

Sheppard, J. *The Redlegs of Barbados.* New York: KTO Press, 1977.

Smith, M. G. *The Plural Society in the British West Indies.* Berkeley: University of California Press, 1965.

Smith, R. T. *Kinship and Class in the West Indies.* Cambridge: Cambridge University Press, 1988.

Stanford, S. *Creating Awareness about Workers' Remittances Flows to Barbados: A Note.* Bridgetown: Research Department, Central Bank of Barbados, 2006.

Stewart, E. C. 1972. *American Cultural Patterns: A Cross-Cultural Perspective.* Chicago: Intercultural Press.

Stoffle, R. "Industrial Impact on Family Formation in Barbados, West Indies." *Ethnology* 16, no. 3 (1977): 253–67.

Stoute, J., and K. Ifill. "The Rural Rumshop: A Comparative Case Study." In *Everyday Life in Barbados: A Sociological Perspective,* edited by G. Dann, 145–67. Leiden: Royal Institute of Linguistics and Anthropology, 1979.

Sutton, C. *The Scene of the Action: A Wildcat Strike in Barbados.* Ph.D. diss., Columbia University, 1969.

———. "Transnational Identities and Cultures: Caribbean Immigrants in the United States." In *Immigration and Ethnicity: American Society—"Melting Pot" or "Salad Bowl,"* edited by M. D'Innocenzo and J. P. Sirefman, 231–41. Westport, CT: Greenwood Press, 1992.

Sutton, C., and S. Makiesky-Barrow. "Migration and West Indian Racial and Political Consciousness." In *Migration and Development: Implications for Ethnic Identity and Political Conflict,* edited by H. I. Safa and B. DuToit, 113–44. The Hague: Mouton, 1975.

———. "Social Inequality and Sexual Status in Barbados." In *The Black Woman Cross-Culturally,* edited by F. Steady. Cambridge: Schenkman, 1981.

Thomas-Hope, E. "Caribbean Skilled International Migration and the Transnational Household." *Geoforum* 19, no. 4 (1988): 423–32.

———, ed. *Perspectives on Caribbean Regional Identity.* Monograph Series no. 11. Liverpool: Centre for Latin American Studies, 1984.

———. "Return Migration and Implications for Caribbean Development." In *Migration and Development in the Caribbean,* edited by R. A. Pastor, 157–73. Boulder, CO: Westview Press, 1985.

Thornton, J. *Africa and Africans in the Making of the Atlantic World, 1400–1800*, 2nd ed. New York: Cambridge University Press, 1998.

Trouillot, M.-R. 1987. *Women and Children in Barbados: A Situational Analysis.* Bridgetown: UNICEF Caribbean Area Office.

———. "The Caribbean Region: An Open Frontier in Anthropological Theory." *Annual Review of Anthropology* 21 (1992): 19–42.

UNESCO. "The Effects of Tourism on Socio-Cultural Values." *Annual of Tourism Research* 4 (1977): 74–105.

Voyages Database. *Voyages: The Transatlantic Slave Trade Database*, 2009. http://www.slavevoyages.org (last accessed 8/4/10).

Watson, H. "Recent Attempts at Industrial Restructuring in Barbados." *Latin American Perspectives* 17, no. 1:64 (1990): 10–32.

Watson, J. L. *Between Two Cultures.* Oxford: Basil Blackwell, 1977.

Watson, K. *The Civilized Island, Barbados.* Bridgetown: Caribbean Graphics, 1979.

Welch, P. L. V. "In Search of a Barbadian Identity: Historical Factors in the Evolution of a Barbadian Literary Tradition." *Journal of the Barbados Museum and Historical Society* 40 (1992): 37–46.

West India Royal Commission. *Report of the West India Royal Commission.* London: HMSO, 1945.

Western, J. 1992. *A Passage to England: Barbadian Londoners Speak of Home.* Minneapolis: University of Minnesota Press, 1992.

Wickham, J. "The Thing about Barbados." *Journal of the Barbados Museum and Historical Society* 35 (1975): 223–30.

Williams, E. *Capitalism and Slavery.* New York: Putnam, 1966.

Wilson, P. "Reputation and Respectability: A Suggestion for Caribbean Ethnology." *Man* 4 (1969): 70–84.

———. *Crab Antics: The Social Anthropology of English Speaking Negro Societies of the Caribbean.* New Haven, CT: Yale University Press, 1973.

Wiltshire, R. *The Caribbean Transnational Family.* Cave Hill: Institute of Social and Economic Research, 1986.

———. "Implications of Transnational Migration for Nationalism: The Caribbean Example." In *Towards a Transnational Perspective on Migration*, Vol. 654, edited by N. G. Schiller, L. Basch, and C. Blanc-Szanton, 175–87. New York: Annals of the New York Academy of Sciences, 1992.

———. *The Status of Jamaican Women in Politics.* Kingston: Three Leaves, 1975.

Withey, S., and R. Abeles. *Television and Social Behavior: Beyond Violence and Children.* Hillside, NJ: Lawrence Erlbaum Associates, 1980.

Wolf, E. R. *Europe and the People without History.* Berkeley: University of California Press, 1983.

Wood, C. H., and T. McCoy. "Migration, Remittances, and Development: A Study of Caribbean Cane Cutters in Florida." *International Migration Review* 19, no. 2 (1987): 251–77.

Worrell, D., ed. *The Economy of Barbados, 1946–1980.* Bridgetown: Central Bank of Barbados, 1982.

———. *Small Island Economies.* New York: Praeger, 1987.